Open Business Innovation Leadership

Open Business Innovation Leadership

The Emergence of the Stakeholder University

Edited by

Aldo Romano

First published 2009 by
PALGRAVE MACMILLAN

Palgrave Macmillan in the UK is an imprint of Macmillan Publishers
Limited, registered in England, company number 785998, of Houndmills,
Basingstoke, Hampshire RG21 6XS.

Palgrave Macmillan in the US is a division of St Martin's Press LLC,
175 Fifth Avenue, New York, NY 10010.

Palgrave Macmillan is the global academic imprint of the above companies
and has companies and representatives throughout the world.

Palgrave® and Macmillan® are registered trademarks in the United States,
the United Kingdom, Europe and other countries.

ISBN-13: 978-0-230-57747-3   hardback
ISBN-10: 0-230-57747-4   hardback

This book is printed on paper suitable for recycling and made from
fully managed and sustained forest sources. Logging, pulping and
manufacturing processes are expected to conform to the environmental
regulations of the country of origin.

A catalogue record for this book is available from the British Library.

A catalog record for this book is available from the Library of Congress.

10 9 8 7 6 5 4 3 2 1
18 17 16 15 14 13 12 11 10 09

Printed and bound in Great Britain by
CPI Antony Rowe, Chippenham and Eastbourne

Contents

Figures

Tables

Foreword

While it has become a cliché to say that "people are our greatest asset," many organizations do not live up to the rhetoric by truly investing in the form of capital that offers the greatest return. You will find little disagreement with the notion that people offer the best (and perhaps the only) source of sustainable competitive advantage—in short, talented and knowledgeable people are the greatest drivers of value for organizations. It's a simple equation: more effective and innovative ways of managing learning, knowledge and wisdom allow to generate more talented people who are able to drive value.

These concepts are not only vitally important, but also quite timely. We are discovering that the concept of knowledge workers is not quite what we thought it was—workers need more than knowledge to contribute; they need skills and the ability to creatively apply knowledge to the workplace. This means that we must re-think what leadership means in a knowledge organization and, more importantly, redefine managerial roles. More than being producers of output or overseers of processes, managers must become leaders of talent. They must be capable of cultivating connections and of leveraging knowledge and learning.

The corporate university concept has been an evolving phenomenon since the beginning. From the 1940s until the 1980s, many organizations created corporate universities, which were little more than expanded versions of training and development departments. As corporate universities proliferated in the 1980s and 1990s, there was a growing understanding that they can contribute more than just training classes. In the first decade of the 21st century, we have seen more integrated approaches to developing people and organizations through a variety of methods.

And that is where *Open Business Innovation Leadership: The Emergece of the Stakeholder University* comes in. As we approach the second decade of this century, Aldo Romano and his colleagues present a comprehensive picture of the most recent trends in human capital development based on the integration of strategic management and organizational learning perspectives. In particular, they highlight the importance of networked learning in harnessing greater efficiencies and greater capacities in both individuals and organizations. By connecting people and organizations in networks, we can exponentially expand the reach and value of learning. Based on the recognized importance of an open and multi-stakeholder perspective of business, the authors lead us to the next step in the evolution of corporate universities, that is, the Stakeholder University.

The stories told in this book leverage the experience of the *Euro-Mediterranean Incubator* in *Business Innovation Leadership* to reveal how innovative models of human capital development can deliver value to organizations, universities and regional economies. Based on the integration of new learning methodologies, cross-disciplinary collaboration, public/private partnerships, and the integration of research, education and professional practice, the Incubator is engaged in implementing a best practice to follow. I had the pleasure of meeting Aldo Romano and his colleagues at the Advanced International Summer School that they run each year in the south of Italy. There I met an engaged team of scholars who were as interested in the practical side of their research as the academic.

I have long believed that an effective corporate university can be the best lever to propel an organization forward. This book contributes to extending the reach of that lever by opening new avenues for exploring a very relevant topic represented by the emergence of an open perspective in the management of learning and innovation as drivers of value.

Mark Allen, Ph.D.
Malibu, California
October, 2008

Mark Allen, Ph.D., is the editor and co-author of *The Corporate University Handbook* and *The Next Generation of Corporate Universities*. He is on the faculty of Pepperdine University's Graziadio School of Business and Management.

Preface

Background and positioning

Business Innovation Leadership is the distinguishing and consolidated brand of the *Euro-Mediterranean Incubator* of *Business Innovation Leadership* at the Scuola Superiore ISUFI, to which the authors of this book belong. The brand is founded on the following pillars and characterizing values of the Incubator (Romano et al., 2001), which consist of:

- the scanning across different disciplines and industries to find emerging conditions, paradigm shifts and opportunities from the competitive landscape of the Net Economy;
- the search for an integration of the various frameworks to link strategic management and entrepreneurship theories of value creation;
- the redesign of organizations' educational environment to increase returns from networks of academic and industrial partners;
- the promotion of non-linear thinking and entrepreneurial behavior to recognize patterns and opportunities;
- the use of learning strategies and processes for knowledge-creation and leadership; and
- the creation of partnerships and strategic alliances with leading academic and business actors at national and international levels.

Why are we talking about *Open Business Innovation Leadership* now?

The key factors underlying the *Open Business Innovation Leadership* concept are value creation and intellectual capital development within boundary-less networks of individuals and organizations. The issues investigated in this book are the result of research activities in two areas at the *Incubator*: *Learning, Innovation and Value Network*; and *Open Networked Management*. The research addresses three areas: (1) developing social capital by addressing all relevant stakeholders; (2) creating value, beyond financial performance, which includes relationships, knowledge creation and innovation processes; and (3) human capital development and corporate learning processes.

What is driving the emergence of the Stakeholder University?

The affirmation of an *open* economy determined landmark transformations at different levels, such as production processes, forms of cooperation and competition, organizational structures and cultural models that have resulted in new challenges for the corporate world. In particular, the exponential growth of knowledge requires: (a) visions and cultural approaches that are no longer based on reductionism, but on cross-disciplinary and holistic approaches; (b) the strategic relevance of Intellectual Capital, and in particular, human capital for growth and competition; (c) non-linear dynamics of innovation as a driver of organic relationships among companies and universities; (d) the view of the Internet as a technological infrastructure of the knowledge economy; and (e) the awareness of deep changes in the demand of advanced education for both young and adult learners and workers, raising the relevance of life-long and "ubiquitous" learning processes.

The complexity of these issues requires a holistic approach to analyze the *creative destruction* effects on management mindsets and roles, human capital development processes and organizational models. It is necessary to address the growing interdependencies and the need of federative models among companies and their suppliers, customers, partners, employees and all the public and private stakeholders concerned in the success and sustainability of the organization. In line with this vision, the Stakeholder University is presented in this book as an emerging philosophy, strategy and model that can embed all those perspectives to drive the *Open Business Innovation Leadership* of organizations.

Target audience

Open Business Innovation Leadership: The Emergence of the Stakeholder University is a book targeting three categories of readers: (a) *business strategists* and *human resource managers*, providing them with a conceptual framework and a set of guidelines for the development of human capital as a key process to lead change in complex environments; (b) *academics* and *business schools*, through insights and best practices for redesigning curricula and learning processes in terms of new approaches to content delivery and competency development; and (c) *practitioners* and *consultants*, providing them with a holistic view of emerging trends in corporate learning, depicting the convergence of management education and the corporate world, and the emergence of the next-generation's learning organizations.

Key features

A key distinguishing feature of this book resides in the word "integration," in three senses:

a. integration of several *sources of evidence*, represented by an extended theory review, the analysis of authoritative industry reports, the study of exemplary company cases, a direct researchers' observation at the company site, and a survey made involving corporate learning and human resource managers;
b. integration of strategic management, organizational learning and technology management *perspectives* in defining the assumptions and the models proposed; and
c. integration of *contributions* provided represented by theoretical models and knowledge systematization, from one side, and guidelines for practitioners from the other side.

Structure and content

The structure of the book includes the following five chapters:

1. *Toward Open Business Innovation Leadership*
2. *The Emergence of a New Managerial Mindset*
3. *Networked Learning for Human Capital Development*
4. *Fostering Innovation by Nurturing Value-Creating Communities*
5. *The Emergence of the Stakeholder University*

The organization of the book follows the logic of preparing the overall rationale and conceptual frame of the *Open Business Innovation Leadership* paradigm (Chapter 1), providing the fundamental pillars and elements of discussion at cultural (Chapter 2), learning (Chapter 3) and organization levels (Chapter 4), with the ultimate objective of creating a definition of the Stakeholder University model (Chapter 5) that addresses the initial assumptions and objectives (arrows are used to represents these links).

Figure 0.1 shows a synthetic framework of chapters and the key issues investigated. A synopsis of each chapter follows.

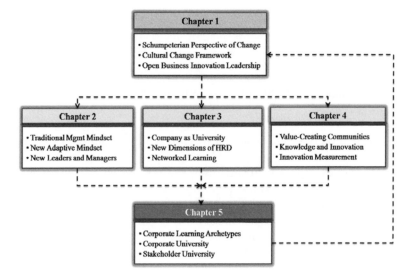

Figure 0.1   Chapters and key contents

In Chapter 1, *Toward Open Business Innovation Leadership*, Alessandro Margherita and Francesca Grippa introduce the key drivers and assumptions at the basis of defining a different cultural framework in management, and define the overall conceptual model. The abstract of the chapter follows.

The chapter starts by analyzing the concept of techno-economic paradigm, and in particular the Information and Communication paradigm, through a threefold economic, sociological and industrial perspective of changes emerged not only at the technology and production levels, but also at cultural level. Systemic changes are indeed referred to four key dimensional changes related to time (proliferation of real-time transactions and reduced life cycles), space (emergence of global business environment and virtual spaces), density (increased connectedness and networks among individuals and organizations), and diversity (emergence of self-organizing agents and closeness to the chaos). These transformations have dramatic effects on the strategic capabilities required to companies to be successful. We claim that a new set of assumptions about how to create value and a new management mindset are needed. These new assumptions should consider organizations as boundary-less, open networks of stakeholders aimed at developing intangibles assets and human capital through learning and innovation. We enclose this vision in a paradigm we call Open Business Innovation Leadership. The chapter provides the conceptual framework of the whole book that has been based on the exploration of key theory contributions as well as on the observation of leading companies (such as 3M, ABB, and Skandia). These are considered as examples of a new management style based on close attention to open communication and relationships, and to create networks of interdependences at individual, intra-organizational and inter-organizational levels.

Chapter 2, *The Emergence of a New Managerial Mindset*, by Aldo Romano, Marco De Maggio and Pasquale Del Vecchio, begins with an analysis of the dynamics that characterize today's markets and industries. The chapter then describes the need to go beyond the linear and deterministic approach to managing corporations.

This chapter focuses on the emergence of a new managerial mindset as the result of the evolution from a linear to a non-linear way of thinking. The disruptive impact of ICTs on the social, cultural and economic dimensions at the global scale required a radical rethinking of traditional management practices as well as of the ways of looking at the world and interpreting reality. The basic management challenge in the early years of the Industrial Revolution was the search for scientific principles for handling men, materials, capital and machines. The faith in a Newtonian and deterministic view of reality led to search the "one best way" for a job to be done or for management to be performed. The organization was conceived as a machine and the approach was clearly mechanistic and linear. A threat to this vision came from the recognition of an interrelatedness of processes and management skills within an organization and the resulting need for companies to adopt a more articulated, dynamic and holistic vision of management, and the need to move from scientific reductionism to embrace complex phenomena. Concepts such as self-organization, fitness and co-evolution become three dimensions of a new perspective on organization and business, and thus three dimensions of new management. The new managerial mindset is based on three key assumptions: a shift in company's goal, from efficiency and profitability to the search of a large space of options; the changing role of the manager, from "cardinal rational actor" to "coach"; and the emerging organizational form as a catalytic network.

Chapter 3, *Networked Learning for Human Capital Development*, by Giustina Secundo, Alessandro Margherita and Gianluca Elia, illustrates how companies transform their learning and human capital development strategies and models to fit the new competitive landscape, with a specific focus on networked learning as a creator of stakeholder value.

The chapter starts with an analysis of time, space, density and diversity-related changes in human capital development strategies and models of organizations. The chapter then investigates the emerging practices in human capital development as a strategic response of companies to fast-changing and hypercompetitive markets and industries. The primary assumption made is that, in parallel with their strategic objectives and actions, leading organizations are also transforming the way people's competencies are being developed. Human capital development processes are evolving to enhance the interconnections at intra and inter-organizational levels, along with the strategic focus and the scope of learning as a cause of competitiveness and value. This chapter addresses the centrality of learning and human capital development in leading companies that behave like educational institutions, to the point of referring to the company as a university. The changing dimensions of human capital development are described in terms of people, processes and strategic purpose that are leading toward the affirmation of new management roles and competency models, new management learning practices, and a wider perspective of learning in terms of focus, scope and interconnections. Finally, the paradigm of Networked Learning is investigated from a technological point of view.

Chapter 4, *Fostering Innovation by Nurturing Value-Creating Communities*, by Francesca Grippa, Attilio Di Giovanni and Giuseppina Passiante, provides a case-based response to the request for a definition of new approaches to developing social capital and new organizational models to stimulate the creativity and innovativeness of organizations.

Within a complex environment, change is endemic to survival and the dynamic capability to continuously learn becomes a critical success factor. Linear management models and hierarchical organizations based on command-and-control have to be replaced with emergent networks and self-organization. To innovate and reinvent the sources of value creation, the challenge for firms is to become learning organizations, acquiring the skills to learn from others and from past experiences at individual, team, organizational and inter-organizational levels. To pursue innovation in an open and systemic perspective, new organizational forms—such as communities of practice or communities of innovation—have demonstrated success in creating the level of flexibility and responsiveness required to continuously reinvent business and promote change. Innovative communities behave as integrated networks and implement a model of knowledge-creation emphasizing the roles of socialization, externalization, combination and internalization processes. The chapter addresses the emerging organizational forms fostering innovation and value creation, focusing on the concept of community. A combination of field-based and desk research is used to validate a conceptual framework and explain how the dynamic capability to continuously learn and share knowledge is at the basis of today's ability to succeed. These ideas are also illustrated through cases such as GE, 3M and Toyota. The case of Finmeccanica is studied—this is a leading Italian industrial group operating globally in the Aerospace, Defense, Energy, Transportation and Security sectors. The focus is on Mindsh@re, a corporate-wide project launched in 2003 with the goal of promoting technology sharing, network management and human capital development.

Chapter 5, *The Emergence of the Stakeholder University*, by Alessandro Margherita and Giustina Secundo, summarizes the main ideas and key assumptions and provides an analysis of the evolution of corporate learning archetypes. A specific focus is given to the Corporate University phenomenon and the emergence of the Stakeholder University as a model to drive Open Business Innovation Leadership.

This chapter begins with an analysis of the evolution of traditional corporate learning archetypes such as training departments, web learning platforms and corporate universities to embrace the key concepts of value creation and stakeholder focus. An analysis is proposed of the Corporate University phenomenon, using both desk and field research. Desk analysis is based on published studies and specialized market data coming from Corporate University Xchange benchmarking reports. Field investigation is founded on a survey of learning officers and other managers involved in corporate learning initiatives at about 50 companies. A set of key variables related to the corporate university are identified and explored to extract the new trends that are bringing to the emergence of a Stakeholder University model. This model has been adopted by leading companies such as Motorola, Cisco and Volkswagen as a strategic response to fast-changing and hypercompetitive markets and industries. The presence in the Stakeholder University of such features as openness, orientation to value creation, integration with strategic company purpose and connectedness with different stakeholders positions the Stakeholder University as enabler of Open Business Innovation Leadership. The chapter ends with a detailed design and implementation roadmap.

Feedback

We are interested in hearing your comments about this book. In times of proliferating management bibles, roadmaps and receipts for success, our objective is to share with the reader our belief that in management, as in life, everything starts with one's inspiring visions and assumptions. We hope you enjoy the journey.

Aldo Romano (aldo.romano@unile.it)
Lecce, August 2008

Notes on Contributors

Marco De Maggio holds a Ph.D. from the *Euro-Mediterranean Incubator* in Business Innovation Leadership of Scuola Superiore ISUFI—University of Salento (Italy), where he is currently a Researcher. In 2007, he was a visiting Ph.D. student at the MIT Sloan Center for Digital Business. His research concerns the development of methodologies for the analysis and management of learning patterns within organizations and communities of practice. Currently, he's involved in the development of an interdisciplinary approach and competence development models in higher and management education (e-mail: marco.demaggio@ebms. unile.it).

Pasquale Del Vecchio holds a Ph.D. from the *Euro-Mediterranean Incubator* in Business Innovation Leadership of Scuola Superiore ISUFI—University of Salento (Italy), where he is currently a Researcher. In 2007, he was a visiting Ph.D. student at the MIT Sloan Center for Digital Business. His research is focused on Social Network Analysis applications to virtual communities enabled by the use of Web 2.0 tools, mainly in Marketing. Currently, he's involved in research activities focused on interdisciplinary and competence-based learning approaches to Business Management (e-mail: pasquale.delvecchio@ ebms.unile.it).

Attilio Di Giovanni holds a Bachelor's Degree in Electric Engineering from the University of "La Sapienza" in Rome, Italy. He is Vice President of Technology Development for Finmeccanica Corporation. His main responsibilities are in the area of technology governance of the Finmeccanica Group. He's worked in management positions within the different companies of the Finmeccanica Group (e-mail: attilio. digiovanni@finmeccanica.com).

Gianluca Elia holds a MSc from the *Euro-Mediterranean Incubator* in Business Innovation Leadership of Scuola Superiore ISUFI—University of Salento (Italy), where he is the coordinator of the research activities in *Learning, Innovation and Value Network*. He is also a Researcher at the Faculty of Engineering of the University of Salento. His research is focused on innovative methodologies, strategies and tools to enhance collaborative learning. He's involved in the management of complex research projects, in collaboration with leading companies, universities and research centers. He had a major role in the design and implementation of the "Virtual eBMS," a technology platform integrating knowledge management and web learning applications. This platform was awarded the "Brandon Hall Research" prize in learning technology in 2006 (e-mail: gianluca.elia@ebms.unile.it).

Francesca Grippa holds a Ph.D. and a MSc from the *Euro-Mediterranean Incubator* in Business Innovation Leadership of Scuola Superiore ISUFI—University of Salento (Italy), where she is currently a Researcher. In 2005 and 2006, she was a visiting Ph.D. student at the MIT Sloan Center for Digital Business. Her research interests include the application of Social Network Analysis to business and learning communities (e-mail: francesca.grippa@ebms.unile.it).

Alessandro Margherita holds a Ph.D. and a MSc from the *Euro-Mediterranean Incubator* in Business Innovation Leadership of Scuola Superiore ISUFI—University of Salento (Italy), where currently he is a Researcher. His research activities have a cross-disciplinary business and technology management focus. He has an interest in the fields of organizational change based on technology adoption and process redesign, and organizational development through learning and competency growth. He's involved in the design and experimentation of innovative methodologies, models and technology platforms to support higher education and corporate learning processes. He also collaborates with the MIT Sloan Center for Digital Business, where he was visiting Ph.D. student in 2006 (e-mail: alessandro.margherita@ebms.unile.it).

Giuseppina Passiante is Full Professor of Innovation Management at the Department of Innovation Engineering of the University of Salento (Italy). She is coordinator of the research area on *Open Networked Business Management* at the Euro-Mediterranean Incubator in Business Innovation Leadership of Scuola Superiore ISUFI—University of Salento (Italy). Currently her research fields concern the management of learning organizations and learning processes in the Net-Economy. Her focus is mainly on the development of Intellectual Capital, both in entrepreneurial and academic organizations. She is also expert in the development of local systems, and complexity in economic systems.

In these research fields she has realized programs and projects, and published several papers (e-mail: giuseppina.passiante@unile.it).

Aldo Romano (Editor and author) is Full Professor of Innovation Management at the Faculty of Engineering and Director of the Euro-Mediterranean Incubator in Business Innovation Leadership of Scuola Superiore ISUFI at the University of Salento (Lecce, Italy). He is also President of DHITECH, a Technological District in the Apulia region and former President of the Italian Technical-Scientific Commission. Aldo Romano's activities have three general areas:

- Research in High Energy Physics at the Department of Physics at University of Bologna and University of Bari (Italy). He has participated in numerous scientific experiments at the European Organization for Nuclear Research (CERN) in Geneva.
- Scientific, cultural, and political commitment to the development of innovation, especially in the south of Italy. In 1981, as Visiting Professor at the Stanford University (California—USA), he studied the phenomenon of Silicon Valley. This experience represented the basis for the foundation of the First Italian Scientific and Technological Park (Tecnopolis Novus Ortus) in 1984.
- Scientific and operative commitment to issues concerning Internet-enabled organizational changes, with special reference to the analysis of the "Digital Divide." This scientific activity has been documented in different books, among which *Creating Business Innovation Leadership* (2001) presents the context and scientific background of the present volume.

Aldo Romano is the author of many books and publications in international journals and leading conference proceedings. In acknowledgment of his scientific achievements, Aldo Romano has been awarded the Gold Medal of Merit for Culture, School and Arts from the President of the Italian Republic.

Giustina Secundo holds a MSc from the *Euro-Mediterranean Incubator* in Business Innovation Leadership of Scuola Superiore ISUFI—University of Salento (Italy), where she is currently a Researcher. Her research interest concerns the emerging trends in management education and human capital creation process in business schools and corporations, with a special focus on the evolution of corporate university phenomenon. She's currently involved in the design and experimentation of innovative methodologies and technology platforms to support higher education and corporate learning processes. These research activities are strictly connected to her involvement in the management of the advanced education programs of the *Incubator,* which involve students coming from Tunisia, Morocco and Jordan (e-mail: giusy.secundo@ebms. unile.it).

1

Toward Open Business Innovation Leadership

Alessandro Margherita and Francesca Grippa

1.1 Introduction

In the last three decades, the transformation processes experienced by industrialized countries radically changed the international economic and social structure. A relatively new approach to interpret and frame the meaning of these changes is provided by the neo-Schumpeterian analysis. This field of the economic literature investigates the dynamic processes of qualitative transformation of economies that are driven by the introduction of various forms of innovations. In particular, the neo-Schumpeterian view assumes the centrality of large technological innovations in determining the dynamics of economic and social systems, and offers tools for understanding long-term fluctuations (Dosi et al., 1988).

Every transformation process results from a progressive emergence and affirmation of a new techno-economic paradigm that defines the "meta-routines" for the economy. A techno-economic paradigm is "a shared common sense model of best technical and organizational practice for the use of that set of pervasive technologies, which provides a generalized quantum jump in productivity and quality" (Perez, 2007, p. 778). What differentiates a technological revolution from a single radical innovation is its pervasive nature and potential to go beyond specific industries, providing generic technologies that transform the entire economic structure. The rise of a new techno-economic paradigm determines the emergence of an interrelated set of innovations at different levels such as production, organizational structures and cultural models.

In the analysis of such large-scale transformations in a modern economy, a particularly relevant interpretative role can be associated to

1

the theory of long waves introduced by the Russian economist Nikolai Kondratieff (1926) to describe regular, sinusoidal and fifty/sixty-year long cycles in the capitalist economy. In the 1930s, Joseph Schumpeter leveraged on Kondratieff's analysis to suggest how, according to the innovation theory, long waves arise from a set of basic innovations that initiate technological revolutions that in turn create leading industrial sectors (Schumpeter, 1934). The decline of industries and forms of employment, accompanied by a process of structural adaptation, represents the core of Schumpeter's theory of long waves in economic development. The long wave theory has been enriched by the contribution of authoritative scholars belonging to the neo-Schumpeterian stream such as Dosi (1982), Freeman and Perez (1988), and Freemen and Soete (1999).

There are some relevant issues that distinguish the original analysis of Kondratieff from Schumpeter's thought, and further, from the renewed insights of neo-Schumpeterian scholars. Understanding this evolution is particularly relevant for the purposes of our investigation.

In Kondratieff's studies, the occurrence of long waves in the world economy in terms of movements in economic variables is not explicitly associated with the role of technical change. In his analysis, the economist only suggested that when a major cycle of economic expansion was underway, inventions that had remained *dormant* could find new applications. The interpretation provided later by Schumpeter is somehow in contrast in that he associated the fluctuations in business activity to the innovation process that was essentially discontinuous due to the nature of entrepreneurial activity. The variations in fluctuations between short, intermediate, and long cycles are thus caused by the varying impacts of different types of innovations. In particular, long cycles are associated with fluctuations in basic innovations (such as steam engine and electricity) that cause surges of investment associated with the *bandwagon* effects of the diffusion of new technologies. The simultaneously creative and destructive effects of technological innovation lead to imbalances and cyclical phenomena in the economy. Economic growth is thus not simply accompanied by the introduction of new products and processes, but it is instead driven by these innovations, and technical change is endogenous to economic progress rather than a marginal and exogenous factor. In his definition of economic development as "the carrying out of new combinations," Schumpeter (1934) presented five "cases" represented by new goods, new methods of production, new markets, new sources of supply, and new organizations of industry. The concept of "new combination" is essentially a matter of organizing ideas and activities into a new configuration. Schumpeter stressed the disruptive character of capitalist enterprise and observed how these new combinations are usually embodied in firms, even though he does not offer deeper analysis of the organization of these new businesses.

Neo-Schumpeterian economists emphasize the role of diffusion of major technological breakthroughs in stimulating economic growth and exhausting older technological systems. New techno-economic paradigms represent systemic changes that are so far-reaching in their effects that they lead to a series of interrelated technological changes and associated effects such as drastic reductions in the cost of many products and services and marked improvements of their features. The diffusion of these innovations involves a complex interplay between technological, economic and socio-political forces. A new techno-economic paradigm can be thus conceived as a "meta-paradigm" (Castells, 2000) that has a dominant influence on the strategies and operations of firms, leading to a reorientation of industrial organization and management.

The effects of the emergence of a new techno-economic paradigm require a multi-perspective analysis of the phenomenon. In the following part of this chapter we refer to three contributions framing three perspectives: that of innovation economists, as described by Freeman and Perez (1988); the sociological perspective provided by Castells (2000); and the industrial economics perspective, as illustrated by Dunning (1997). The following table (Table 1.1) synthesizes the contributions described above.

Among neo-Schumpeterians, the contribution given by the work of Christopher Freeman and Carlota Perez (1988) is particularly relevant. The authors provide an *innovation economics* view when they refer

Table 1.1 A multi-perspective view of techno-economic paradigms

Perspective	Contribution	Key concepts
Economics of Innovation	Freeman and Perez, 1988	• systemic innovation • innovation principles
Sociology	Castells, 2000	• informationalism • network society • collapse of time and space
Industrial Economics	Dunning, 1997	• evolution of capitalism • structuralist-evolutionary view • global industries

to a techno-economic paradigm as to a combination of interrelated products and processes, and technical, organizational and managerial innovations. These innovations are able to cause quantum jumps in productivity and create a wide range of investment and profit-making opportunities. In this sense, Kondratieff cycles are not an exclusive economic phenomenon, but the expression (measurable in economic terms) of changes in the behavior of the entire socioeconomic and institutional system that affects cultural models and assumptions. This consideration represents a key principle adopted in our analysis.

Freeman and Perez identified five long cycles, associated with five different techno-economic paradigms: early mechanization (1770–1830); steam power (1830–80); heavy engineering (1880–1930); Fordism (1930–80); and the Information and Communication Technologies (1980–present). The evolution of the different cycles is investigated by the two economists by describing how a set of key variables have been transforming over time, such as key production factors, forms of organization, cooperation and competition, technological leaders, national/international regulatory regimes, and also the presence of innovative entrepreneurs, engineers, political economists and philosophers. With reference to these variables, the *Information and Communication Technology* paradigm is characterized by the following key features:

- computers, robotics, telecom and electronics as main sectors;
- information as key production factor and microchips as key resource;
- pervasiveness of information technologies and their effects;
- systems/process flexibility and networking as key organizational logic;
- integration of services and manufacturing;
- horizontal integration, factory as laboratory, collaborative research;
- Japan and USA as leaders, emerging Latin America countries;
- Schumacher as an example of a philosopher and Kobayashi as an innovator.

Carlota Perez (2007) describes the "quantum jump in productivity and quality" as an integrated effort to overcome the resistance of those who had adopted and practiced within the previous paradigm. As a result of the emergence of a new paradigm, "common sense innovation principles" arise. Table 1.2 shows the interrelated set of new technologies, industries, infrastructures and innovation principles/routines that have emerged as a consequence of the new techno-economic paradigm.

Table 1.2 Industries, infrastructures and paradigms of the new technological revolution

New technologies and new/redefined industries	New/redefined infrastructures	Innovation principles/routines
• Cheap microelectronics • Computers, software • Telecommunications control instruments • Computer aided biotechnology and new materials	• World digital telecommunications (cable, fiberoptics, radio and satellite) • Internet/Electronic mail and other e-services • Multiple source, flexible use, electricity networks • High speed physical transport links	• Information—intensity (micro-electronics based ICT) • Decentralized integration/network structures • Knowledge as capital/intangible value added • Heterogeneity, diversity, adaptability • Segmentation of markets/proliferation of niches • Economies of scope and specialization combined with scale • Globalization/interaction between the global and the local • Inward and outward co-operation/clusters • Instant contact and action/instant global communications

Source: Adapted from Perez (2007).

Like other technological revolutions, Information and Communication Technology determined the emergence of a new organizational logic applied within existing, redefined and new industries and markets. The surge of development propagated after each technological revolution is the product of the continuing essential transformation of both the techno-economic and the socio-institutional spheres of the social system. Thus, a "quantum jump" emerges as consequence of the process by which a technological revolution and its techno-economic paradigm spread across the economy, generating structural changes in production, distribution and consumption, generating profound societal and cultural changes.

The great transformations in production and economic models and structures are not the unique effects caused by the affirmation of a new paradigm. The emergence of new thought leaders and philosophers is indeed one of the signs of the pervasive impact of innovation on the entire economic, social and cultural system. There is a need to consider a *sociological perspective* in the analysis of change as well. In his landmark work on the Network Society, Manuel Castells (2000) illustrates a multidimensional revolution and the rise of a new mode of development referred to as "informationalism." Castells went beyond the investigation of the role of globalization in making the different world economies work as a unique entity in real time and the role of efficient knowledge elaboration and application as determinant of productivity and competitiveness of economic agents. The rationale of the network society resides in the fact that networks become the prevalent form of organization of economic and human activities and a global net of interconnections among individuals and institutions take shape and are continually developed, determining a set of related effects:

- economic activities become organized and managed on a global scale;
- alliances are the fundamental form for competing;
- workplace and processes become increasingly flexible and dynamic;
- a culture of *virtuality* emerges based on pervasive, interconnected, and diversified technologies; and
- fundamental assumptions about life, space and time change significantly.

Information and Communication and network paradigms give rise to a new socio-economic system, characterized by a different role of companies and organizations, and a distinct set of relationships and interdependencies among suppliers, customers and partners, as well as among employers and employees. This new scenario also entails sweeping changes in social institutions, culture and personal values.

The properties of the new techno-economic paradigm leads to the emergence of new, decentralized organizational structures enabled by technology, but centered on human values. At the same time, the "gale of creative destruction" will lead to a shift from "command-and-control" management to "coordinate-and-cultivate," requiring new skills to succeed (Malone, 2004). Just as the printing press allowed a larger number people to participate in the politics of their times, so will communications technologies and the Internet enable workers to perform their jobs acting as more active decision-makers.

We discussed so far the innovation economics and the sociology perspective. A third dimension we mentioned at the outset is

Table 1.3 Phases of evolution in modern capitalism

Dimension	Entrepreneurial capitalism	Hierarchical capitalism	Flexible capitalism
Period	*(1770–1875)*	*(1875–1980)*	*(1980–present)*
Markets	small, fragmented, local	national/international	global and integrated
Cooperation and Competition	single entrepreneurs, small companies	oligopoly	dynamism and hyper-competition
Organization	small organizations	hierarchies	strategic alliances
Key Resource	natural resources	physical capital	tangible/intangible assets
Asset Mobility	low	medium	high for firm-specific assets
Government Role	limited involvement	welfare state	participation and support
Cross-national Integration	financial markets	discontinuous	high interconnection
Hegemonic Power	UK	USA	None

the *industrial economics view*. At this purpose, the analysis of Dunning (1997) provides some insightful considerations about the emergence of a different concept and practice of capitalism. The new capitalism, flexible and based on alliances, is sensibly different from that of only 30 years ago. Dunning identified three main stages in this evolution (Table 1.3): the phase of *entrepreneurial capitalism* (characterized by the presence of small and independent companies); *hierarchical capitalism* (big companies driven by mass production and economies of scale); and *flexible capitalism* (networks of innovation-driven companies operating at national, regional and global levels).

Flexible, or *alliance* capitalism, is founded on the adoption of ICT and specifically on the Internet as socio-technological platform and is characterized by the following features:

- presence of global, dynamic and hypercompetitive markets;
- networks of companies based on strategic alliances;
- key resources are intangible assets such as knowledge and people competencies;
- low mobility for location-specific assets and high mobility for firm-specific assets;

- less regulation-oriented governments supporting markets;
- high cross-regional and cross-organizational integration; and
- no hegemonic power of countries.

The perspective of modern business as networks of alliances is one of the conceptual pillars of this book. Another interesting characterization about new capitalism is also provided by Castells: "this is a brand of capitalism that is at the same time very old and fundamentally new. It is old because it appeals to relentless competition in the pursuit of profit, and individual satisfaction (deferred or immediate) is its driving engine. But it is fundamentally new because it is tooled by new information and communication technologies that are at the roots of new productivity sources, of new organizational forms, and of the formation of a global economy" (Castells, 1999, p. 10).

In his book *The Future of Work*, Thomas Malone (2004) proposed a parallel between the evolution of society throughout history, going from decentralized and unconnected bands to centralized kingdoms to decentralized and connected democracies, with the evolution of businesses in the 20th century. The early decades of the 1900s were characterized by small and local businesses and, around 1950, there was an emergence of large and centralized corporations. The way of doing business in the new millennium is through mechanisms such as empowerment, outsourcing and networked organizations that allow higher complexity management through increased interdependence. Each stage requires more communication and more coordination efforts and has potential benefits over previous periods (Malone, 2004).

In the new capitalism emerging in the age of the Internet, businesses are growing decentralized, building newer environments where "workers seek advice instead of approval." Empowered by new technologies, knowledge workers have the opportunity to be part of important decisions.

The emergence of the Information and Communication paradigm, the rise of a network society and the evolution toward the flexible or alliance capitalism represent three phases of a unique phenomenon: the affirmation of a new era in the world economy and business. In particular, we want to highlight here the impact that these structural changes have in terms of competitive principles and drivers. A recent contribution here comes from Tapscott and Williams (2006), who identified in openness, peering, sharing and acting globally the new principles that inspire today's competitive paradigm. Besides, factors like faster technology changes, shortening product life cycles and converging industry boundaries change the *strategic capabilities* that are relevant as drivers of

competitive advantage and leadership. In particular, today it is fundamental for organizations to:

- anticipate and adapt readily to environmental changes;
- accelerate the development of new products, processes and services;
- expedite the transfer of individual and organizational knowledge;
- learn more effectively from the past and from the environment;
- shorten the time needed to implement strategic changes;
- stimulate continuous improvement organization-wide;
- attract best human resource and constantly develop people at all levels; and
- stimulate commitment and creativity.

Organizational capabilities are also founded on the ability to define
simple strategies with limited number of guidelines that focus attention
and efforts into specific directions to face complex business environments and dynamics (Eisenhardt and Sull, 2001). There are several
cases of companies leading the change by adopting strategic approaches
based on simple rules like Cisco's "boundaries rules" for acquiring new
companies (it must have no more than 75 employees, and 75% of
them have to be engineers). Competing in a diversified and complex
landscape requires a strategy that is "diverse." Microsoft, for example,
adopted a dynamic strategy that does not follow Porter's approach of
"do an industry analysis, pick a strategic position and execute." It does
not even mirror the resource-based view that teaches to "examine the
core competencies and build off of them." Its unpredictable and proactive strategy looks more similar to the "creation of relentless flow of
competitive advantages" that are connected together to form a semicoherent strategic direction (Eisenhardt and Sull, 2001).

Developing these capabilities requires a new perspective about
economy and business, and a new set of assumptions about how to be
successful. A *different cultural mindset* is needed that embraces the ability to compete on the edge, to enhance the processes of individual and
organizational learning, and to pursue a logic of stakeholder value creation as the real foundation of success.

1.2   Setting the frame for new cultural frontiers in management

In the emerging business realm, markets and companies both contribute to enacting processes of creative destruction and the rise of
a completely new role of companies in society, new relationships

employers-employees, and new functions and roles of management itself. This asks for a redefinition of current dominant cultural models about key aspects such as business purpose and value creation. We try here to apply the Schumpeterian perspective and the threefold view about change described in the previous section.

Historically, the Schumpeterian view has been mostly ignored in discussions focused on development policies in management. The need to investigate new cultural frontiers in the analysis of development and innovation is an issue previously debated (Romano and Passiante, 1996); in particular, the importance of cross-cultural and cross-disciplinary approaches to analyze technology, society, organization and economy as a holistic phenomenon.

In our attempt to define a roadmap for developing a new cultural mindset, we move from the analysis of relevant changes related to four key dimensions of the economic and business scenery: *time, space, density* and *diversity*.

Time (narrowing): Economic and business activities are more and more characterized by real-time transactions enabled by ICT; moreover, the frequency of changes is increased by reduced life cycles of technology and innovation, resulting in reduced life cycles of products, markets and key competencies of people.

Space (widening): The scope and geographical distribution of economic and human activities causes the emergence of a truly global business environment; "virtual spaces" and organizational proximity take the physical place, reducing the boundaries among agents and organizations. Estimates suggest that between 20 percent and 25 percent of research & development activities undertaken by the largest global corporations are located outside their home countries. At the same time, as companies' intangible assets have increased their mobility across national borders, the location of their creation and use is more and more influenced by the presence of "spatially immobile clusters of complementary value-added activities." The new globalized economy is characterized by the paradox of the presence of "sticky places within slippery space" (Dunning, 1997).

Density (widening): The increased interconnections inside and among organizations determines the appearance of integrated networks as the most innovation-oriented organizational structures. Business processes are increasingly more interconnected between firms, regions, and countries, in a boundaryless space in which "networks of locations are more important than hierarchies of places" (Castells, 2000). Firms recognize the importance of being interconnected to achieve a sustainable advantage, as the case of Toyota demonstrates. Toyota and its suppliers have implemented a "dynamic learning capability" and learn at a faster rate than competitors. Toyota has created a strong network identity with rules for participation and entry into the network, motivating members to share important knowledge while preventing spillovers to competitors and free-riding (Dyer and Nobeoka, 2000).

Diversity (widening): The proliferation of diversified and self-organizing agents and organizations with highly specific and independent behavior causes the emergence of a complex economic and business scenario whose state in many cases can be considered close to the chaos. As demonstrated by the emergence of business ecosystems, agents co-evolve their capabilities and roles in an economic community supported by interactions among individuals and organizations including suppliers, lead producers, competitors and other stakeholders (Moore, 1993).

Assuming this four-dimension framework as our reading lens, concepts such as ICT, reduced life cycles, real-time and global business processes, virtual spaces, interconnections, networks, self-organizing agents and chaos provide the key *conceptual framework* in which we investigate the evolution of economy, organizations, society, and the dominant management culture. In parallel with the affirmation of a new techno-economic paradigm, we highlight here the emergence of a new cultural paradigm: the evolution from a traditional mindset, based on closed and hierarchical organizations aimed at appropriating value and tangible assets as key success factors, toward a new managerial mindset that considers organizations as boundary-less and open networks that create value and develop human and social capital as the foundation of success.

In the analysis of this evolution in managerial culture and assumptions, it is of relevance to mention the concept of *visible hand*, introduced by Alfred Chandler (1977) as a response to the *invisible hand* of Smith (1776) to describe the managerial revolution related to the emergence of the modern large-scale business enterprise and its professional management. The underlying assumption was that the world is linear, static and highly rational. From this perspective, there is one best way of solving problems and a set of tools are available for managers whose decisions, actions and the related effects are thus pretty much *visible* and recognizable. Following this logic, key principles are technical and professional hierarchies, managerial hierarchy, administrative coordination, economies of scale, evaluation of financial performance, separation between shareholders (short term financial expectations) and managers (long term development).

This Newtonian (deterministic and based on cause-effect relationships) view of the world has given shape to a paradigm that for many decades has oriented management meaning and practice, a management paradigm based on the rigid definition of organizational strategies, structures and systems (Ghoshal and Bartlett, 1997). The linear way of thinking about management is no longer acceptable and this results also in a growing interest in the application to management of complexity, chaos, quantum physics and biology theories (Baets, 2006; Clippinger, 1999). A distinguishing feature of highly flexible firms is a change culture that helps resisting to functional specialization that restricts the flow of ideas and reduces the sense of commonality of purpose (Teece, 2000). A statement by the CEO of Intel, Andy Grove, represents this spirit and the need for organizational flexibility that highlights the need for organizations to anticipate the unexpected and make order from the disorder, planning in a way to shape a flexible organization that is capable of responding to unpredictable events (Burgelman and Grove, 2007).

Companies are asked not merely to adjust or adapt as in the past but to confront the need for transformational changes, overcoming the logic of restructuring and engineering that is still dominant in the current managerial mindset. The emerging cultural framework is based on the recognized centrality of pursuing a consistent strategic purpose, enhancing human capital potential and process excellence. From companies viewed in market terms as closed economic entities focused on efficiency, the new vision of company is in organizational terms as a social institution focused on innovation and collaboration to create value for its network of stakeholders. Peoples' competencies, initiative and creativity become a cornerstone of success, as well as the integration of distributed knowledge and expertise in a process of continuous organizational learning and action (Ghoshal and Bartlett, 1997).

Providing people with the tools to be "more intelligent" enables individuals, groups and organizations to connect to a widening circle of others. Despite this potential growth of productivity, different studies on teleworking have shown that such technological changes may produce mixed results: they lead to higher levels of productivity, improved working-time arrangements and new employment opportunities; but at the same time they might create more isolation, marginalization and stress for others.

In this book, we enclose this vision in a paradigm we define as *Open Business Innovation Leadership*. The theoretical foundation of this idea is represented by our previous attempt to define a holistic framework for the innovation of the business concept, that we defined "Business Innovation Leadership." The underlying assumption of this framework, and the evolution toward a wider perspective of openness and value creation as foundations of leadership, are described in details in the next section.

1.3   Toward open business innovation leadership

The purpose of defining a new business management and leadership paradigm as a response to pervasive organizational and technological changes is not new for us. In this endeavor, we moved from a consideration: the new competitive environment, and especially the centrality of innovation management as the striking feature of contemporary business, presents a challenge to conventional theories and requires new interpretative approaches proposing a shift in the unit of analysis of innovation that becomes the holistic view of the business itself rather than simply a product, a process or a technology (Hamel, 2000).

To this end, we introduced the concept of *Business Innovation Leadership* (Romano, Elia and Passiante, 2001) that is the capability to exploit the business opportunities deriving from technology and innovation, by reconfiguring the strategic assets of the organization, and particularly the components of Intellectual Capital, that is, human, structural and social capital. This formulation was based on a set of background assumptions.

First, we considered how the need for a holistic business innovation framework integrates a "technological" view (Kalakota and Robinson, 2001) with an "organizational" (Venkatraman and Henderson, 1998) and a "strategic management" view (Eisenhardt and Sull, 2001). From this perspective, we moved from the analysis of factors such as the explosion of digital connectivity and the rapid emergence of universal standards for communication that have boosted the Schumpeterian "creative destruction process" (Schumpeter, 1934). The role of the Internet as a general purpose technology or platform technology (McKnight, Vaaler and Katz, 2001) has been investigated as the main driver of the New or Internet Economy, defined as an innovation-driven economy. In the new economic and business scenery, innovation is ubiquitous and the key strategic challenge is managing and leading it. The essence of the firm in the Internet Economy is the ability to create, transfer, assemble, integrate, protect and exploit knowledge assets. Knowledge management processes can be seen as a "dynamic capability" of a firm, its ability to reconfigure and protect knowledge, competence and complementary assets and technologies to achieve sustainable competitive advantage (Teece, 2000). A fundamental organizational issue we analyzed is the importance of linking the innovation potential and the effectiveness of change management of an organization with the leadership attitude inside the organization. Change and leadership are indeed inseparable since leadership is the ability of people in an organization to initiate and to sustain significant change and to work effectively with the forces that shape change (Senge, 2000). Leadership is about constant development and innovation and it is the capacity to create intangible assets and deploy them inside the organization (Skyrme, 2000). Finally, from a strategic management point of view, we assumed the importance of organizational flexibility as the ability to compete on the edge (Eisenhardt and Brown, 1998) and locate constantly changing sources of advantage rather than strategizing on clear industry boundaries or competition.

From the formulation of Business Innovation Leadership in 2001, many relevant contributions have highlighted the centrality of principles such as collaboration, distributed knowledge and leadership, and learning interrelations among individuals and organizations as the pillars of a boundary-less perspective of value creation. "Open Innovation" (Chesbrough, 2006b), illustrates that because useful knowledge is no longer concentrated in a few large organizations, business leaders must adopt a new, "open" model of innovation and look outside their boundaries for ideas and intellectual property they can bring in. "Open Business Models" (Chesbrough, 2006a), makes one step further by explaining how to make money in an open innovation landscape, also leveraging on compelling examples such as Procter & Gamble (Connect and Develop initiative) and IBM. In "Wikinomics," Tapscott and Williams (2006) provide a case-based description of the new economic landscape that they characterize as based on four main principles: openness, sharing, peering and global acting. The larger picture in which these contributions are positioned is the emergence of a new technological and sociological paradigm described under the paradigm of Web 2.0 and which represented a real revolution for the traditional equilibrium in business and human activities worldwide.

The transformation of world business in the sense of an increasing openness of production, decision making, knowledge sharing and creation, innovation and leadership processes suggested us to incorporate in the concept of Business Innovation Leadership three important characterizations that address the concerns of this book:

1. The need for organizations and managers to develop a new mindset that incorporates the changing competitive paradigms, strategic levers and drivers of success.
2. The need of a new perspective about human capital development in terms of peoples' competencies and roles, learning processes and approaches, and ultimate strategic purpose to pursuit.
3. The recognized centrality for an organization to develop social capital and stakeholder value by adopting an integrated organizational learning and innovation model.

Open Business Innovation Leadership can thus be defined as the *strategic capability of an organization to create sustainable value for its stakeholders based on networked innovation, learning and human capital development processes. Ultimately, Open Business Innovation Leadership is the key driver of stakeholder value creation and it can also be conceived as Stakeholder Value Leadership.*

This book has the ultimate purpose of discussing the three distinguishing aspects of Open Business Innovation Leadership and integrating them with the Stakeholder University model, which we identify as an integrative perspective. The next section concludes this chapter and introduces the research questions that are posited in the remaining parts of the book.

1.4 Conclusion

The emergence of a new techno-economic paradigm determines transforming changes that can be investigated at the economic, industrial and sociological levels. From a Schumpeterian perspective, the introduction of a new structure results in a process of creative destruction whose main concern, in the economic and business context, relates to the emergence of new organizational models, competitive paradigms and a different cultural mindset. Today's business realm registers a new role for companies in society, new relationships among employers and employees, and new functions and roles of management itself. In the frame of the stakeholder-oriented and value-creating organization, we thus posit the following key questions that will elucidate our study:

- *Which new managerial cultures and mindsets are emerging as a response to major changes in economy and business?*

- *How are corporate learning and human capital development processes evolving to incorporate a value-creation and stakeholder-oriented focus?*
- *Which are the new organizational forms that can foster innovation and value creation in companies?*
- *How have corporate learning models evolved to enhance focus, scope and interconnections, giving rise to the emergence of the Stakeholder University?*

The answer to these questions is based on both an extended review of relevant literature and the analysis of success cases. In particular, we focus on the exemplary cases of organizations (such as McKinsey, Motorola, 3M, Skandia, Andersen, Kao, ABB) that recognize the importance of investing in people, through an intelligent collection of human resources and a view of companies as "universities" (Ghoshal and Bartlett, 1997). These organizations facilitate flows of information to better support productivity and innovation, enhance lateral knowledge-sharing based on trust, openness, equity, and shared values, create continuous value through innovation and collaboration, create integrated networks to sustain collective intelligence, enhance relationships employers-employees, and pursuit process excellence. These cases are representative of a successful style of management that includes close attention to open communication and relationships, and to creating webs of interdependences at individual, intra-organizational and inter-organizational levels. Besides the analysis of literature and cases, a direct researcher observation and a survey involving corporate managers provided the theoretical and empirical foundation of our analysis.

The next chapters will explore concepts such as management function and roles, individual and organizational learning, innovation communities and networks, and human and social capital development. In this chapter we provided the overall picture in which all those issues are positioned and to prepare the grounds for an exploration that we hope to be stimulating and insight-building.

References

W. R. J. Baets (2006) *Complexity, Learning and Organizations: A Quantum Interpretation of Business* (London, UK and New York, NY: Routledge).

R. A. Burgelman and A. S. Grove (2007) "Let Chaos Reign, Then Rein in Chaos—Repeatedly: Managing Strategic Dynamics for Corporate Longevity," *Strategic Management Journal*, 28(10) pp. 965–79.

M. Castells (2000) *The Rise of the Network Society* (London, UK: Blackwell).

M. Castells (1999) "Information Technology, Globalization and Social Development," UNRISD Discussion Paper, 114.

A. D. Chandler (1977) *The Visible Hand: The Managerial Revolution in American Business* (Boston, MA: Belknap Press).

H. Chesbrough (2006a) *Open Business Models: How to Thrive in the New Innovation Landscape* (Boston, MA: HBS Press).

H. Chesbrough (2006b) *Open Innovation: The New Imperative for Creating and Profiting from Technology* (Boston, MA: HBS Press).

J. H. Clippinger (1999) *The Biology of Business: Decoding the Natural Laws of Enterprise* (San Francisco, CA: Jossey Bass Publishers).

G. Dosi (1982) "Technological Paradigms and Technological Trajectories," *Research Policy*, 2(3) pp. 147–62.

G. Dosi, C. Freeman, R. Nelson, G. Silverberg and L. Soete (eds) (1988) *Technical Change and Economic Theory* (London, UK: Columbia University Press).

J. Dunning (1997) *Alliance Capitalism and Global Business* (New York, NY: Routledge).

H. J. Dyer and K. Nobeoka (2000) "Creating and Managing a High Performance Knowledge-Sharing Network: The Toyota Case," *Strategic Management Journal*, 21(3) pp. 345–67.

K. M. Eisenhardt and S. L. Brown (1998) *Competing on the Edge. Strategy as Structured Chaos* (Boston, MA: HBS Press).

K. M. Eisenhardt and D. N. Sull (2001) "Strategy as Simple Rules," *Harvard Business Review*, January, pp. 107–16.

C. Freeman and C. Perez (1988) "Structural Crisis of Adjustment. Business Cycles and Investment Behavior," in G. Dosi, C. Freeman , R. Nelson, G. Silverberg and L. Soete (eds) *Technical Change and Economic Theory* (London, UK: Columbia University Press).

C. Freeman and L. G. Soete (1999) *The Economics of Industry Innovation* (Boston, MA: MIT Press).

S. Ghoshal and C. A. Bartlett (1997) *The Individualized Corporation* (New York, NY: Harper Collins).

G. Hamel (2000) *Leading the Revolution* (Boston, MA: HBS Press).

R. Kalakota and M. Robinson (2001) *E-Business 2.0: Roadmap for Success* (Boston, MA: Addison-Wesley-Longman Inc.).

N. D. Kondratieff (1926) "Die Langen Wellen der Konjunctur," *Archiv für Sozialwissenschaft und Sozialpolitik*, 56(3) pp. 573–609.

J. F. Moore (1993) "Predators and Prey: A New Ecology of Competition," *Harvard Business Review*, 71(3) pp. 75–86.

T. W. Malone (2004) *The Future of Work* (Boston, MA: HBS Press).

L. W. McKnight, P. M. Vaaler and R. L. Katz (2001) *Creative Destruction* (Boston, MA: MIT Press).

C. Perez (2007) "Finance and Technical Change: A Long-Term View," in H. Hanusch and A. Pyka (eds) *The Elgar Companion to Neo-Schumpeterian Economics* (Cheltenham, UK: Elgar).

A. Romano and G. Passiante (1996) *Il Mezzogiorno Chiama Schumpeter* (Roma: RIREA).

A. Romano, V. Elia and G. Passiante (2001) *Creating Business Innovation Leadership: An Ongoing Experiment* (Napoli: Edizioni Scientifiche Italiane).

J. A. Schumpeter (1934) *The Theory of Economic Development: An Inquiry into Profits, Capital, Credit, Interest, and the Business Cycle* (Boston, MA: HBS Press).

P. Senge (2000) "Reflection on a Leader's New Work: Building Learning Organizations," in D. Morey, M. Maybury and B. Thuraisingham (eds) *Knowledge Management: Classic and Contemporary Works* (Boston, MA: MIT Press) pp. 53–59.

D. J. Skyrme (2000), "Developing a Knowledge Strategy: From Management to Leadership," in D. Morey, M. Maybury and B. Thuraisingham (eds) *Knowledge Management: Classic and Contemporary Works* (Boston, MA: MIT Press) pp. 61–83.

D. Tapscott and A. D. Williams (2006) *Wikinomics* (London, UK: Portfolio).

D. J. Teece (2000) *Managing Intellectual Capital* (Oxford, UK: Oxford University Press).

N. Venkatraman and N. Henderson (1998) "Real Strategies for Virtual Organizing," *Sloan Management Review*, 40(1) pp. 33–48.

2
The Emergence of a New Managerial Mindset

Aldo Romano, Marco De Maggio and Pasquale Del Vecchio

2.1   Introduction

The last two centuries have been marked by many significant paradigm shifts, related to changes in concepts and their interpretations.

Several technological innovations made production and communication more efficient, and allowed a wide network of interactions among people, organizations and systems to grow and spread worldwide. A complex "system of systems" (Heylighen et al., 2006) was built, characterized by interdependence among the economic, social, technological and ecological dimensions.

Accordingly, the growing complexity called into question faith in the scientific method that focused on analysis and isolation, and relied on the capability to isolate information about phenomena.

The dawn of the new century drove a rethinking of organizations and posed new questions about the shape of a new managerial mindset.

In an era of change and uncertainty, there is a need for reinterpreting management and for a new reading of managerial theories, toward the discovery of principles and values able to guide the creation of a new manager profile.

The management of new organizational forms calls for a radical innovation in the process of developing new leadership capabilities.

Section 2.2 of this chapter presents the analysis of the turbulent dynamics that characterize today's markets and industries; they determine, as described in Section 2.3, the need to go beyond the classic deterministic approach to managing corporations. Section 2.4 presents the context and the conditions enabling the emergence of the new managerial mindset, as the result of the evolution from a linear to a non-linear way of thinking. The rise of a new manager profile, as described in Section 2.5, is introduced as the necessary response to the challenges posed by a new managerial culture.

2.2   The environmental change and the new business scenario

2.2.1   A multidimensional approach to change

Environmental change is of great interest to management scholars and has become a key element in theoretical approaches that deal with specific organizational processes, like competitiveness and innovation and its effects on organizational performance (Suarez and Oliva, 2005; D'Aveni, 1994; Christensen, 1992; Tushman and Rosenkopf, 1992).

In an attempt to assess the impact of the environment on companies' performance, organizational theorists have proposed different characterizations of environmental attributes affecting firms, providing a complex multidimensional approach. Suarez and Oliva (2005) proposes a simplified focus based on empirical evidence, which highlights three basic environmental attributes (Dess and Beard, 1984): *munificence*, intended as the sustainability of growth that an environment could support; *dynamism*, referring to the rate of environmental unpredictability and instability; and *complexity*, which is the level of skills, knowledge and capabilities used to process information that managers apply to succeed in the environment.

Along these three dimensions, many scholars have investigated the characteristics of environmental changes and the relationship between the degree of change and the organizational evolution and adaptation.

Moving from the work of Wholey and Brittain (1989), Suarez and Oliva (2005) suggested a set of attributes of environmental variation, to provide a comprehensive treatment of environmental change. According to the authors, this process is characterized by the required granularity to embrace different insights coming from the literature. As a result, they proposed a framework to interpret the emerging business scenario, consisting of the following four dimensions:

- *frequency*, intended as the number of environmental disturbances for unit of time;
- *amplitude*, which is the magnitude of the deviation from initial conditions caused by a disturbance;
- *speed*, the rate of change of the disturbance; and
- *scope*, the variety of environmental dimensions affected by simultaneous disturbances.

Table 2.1 Attributes of change and resulting typology

Type of Environmental Change	Frequency	Amplitude	Speed	Scope
Regular	Low	Low	Low	Low
Hyperturbulence	High	Low	High	Low
Specific Shock	Low	High	High	Low
Disruptive	Low	High	Low	Low
Avalanche	Low	High	High	High

Source: Adapted from Suarez and Oliva (2005).

The variations in the four attributes lead to five symbolic cases of particular interest, as shown in Table 2.1.

Regular change happens continuously, in environments that experience a latent incremental change. These environments are relatively stable, and the direction of their evolution is relatively predictable. In this context, planning and positioning are the basic strategies of the business actors who perform in this sector.

Hyperturbulence represents environments in which frequent high speed changes happen, involving only one or a few dimensions. Such environments are affected by new dynamics altering the industry pace, and where the intensity of each perturbation is so modest that the firms' need to adapt to new conditions requires a low effort (D'Aveni, 1994).

Specific shock refers to rare, rapid and intense changes that have limited dimensions of impact. A typical example of this sort of change is deregulation interventions, which, at a national or local level, radically change the rules of the "game" within limited geographical areas.

Disruptive change embraces changes that are not frequent and develop gradually; they are linked to specific sectors, requiring new sets of skills and are not easily integrated by the industry players.

Finally, *avalanche change* is a change that is not frequent but is intense, fast and, above all, simultaneously affects several dimensions of the environment.

This kind of change implies a radical rethinking of traditional managerial practices in different dimensions of life; it brings a complete shift in the way of life and of representing the reality. It represents the rising of a new paradigm.

2.2.2   The growing openness of economies and markets

The radical changes that took place during the last decades have significantly transformed the macro-economic and organizational environment by reducing the national barriers to market, enhancing the volatility of capital, and facilitating the rising of new global players.

The emerging scenario in this period is extremely different from the past, as it is characterized by new competitive dynamics: the growing openness of the economy drives a new logic of competition and facilitates the rising of new economic "giants" like Asia and Latin America.

In a recent report (2008) about the emerging trends in the world global economy, Elmeskov, the Acting Head of the OECD Economic Department, introduces the main challenges that the economic and political actors are called to afford in such a scenario, balancing a policy of openness and protectionism. In his conclusions he points out: (a) the need for a more flexible labor-market; and (b) the improvement of workers' education.

In his analysis, Elmeskov (2008) highlights the positive outcomes of the process of opening of national economies and markets: according to him, the nature and form of globalization is visibly changing, as increasingly it is characterized by the "internationalization of innovation."

According to Bravo-Castillo (1998), the process of globalization and opening of economies and markets is the final result of three changing factors: the rapid acceleration of trade and production processes; the growing availability of capital; and the higher value and mobility of assets like knowledge and information flows. Technology, trade and capital mobility, strategic alliances and networked organizations, are identified as the main variables affecting the degree of the integration of the national economies.

The large diffusion and adoption of ICTs have been generally defined as the main factor enabling the new global trends (Romano et al., 2003), the main source of the shift in the evolutionary path of the contemporary capitalism.

According to Kobrin (1997), the emerging economic landscape on a global scale is:

- *broader*, in terms of the encompassed national markets;
- *deeper*, for the density and velocity of the interactions, the flow of trade and investment; and
- contains *multinational* enterprises operating across national markets.

Dunning (1997) offered an exhaustive interpretation of the evolutionary path of capitalism. According to him, capitalism moved from a hierarchical form, characterized by relatively stable markets based on physical resources, to a new form of flexible capitalism (or alliance capitalism), characterized by highly competitive and dynamic markets, local and global, centered on intangible assets in the value-adding processes.

Romano (2003) pointed out the most significant factors behind the phenomenon of discontinuity charactering the capitalism evolutionary path; accordingly they are:

- the increasing complexity and specialization of economic activity;
- the growing interdependencies of many product markets;
- the accelerating movement toward an innovation-driven economy;
- the widening of the territorial boundaries of firms;
- the increased significance of created assets in the value-adding process;
- the evolvement of new institutions and organizational forms; and
- the re-evaluation of organizational cultures and behavioral norms.

On February 2008, Peter Mandelson, EU Trade Commissioner, pointed out the consequences, both negative and positive, of the opening process of economies and markets. Whether his analysis is limited to the European context, he outlined some easily generalized conclusions. He identified some challenges represented by the capability to afford and manage some main critical issues like environmental costs, the painful adjustment in the labor-market due to the technological changes, and the risks associated to the global dimension of financial markets. Mandelson concluded his contribution by stating that the openness force is not the "panacea for economic development," but it doubtless represents a "powerful transformative force."

2.2.3   Pre-industrial, industrial and post-industrial mindset

Organizational studies during the last century addressed the challenge of both analyzing and interpreting a reality in the context of continuous, rapid change. Accordingly, that includes reconfiguring the theoretical background behind management practices.

Substantial uncertainty and instability and the evolution of organizations' social and cultural environment resulted in some theoretical interpretative approaches, aimed at reconsidering the traditional thinking models.

While new forms of organizations are emerging, management philosophy feels the need to fit into the new age, to surf the "mental revolution" for both management and organizational design (Duncan and Van Matre, 1990).

To understand the rate of this revolution, it is necessary to investigate the development of management thought and practices, discovering which perspectives survived until now.

Though "management" is an evolving discipline, many organizations and managers still adopt the results of its first developments. The primary assumptions and principles around which the Classic Management corpus was designed, like the division of work by tasks, conceptualized in 1776 by Adam Smith, is still a basic method of work organization (Robbins and Coulter, 2003).

The management structure and systems proposed during the 19th and 20th century by Weber, Fayol, Taylor and Drucker established a managerial paradigm able to endure until now, even if it was conceptualized in a period characterized by a slower perception of time, less aggressive competition, long phases of stability and a primordial development of Information Science (Murphy, 2003). Although the organizational environment continued to change, such theoretical concepts are still the basis for efficiency gains in many organizations.

The stages of evolution of management thought relies firstly on the diverse needs of individuals and groups in society; then on the stage of evolution of each society in time and space; and finally on the different kinds of organizations emerging in different places or periods.

In 1980, Alvin Toffler pointed to a consideration about the evolution of the world's societies. The central theme of his research is that human history clearly fits patterns. Looking back to the past, he highlighted three categories of waves in the actions of societies (Murphy, 2003) that he considered the main three waves of change in civilization, societies and economies. These phases shaped three waves in the evolution of the organization of work, corresponding to the Pre-Industrial, Industrial and Post-Industrial Ages. Accordingly, they outlined two shifts in the ways of managing organizations (Kruger, 2003).

All countries have experienced in different periods an agricultural and mining age, characterized by large familiar communities and a cyclical sense of time. In that time, people were generalists, able to do many things; business was simple and the valued commodity was land. The information available to people during this First Wave was limited to what they were able to learn or experience. In pre-industrial times, the work organization was dominated by small industries, where handicrafts were made to supplement farm income. It represented a "domestic system" of production (George, 1972).

The rising of the Second Wave started with the invention of power-driven machinery that dramatically transformed the production process. A "factory system" was conceived to gather machinery and workers in the same place, with the goal of maximizing profits for the factory stakeholders.

Adam Smith himself had predicted in 1776 what was going to happen in the Second Wave. He forecasted an increasing division of labor as the answer to the growing extent of markets. But he was unable to imagine the organizational consequences of this division as he was a believer in the power of the "invisible hand" of the market to coordinate economic activity (Langlois, 2003). The economy emerging at the end of the 19th century made it necessary for an internal and administrative coordination of work and organizations: the new technologies and the growing markets led the "visible hand" of managerial coordination to prevail on the "invisible hand" of markets (Chandler, 1977).

The first elements of a paradigm shift in the organization of work became clear at the beginning of the Industrial Age as shown in Table 2.2.

The goal of the mass production, enabled by the availability of a new technology, required the generalist workforce coming from land and handicraft to specialize on the competences needed for performing a specific task in the production process. Ensuring the effective performance of one single task became the aim of the worker, substituting the entrepreneurial spirit with individual jobs. Specialization was to be achieved through training activities, against the traditional experiential

Table 2.2 The evolutionary path in the organization of work

	The organization of work		
	Pre-Industrial	**Industrial**	**Post-Industrial**
Production Goal	Individual Customization	Mass Production	Mass Customization
Workforce Competence	Generalist	Specialist	Generalist
Workforce Attitude	Entrepreneurship	Task-Performance	Entrepreneurship
Competence development	Experience	Training	Experience
Control Mechanisms	Self-Organization	Centralization of control	Self-Organization
Organizational Form	Community	Bureaucracy	Community

way of acquiring new knowledge. The new productive structures, more and more vertically organized, counted on the centralization of control to ensure the effective achievement of the task. The community-based social structure evolved toward hierarchies and bureaucracies, with a straight differentiation of roles and positions.

These factors gave "management" a relevant role: in a slow, stable and predictable economic world, managers became able to answer to the need of *planning, organizing, leading and controlling* the production, and the workforce, moving toward the goal of growing production and increased profits (Robins and Coulter, 2003). These elements generated a new managerial mindset.

What happened at the end of the Industrial Age?

At the end of the 20th century, a new technology replaced the disruptive effect of the introduction of the power-driven machinery: the diffusion of ICT, together with the rising of the contingent factors of the "avalanche change," provoked a new paradigm shift in the organization of work.

An aspect of the arising epistemology in the representation of emerging organizations relies on this evidence: under new different conditions, the organization of the work called for the restoration of several ancient principles by:

- making *mass customization* the primary goal of production;
- intending the workforce to become adaptable to *generalist* profiles;
- requiring competencies to be developed under the exploitation of the value of *experience* intended also as learning experience;
- retrieving *self-organization* of work and the entrepreneurial attitude toward jobs; and
- revaluing the *community* dimension of working and collaboration.

Table 2.2 represents these issues

This rediscovery of some aspects of the Pre-Industrial Age organization of work merited consideration under new, unprecedented conditions. The rising of the Third Wave represented by the Post-Industrial Age tracked a structural revolution as profound as that of the 19th century.

The driving forces of the economy are still population, income and economic integration, but transportation and communication technologies of the early industrial revolution are now substituted by computer, internet, and digital technologies. Together with the reduction

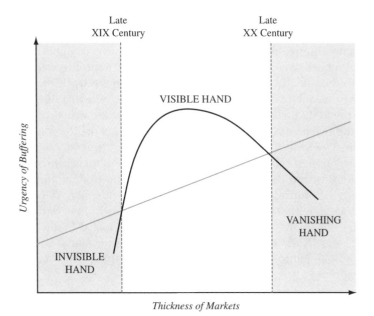

Figure 2.1 The vanishing-hand hypothesis.
Source: Adapted from Langlois (2003).

of technological and legal barriers to trade, they made production more and more coordinated by trading on thicker markets.

These new conditions made the Smithian forces prevail again over the Chandlerian ones. Management maintained its principal functions, but the mechanism of coordinating production evolved into a new equilibrium, more imbalanced in the market. The new equilibrium called the "visible hand" into question, and saw it "fading into a ghostly translucence" (Langlois, 2003, p. 3).

The "Vanishing Hand" hypothesis (Langlois, 2003) describes this evolution in the context of internal and external coordination of production. Developed by Richard Langlois in 2003, the model represented in Figure 2.1 is a function of:

a. *Thickness of Markets*: It is driven by exogenous factors like population, income and the height of technological and political trade barriers; and
b. *Urgency of Buffering*: Intended as the degree to which the production technology is complex, sequential and high-throughput.

The straight line indicates the boundary between markets and firms in the coordination of production; the area below the line shows that buffering through market is less costly and the preferable choice.

The model shows that the passage from the first to the second and third waves saw over time two trends: (1) the market getting thicker; (2) the urgency of buffering levels, grown in the Industrial Age, declining over time for the next period. These trends are explainable with the improvements in coordination technology, and the lowering of the minimally-efficient scale of production (Langlois, 2003).

It is doubtless that the roots of modern theory of management are to be found within the industrial age. During this period, almost all the managerial principles were generated that have endured until now, and continue to represent the basis for each development in organizational studies. The managerial mindset of the age dominated by the "visible hand" was clearly fitting the economic and organizational conditions of the time. But looking at the age of the "vanishing hand" one question arises:

"What should be the features of the managerial mindset of the Post-Industrial Age?"

The next sections will analyze the Industrial Age managerial mindset, highlighting developments and limits of the main theoretical contributions.

Following, the emerging managerial mindset of the Post-Industrial Age is identified. The aim of the analysis is to describe the role and the profile of the manager of the current times. It investigates the set of competencies that has to develop and the current trends and methodological approaches to the managerial competencies development.

2.3   The management paradigm of the industrial age

2.3.1   The traditional managerial culture

In the slow world of the 19th century, not yet connected by efficient transportation systems, the shift in the way of production through machinery inspired a consideration about the wealth of countries, at both the community and individual level.

The work of Smith (1776) represented in the "Wealth of Nations," pointed out a positive correlation between the pursuing of individual interest and the promotion of community's good: according to him, in free markets the principle that he called "the invisible hand" made it possible for individuals to maximize revenue for themselves by maximizing the total revenue of society as a whole. The principle was based on the Newtonian view that the whole richness was equal to the sum of individual revenues.

The Industrial Age ushered in an era of mechanized processes that allowed organizations to gain the economic advantage of high productivity levels through the division of work, by increasing each worker's skill and dexterity, and by saving time of changing tasks and costs of training people for different practices. With the Industrial Revolution, the substitution of machine for human power definitely focused large and efficient factories and power driven equipment as the locus and the way of manufacturing.

This implied a new sense of organization, and required new managerial skills: as the factories grew in dimension and equipment, managers were needed to forecast demand, ensure the right quantity of material for the production process, assign task to people, coordinate them, guide and control workforce and the correct use and maintenance of the machines.

The development of a formal theory of management was the answer to the need of managers to find codified management practices to govern larger corporations. The role of the manager was designed around four main "Managerial Functions" (Robbins and Coulter, 2003):

1. *Planning*: Defining the goals, establishing the strategy, and developing plans to coordinate the organization's activities;
2. *Leading*: Directing all the members of the organization, making the rules to be respected, and resolving conflicts;
3. *Organizing*: Determining and assigning the tasks, pointing what needs to be done, how it must be done, and who as to do it; and
4. *Controlling*: Monitoring the accomplishment of the individual work within the organization, matching the task performances with the expected results.

Accordingly, three main perspectives guided the early conceptualization of Management Theory that can be considered the Classic Management Approach as shown in Figure 2.2.

1. the improvement of *productivity* and *efficiency*, which called for a Scientific approach to Management;

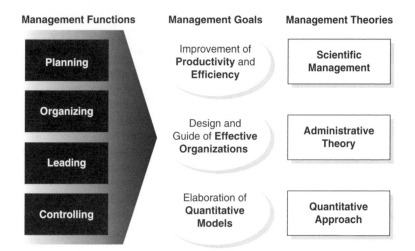

Figure 2.2   Industrial age management conceptualization.

2. the design and guide of *effective organizations,* requiring a focus on the administrative perspective of Management; and
3. the elaboration of *quantitative models,* following an approach able to translate the organization's activities in measurable aspects and outcomes.

1. *Scientific Management.* The basic challenge facing management during the early years of the Industrial Revolution was the search for rational, scientific principles for handling men, materials, capital and machines. On one hand, the clear focus on productivity and profitability presented the risk of low worker motivation. On the other one, the positive faith in the Newtonian deterministic view of reality made reasonable the search for the "one best way" for a job to be done, or for the management to be performed. At the end of the 19th century, Frederick Taylor, moving from his personal experience, as worker started investigating the creation of a "Science of Work." He became universally recognized as the father of *Scientific Management,* a discipline containing the guiding principles for improving production efficiency. His basic assumption was that the scientific selection, training and development of workers, and the application of economic incentives, could provide the best solution for the achievement of production efficiency. People were functional to the firm's goal, but they knew only what they were going to do. Furthermore, the logic of efficiency made it clear that

specialization and *task orientation* could ensure the best performance of each worker. The organization was conceived as a machine. The approach was clearly *mechanistic*.

2. Administrative Theory. While scientific management took a micro approach, the early part of the 20th century saw the development of macro issues, a body of knowledge that emphasized broad administrative principles applicable to large organizations. The design of effective organizations was the central focus of the intellectual analysis of organizations made by Weber (1947), at the beginning of the 20th century. His conceptualization was aimed at designing the ideal type of organization, what he called an "Ideal Bureaucracy." The concept of bureaucracy embraced rational and structural characteristics of a mechanistic organization, like the hierarchical structure, technical competence, rules and regulations, and impersonal relationships. Following his model, job positions were based on rational-legal authority, linked by a formal chain of command, essential for a rational control of employees' behavior.

Some of the principles described by Weber were also stated in formal Principles of Management by Fayol (1949). He leveraged on his 30 years management experience to describe management as a universal set of functions that included planning, organizing, commanding, coordinating and controlling.

The insights from the work of Weber and Fayol, named *Administrative Theorists* (Robbins and Coulter, 2003), represent an attempt to formulate an ideal organization design and the right model of the manager rule.

They interpreted a reality that is still far from expressing the organizations' need to respond quickly to an increasingly dynamic environment by boosting the individual creativity of workers. But the importance of their contribution is doubtless: it relies on the identification of rules and practices to refer to. Despite the shift in environmental conditions, and the growing speed of change in today's organizations, some successful flexible organizations like General Electric or Cisco Systems adopt and apply some bureaucratic mechanisms to ensure the efficient and effective employment of resources.

3. Quantitative Approach. During the 20th century, the search of a rational approach to management brought to the development of quantitative techniques to support decision making. The *Quantitative Approach*, also labeled as *Operation Research*, arose from the application of mathematical and statistical models to military issues during the World War II, and then to business problems. Optimization and information models, and then computer simulations, became a basic tool for managers in large companies, to support the decision making process. One of the main corporations to experiment these techniques during the 1940s was Ford Motor Company.

The natural field of application for this approach was the area of Operation Management, aimed at identifying the optimal allocation of resources, at guaranteeing the precise and efficient scheduling of work, at defining the optimal level of inventory. These applications were allowed by the predictability of the business world variables, like the trend in demand, the future production level of equilibrium, the price level of materials and products. In a predictable world it became a "science of management."

The common streams to all the contributions to the Classic Management approach of the Industrial Age were represented by the rational view of world, and by the consideration of the manager as the cardinal rational actor able to:

- collect the right complete information;
- weigh alternatives;
- make decisions; and
- translate the strategy into action.

Accordingly, the perspective of the early management conceptualization looked at the organization as a "machine," suitable to be managed in a linear rational way. This is what we call "Mechanistic" organization.

2.3.2   The features of mechanistic organizations

Management literature defines the organization as "a deliberate arrangement of people to accomplish some specific purpose" (Robbins and Coulter, 2003, p. 16). According to this assumption, three dimensions emerge to define an organization: first, a distinct "purpose," most often expressed in terms of goals to be accomplished; second, the human dimension of the group of "people" performing the activities required to achieve its goals; third, the "deliberate structure" adopted by organization's members, required to clarify the members' work relationships (Hage and Aiken, 1967; Robbins and Coulter, 2003). Though these three features have been always considered as the organizations' roots, their conceptualization changed over time.

The metaphors used by Charlie Chaplin in his movie *Modern Times* (1936) are a good representation of one of the most important organizational structures at the beginning of the 20th century, designed around the requirements of the Fordist production systems

(Galanopoulos, 2008). The movie's main character is a factory worker, employed on an accelerating assembly line that brings him to suffer a mental breakdown. Henry Ford was clearly aligned with the Taylor's management theory, broadly known as "scientific management." He tried to improve his car factory's productivity by applying the Taylorist perspective with the aim of reaching the mass production (Litter, 1982). Furthermore, he introduced three revolutionary innovations that informed the organizational culture of the following era (Galanopoulos, 2008):

1. the choice of the *"unique best way"* through the rationalization of work principles (Buchanan and Huczynski, 2004): the work consisted of simple repetitive tasks to be performed in scheduled time in order to be efficient;
2. the use of *single-purpose machine* (Buchanan and Huczynsk, 2004) called "farmer machines" that required just a short phase of workers' training; and
3. the introduction of the *assembly line* allowed by a high degree of standardization of commodities, which enabled Ford to control the production by increasing the speed of the line (Salaman, 1985).

In this context, the flow of information and the decision-making process was completely dominated by bureaucracy. Discipline and obedience made the roots of relationships among the different levels of the hierarchy. Compared with the expectations of its historic and economic context, the Fordist organization structure represented a successful and effective system, able to guarantee in a period of stability high levels of productivity (Litter, 1982; Galanopoulos, 2008).

The stable environment of the Fordist period supported the development of the classic "Mechanistic Organization," similar in some ways to the bureaucratic structures that found their basics in efficiency and predictability. The label "mechanistic" clearly suggests an organizational structure made up like a machine, where each component performs only what it is designed to do (Barnett and Hofler, 2006). The mechanistic formalization implies that processes and procedures are to be administratively authorized: each variance must be brought under control in order to support and increase predictability, and finally to improve efficiency. Environmental and technological stability enable a clear definition and differentiation of work, where specialized job positions identify the needed skills, the task methodology and the procedures to be used (Barnett and Hofler, 2006).

The Ford system was called into question very soon. During the 1930s, it appeared to be less effective if compared to the innovative organization at General Motors (GM). The new organizational structure of GM had allowed Alfred P. Sloan to reposition the car company through the creation of a five-model product line, developing what remains the multi-product or M-form organizational structure. Such a structure was characterized by different operating divisions devoted to different products or markets, showing the positive effect of the decentralization of administrative control (Womack, Jones, and Roos, 1990).

In the early 1960s, starting from the observation of the misalignment emerging between real organizational experience and classical management perspectives, organizational studies were devoted to define a new sustainable organizational structure, able to reach success and sustainability.

The study about the structural dimension of organizations saw, especially during the 1960s and 1970s, a huge amount of contributions from the Contingency Theory (Lawrence and Lorsch, 1967; Burns and Stalker, 1961). They assumed as a common base the belief that structure and operation of an organization are dependent on situational variables, like environment and technology. It makes it hard to develop general principles applicable to organizations any-time and any-place (Waldersee, Griffiths and Lai, 2003; Scott, 1987).

Contingency theory arose with the aim of explaining the relationships and the "functional fit" between the external environment of the organization and its internal structure. Different studies in the "contingency field" provided evidence of the impact of several categories of contingent factors, the most prominent ones were related to the following variables (Waldersee, Griffiths and Lai, 2003):

- *Uncertainty* (Burns and Stalker, 1961);
- *Technology* (Woodward, 1965);
- *Size* (Blau, 1970); and
- *Strategy* (Chandler, 1962).

The main premise of contingency theory was that organizational success was dependent on the "fit" between the contingent factor and the organizational structure. It encouraged many organizational theorists to define the characteristics of successful organizations, as related to the more and more rapid change at environmental and technological levels. The attempt was to develop a taxonomy of organization structures related to different external and internal conditions.

In 1961, Burns and Stalker analyzed the organization structure of twenty firms in Scotland and England, chosen among the sectors of rayon mill, engineering, medium and high tech electronics, facing different technology and environment conditions. The attempt of their work was to track a continuum evolutionary trend in organizational structures according to the predictability and stability of the environment in order to provide a complete systematization of the representations of organizational forms (Waldersee, Griffiths and Lai, 2003).

The Fordist organization was placed at one of the extreme positions in such a continuum of high predictability and stability. They defined it the "Mechanistic Organization."

According to the main findings of their work, the main features of the Mechanistic Organization can be summarized under the following dimensions (Burns and Stalker, 1961):

1. *Task Distribution*: The assembly line of the Fordist organization required the *specialized differentiation* of *functional tasks*. It allowed workers to perform at best only one phase of the production process, without taking into account the overall goal of the organization.
2. *Task Nature*: Each individual task was extremely abstract; it was intended to be pursued with specific techniques.
3. *Task Definition*: For each level in the hierarchy the individual tasks were determined by the immediate superiors, who assigned and redefined time and modes of the expected performance.
4. *Task Scope*: For each functional role a precise definition was required of rights and obligations of workers, and of the technical methods to be followed for the specific task.
5. *Structure of Control*: Hierarchy ensured a centralization of control, based on the recognition of authority of the higher level organization members.
6. *Knowledge Location*: Since workers were employed only in performing one segment of the whole production, they didn't need to process internal nor external information. The location of knowledge was concentrated at the top of the hierarchy, reinforcing the bureaucratic structure of the organization.
7. *Communication Direction*: The communication was intended to be mandatory between superior and subordinate according to the vertical distribution of roles.
8. *Governance for Working Behavior*: The organizational culture was based on a one direction flow of instructions and decisions issued by superiors. The workforce was not involved in the strategic decisions of

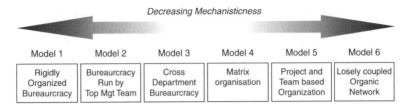

Model 1	Model 2	Model 3	Model 4	Model 5	Model 6
Rigidly Organized Bureaurcracy	Bureaurcracy Run by Top Mgt Team	Cross Department Bureaurcracy	Matrix organisation	Project and Team based Organization	Losely coupled Organic Network

Figure 2.3   Trends in organizational structure.
Source: Adapted from Borgatti (1996).

the top management, so they didn't require workers to develop any managerial or entrepreneurial attitude.

9. *Values*: The values of the organization were the loyalty to the concern and the obedience to superiors.

Leaving on one hand the model of the mechanistic structure, the continuum identified by the "decreasing Mechanisticness" saw six organizational models (Borgatti, 1996), represented in Figure 2.3.

On the opposite side of the Mechanistic Organization there is the model named "Organic." More suitable for unstable, turbulent and changing environmental conditions, it identifies organizations able to re-shape themselves to address new problems and tackle unforeseen contingencies. This new form is characterized by a fluid organizational design based on flexibility, adaptation and job redefinition principles, emphasizing lateral communication against vertical hierarchy (Cravens, Piercy and Shipp, 2005).

A comparison between the two extreme organizational structures along with twelve parameters is presented in the Table 2.3.

The work of Burns and Stalker showed that organizations moving into an unstable, changing environment in the 1960s were forced to reshape their main features, moving far from the mechanistic vision of the classic organizational approach.

Accordingly, in a changing environment the distribution of specialized functional task is replaced by the collaborative contribution of specialized knowledge and experience toward the achievement of a common goal. The nature itself of the task changes in a more realistic way, pointing to the importance of the overall organization goal as the main concern for each single worker. The task is not simply assigned: it is shared and continuously redefined through the interaction with others.

Table 2.3 From stable to changing environment: Mechanistic versus organic organizations

	Stable Environment	**Changing Environment**
Organization Form	Mechanistic	Organic
Tasks Distribution	Specialized differentiation of functional tasks	Contributive nature of special knowledge and experience
Task Nature	Abstract nature of differentiated individual tasks	"Realistic" nature of the individual task consistent with the overall concern
Tasks Definition	Vertical definition, by hierarchical superiors	Continual redefinition through interaction with others
Task Scope	Precise definition of rights and obligations	Shedding of "responsibility"
Structure of Control	Hierarchic, contractual	Network, presumed Community of interest.
Knowledge Location	At the top of the hierarchy, with the reconciliation of distinct tasks	Anywhere in the network
Communication Direction	Vertical communication	Lateral communication
Governance for Working BEHAVIOR	Instructions and decisions	Information and advice
Values	Loyalty to the concern and obedience to superiors	Commitment to the concern's task

Source: Adapted from Burns and Stalker (1961).

Centralized control leaves room to a distributed one, exerted in a networked, community dimension, where each worker takes responsibility for his own contribution to the general performance. In a more open economy and market, the organization continuously processes internal and external information, at whichever level, letting knowledge be located anywhere in the network.

Communication is no more vertical but lateral, among people of different rank, following the concern of consultation more than command. Governance guides the working behavior on information and advice more than by instructions and decisions. The overall organizational goal is shared and the workforce is committed in the overall organization growth.

The new conditions of the environment, the growing turbulence and the speed of change, the loss of stability and predictability, started during the middle of the last century to force organizations to reshape themselves. Under the view of Organizational Studies, the evidence arises of a natural evolution of organizations toward new and adaptable structures. They require managers to put into question their way of conceiving their role, to investigate new areas of engagement, new means of dealing with uncertainty and instability, to focus on information, culture and values.

2.3.3   The drivers for strategic decisions: Stability and predictability

The management of the Industrial Age celebrated the rationality of managers, especially the ones involved into the strategic decision process.

The main theoretical models developed during the last century rely on the capability of the manager to collect the right and complete information about the firm's internal as well as external environment, to weigh alternatives and to compose the decisions in a consistent strategy to translate into action.

Three strategic approaches developed during the 20th century, and still widely applied today, are recognized as the pillars of strategic management:

1. Porter's *Five Forces* (Porter, 1980);
2. *Core Competence* framework (Prahalad and Hamel, 1990); and
3. *Game Theory* (von Neumann and Morgenstern, 1947).

They can be synthetized as follows:

Five Forces. The model of Five Forces developed by Michael Porter has represented for the strategists of the last twenty years of the 20th century a fundamental tool for analyzing an organization's industry structure in its strategic processes. It is based on the premises that a firm's strategic approach has to offer them the possibility of grasping all the opportunities and reinforcing the threats of the organizations according to the external context. It also assumes that the competitive strategy can be based on an understanding of industry structure and the way it changes. Porter identified five competitive forces by which it is possible to cover every industry and market. The premise behind this approach is that the objective of corporate strategy should be to modify these competitive forces in a way that improves the position of the organization.

The stability and cyclical growth of the markets are the main assumptions behind the Five Forces model. In a historical context characterized by such stability, the primary corporate objective is represented by the guarantee of a firm's profitability to defend the acquired positioning. The strategy has to be optimized in relation to the external environment and its main forces; the analysis of the industry structure represented the main performance driver of the model. At that time, the process of development and growth in most industries could be considered stable and predictable, if compared with the current markets' dynamics. The strategy was executed pushing the organization toward the expected position in a selected target market. The assumptions behind the Five Forces model were:

- the existence of a classic perfect market with a relatively static structure;
- a competitive analysis applicable only on market with a simple structure; and
- an idea of competitive position to achieve only over other competitors, suppliers and customers.

Core Competence. Within the dominant managerial paradigms in the 20th century, the strategy domain of "Core Competence" refers to the focus on the internal key factors that allow a company to gain a sustainable advantage.

During the last two decades, the wide conceptualization of "core competence," and the attention to the internal organizational dimensions as the locus of the sources of companies' success, traditionally spans through several theoretical domains, including the resource-based (Penrose, 1959; Wernerfelt, 1984; Barney, 1991).

Although the most common references for the core competence perspective are Prahalad and Hamel (1990), the concept appeared already in the 1970s for the similarity to that of "distinctive competence," first introduced by Andrews (1971) (Collis, 1991, p. 51), and previously drafted by Selznick (1957) and Ansoff (1965). "A firm's core competence is defined as the vector of the irreversible assets along which the firm is uniquely advantaged. Although the vector is multidimensional, reflecting the entire system of tangible and intangible resources that the organization has in place, it is commonly represented on a single plane" (Collis, 1991, p. 51).

What the different definitions of core competence have in common is well represented by the path-dependency of such a vector (Leonard-Barton, 1992), which is intended as the consequence of the accumulation of historic actions and investments; in this sense core competence is considered not as a future investment, but as being pre-determined by the past.

According to the empirical study conducted in 1998 by Mascarenhas on 12 multinational companies (Mascarenhas et al., 1998), three types of core competencies have been identified: superior technological know-how, reliable processes and close relationship with external parties.

Other scholars have proposed that the core competence concept consists of three components (Wang et al., 2004)—marketing, technological and integrative competencies—and measured the effects of the components on the performance of firms.

The recognized attributes of a core competence are clearly expressed (Prahalad and Hamel, 1990; Hamel and Prahalad, 1994) as follows:

1. It must contribute significantly to the perceived customer benefits of the end product.
2. It should be competitively unique, and, as such, it must be difficult for competitors to imitate.
3. It provides potential access to a wide range of markets. That is, the competence should give access to new product arenas, arrayed from its current embedded products.

The approach, as well as the related Resource Based View of the firm (Barney, 1991; Grant, 1991) that focuses on the critical dimensions of core competencies, as of resources to be leveraged, rely on the same assumption: the management even in incrementally changing markets is able to understand market trajectories sufficiently well, and to apply the core competencies, or the strategic resources, in a timely and effective way (Davis and Eisenhardt, 2004; Helfat, 1994; Dosi, 1988).

Game Theory. Born as a branch of the applied mathematics, Game Theory has represented a radical change in conceiving the managerial practices. Theorized by von Neumann and Morgenstern (1947), the main assumptions behind the Game Theory are that all the actors are rational in terms of Expected Utility Theory; all the specifications of the game are also known. This implies that the option with the greatest utility is one that a rational actor will choose. The main characteristics of the theory are:

- *Completeness*: If there are two alternatives, an agent will prefer neither A nor B; the agent is disinterested between A and B;
- *Transitivity*: If an agent prefers A over B and B over C, he will also prefer A over C; and

- *Context-free ordering*: If an agent prefers A over B, he will still do this when additional alternatives (C, D) are available.

The main application of the Game Theory model to business management is represented by the hypothesis that the market can be seen as a dynamic oligopoly. The studies on the possible applications of game theory have conducted researchers to develop new models of interpretations. One of the most famous, the *Nash Equilibrium*, is a solution concept of a game involving two or more players, who are expected to know the strategic choices by which the other players can reach their optimum, and no player is motivated to gain by changing only his own strategic position (i.e., by changing unilaterally).

Even if, under different perspectives, the main insights about the Game Theory can be considered an idealized abstraction of the reality, and a normative more than a descriptive theory, the statistical perspective of the model allowed to obtain only temporary results and to reach a position of competitive advantage limited in time. It is evident that the limitation of the temporary dimension is surely one of the most critical characteristics of the model. The hypothesis of designing and executing strategic activities planned for a relatively short period, as well as the statistical and mathematical perspective offered, seems to allow the application of the game theory model also at the current socio-economic scenario.

2.3.4 Limitations of the linear approach to business management

The Managerial Mindset arising during the Industrial Age showed the characteristics of the intellectual outcomes of the first part of the 20th century, dominated by stability, predictability and certainty.

Early management theories were founded on the following epistemological assumptions:

1. The understanding of business relied on the decomposition of the whole business concept in its components and their fundamental features. Accordingly, business management resulted to be the "sum" of different separated areas, namely the managerial disciplines, covering quite all the different aspects related to the functional areas of an organization (*reductionism*).
2. The certainty and stability of the environment, the relative closeness of economies and markets, and the length of change cycles built faith in the predictability of events in the business context, and in the strong relationship between cause and effect. Organizations

could grow without any limitation, by developing vertical interrelations and hierarchical structures, and counting on a fixed and strong division of roles. Looking at the past was enough to forecast future events (*determinism*).

3. The observation of events within organizations made managers able to gather complete information about the business system. They can perform their tasks by counting on internal analysis, letting them feel sure of holding the overall knowledge needed to drive organizations along the best path of efficient production (*correspondence theory of knowledge*).

4. The capability to collect complete information made managers rational actors, able to choose always the option that maximizes the organization's *utility*, the most suitable solution, the "one best way" to manage (*rationality*).

Reductionism; determinism; correspondence theory of knowledge; rationality: Together they represent the dimensions along which the management paradigm of the Industrial Age was built, but describe also an approach that was common at the time.

The historical period of the early industrialization saw the classical mechanics, proposed by Newton and developed by Laplace, as the foundation of science; the paradigm to which each other discipline could be reduced. Its logic was promising for the coherence, the simple premise and the apparent completeness (Heylighen, Cilliers and Gershenson, 2006).

The first conceptualization of management was developed as the majority of scientific models, in the attempt to follow a scientific approach. Almost all of them implicitly rely on a "classical" or Cartesian mode of thinking that is expressed clearly in the classical or Newtonian mechanics, by which they shared the basic assumptions (Heylighen, 1990).

In a comprehensive work of 2001, Chen and Wang synthesized the main limits affecting the traditional approach to business management, if compared to the growing complexity and turbulence of the environment of the last decades (Chen and Wang, 2001).

The reductionist perspective of the scientific approach had allowed a separated, not systemic, reading of the business management corpus as composed by strategic, marketing, organizational, financial and human resource management. Each one of the mentioned fields had shown to be affected by a too rational and deterministic view of business.

The traditional approach to *Strategic Management* identified the main factors affecting firms' profitability in the environment forces and industrial structures. The analysis of the environment in which the firm was embedded, as theorized by Porter and Ansoff, was useful in planning business objectives and strategies but showed its limitations in the design of long-term strategies.

In the core competences approach, Chen and Wang (2001) observed that the firm's competitive positioning was more focused on the internal competencies and capabilities, compromising sometimes the firm's capability to answer to rapid market changes, and becoming often a source of rigidity for the creation of routines. In a context where technology and market's forces could be very hard to predict, the competition became played on the timing of reaction and the pro-active capabilities sides.

At *Marketing Management* level, the temporal perspective could represent a great limit: the traditional composition of the marketing mix, declined in its product, price, place and promotion dimensions (McCarthy, 1960), is even now a valid basis for the implementation of a marketing strategy; it becomes a limited perspective when facing the growing process of customers' empowerment. The large diffusion of the Internet, and in most recent times of a new generation of web technologies, have impacted significantly on the market dynamics, allowing the customers to have instantaneously all the information they need, to compare products and prices, and also to be creator of their own products. Defined as *"lead users"* (Von Hippel, 2005), they have the capability to create new products, as well as the profitability they can offer; this has to be the main goal of the new marketing approach.

Characterized by the growing reduction of barriers between the internal and external firm's environment, the traditional organizational forms—such as functional, multidivisional and matrix—don't seem to respond well to the needs of a scenario characterized by the enlarging physical dispersion and the growing importance of the knowledge assets. The traditional *Organizational Management* appears to be limited in grasping the benefits coming from the perspective of extended enterprises. In such contexts, a new type defined as "C-form organization" (Chen and Wang, 2001) is emerging, mainly in some knowledge intensive enterprises, such as the software industry.

About the *Financial Management* perspective, the main limits registered are a consequence of the relevance of knowledge as the most valuable asset and a fundamental parameter to assess the firms' productivity. The measurement of the financial results, as well as the level of profitability of firms, is still an important indicator of their performance, even if new metrics to evaluate the non financial results are rising.

The traditional *Human Resource Management* is no longer sufficient in gaining the competition in the new scenario, where the human resources are called to play a more important role in affording the competitive challenges. The survival of a firm in the current competitive landscape results from their ability to continuously renew themselves, to emphasize the knowledge and information available, to facilitate the development of relationships aimed to energize the teams, and to facilitate the creation of a pleasant workplace. Far from being conceived as a cost, they become the strategic asset for the organization's success as well as the soul of the organization and the organization itself, where the virtualization of work and space allow the structure to fall down and people to interact collaboratively in a flat dimension.

Culture, Organization, Strategy—all the dimensions of a managerial paradigm that characterized an entire era, and are still shaping the thought and the mode of some enduring ways of managing organizations—appeared not to be prepared for what we called an "avalanche change."

When a paradigm is no longer able to interpret reality, a new paradigm arises. At the end of the 20th century, the scientific interpretation of business inspired by the linear logic of Newtonian reasoning left room to the research of a new representation of Business reality, shifting toward an approach able to encompass the uncertainty and indeterminacy of the emerging world, turning to physics, quantum mechanics, non-linear dynamics and complexity (Heylighen and Joslyn, 2001).

2.4   The emergence of a new managerial mindset

Common methods for analyzing markets, economies and enterprises are based on linearity principles. The whole is the sum of the parts and the future is a linear projection of the past: these are some of the most representative assumptions of such a way of thinking (Clippinger, 1999). The paradigm shift from a linear to a non-linear view of the world exposed a problem in the interpretation of reality: very few things in nature as well as in business behave in a linear fashion. The work of Clippinger (1999) clearly states the issues that managers are trying to afford today, using three questions:

1. *How can you manage when you cannot control the single parts of your system or the resources?*

2. *How can you manage when the future is too uncertain and too unstable to plan for?*
3. *How can you manage the consequences of changes?*

None of the classical conceptualizations of management could adequately address any one of the present issues. A new perspective of management should be designed that moves far from the research for perfect information and control. Control couldn't be imposed but should be emergent. Perfect information is hard to acquire in a continuous changing market or industry. The only goal managers should aim for is the creation of the right conditions and contexts for achieving a range of desired outcomes.

The emerging Managerial Mindset should overcome the reductionism and the linear vision of business.

2.4.1 A holistic view of business

A first attempt to challenge the reductionism approach of the Industrial Age came from the Systems Science (Smuts, 1926), mainly by the application of a holistic approach to management.

The assumption that events in one part of a system or organization usually create collateral effects in other parts is currently recognized as an obvious statement. Within the Industrial Age managerial mindset, from the late 19th century to the middle of the 20th century, the assumption was not so trivial, until individuals from other disciplines started investigating the activities in the workplace. The knowledge from their disciplines started to transform management concepts into those we have today.

The work of Hamel (2000) focuses on the business concept as the unit of analysis in business management. In such a merging, "holistic" picture, different views of business come from different disciplines, like marketing, strategic management and organization theory.

The originality of this business concept model relies on an integrative perspective resulting from the dynamic combination of three dimensions:

1. Four major *"Components"*: The *customer interface*, representing the marketing perspective of an organization; the *core strategy* and the *strategic resources*, as related to the strategic management issues; and the *value network*, containing the organization theory related issues.
2. Three *"bridges"* that link components: *Customer benefits; configuration*, referring to the linkages between competencies, assets and processes

and how they are managed; and *company boundaries*, referring to the decisions an organization takes along its activity and the interaction within its network.

3. Four *"factors"* affecting company profitability, and related to the *efficiency*, the *uniqueness* of the business model, the *fit*, intended as the consistency among the components of the business model, and the *profit boosters*.

The integration in a holistic view of the business concept has often been driven by the "value creation" perspective. Beyond the main theoretical frameworks aimed at representing the process by which organizations create value (Amit and Zott, 2001), the business model concept could be intended as the representation of the distinctive way an organization achieves its goals. It also appears as a useful means to develop frameworks that help managers to capture, understand, communicate, design, analyze and change the business logic of their firm.

Osterwalder et al. (2005) presents the business model as a building plan supporting the design and implementation of the business structure and systems that will constitute the operational and physical form of the company. Catching the relationship among strategy, organization and culture—and taking into consideration the external pressures, like competitive forces, social and technological change, customer opinion and legal environment, during the last decade—the business model has been adopted in order to develop a holistic picture of business as a whole. It has also allowed business to overcome the traditional segmentation in disciplinary areas and functions.

The main functions that the literature proposes for the business model concept are (Osterwalder et al., 2005):

1. *Understanding and Sharing.* Business models help to represent in a visible and understandable way the vision of the business. Though in an organization it could be a simplified representation, it has the strength to describe explicitly complex conceptualizations (Linder and Cantrell, 2000).

2. *Analyzing.* Since the business model is a representation of the business concept of an organization, it supports the analysis the business logic of companies (Stähler, 2002).

3. *Managing.* Describing holistically the logic architecture of a business, and the way by which organizations create value, the business model concept supports management in aligning strategy, business organization and technology (Lechner and Hummel, 2002).

In its business model conceptualization, Afuah (2003) provides an additional interpretation. According to him, a business model is a money-making framework for firms moving toward the implementation of a new strategy; or the attack of an existing industry by performing some or all of the activities of the industry's value chain. In developing such a strategy—differently, effectively or efficiently—it is able to gain a better position and to offer customers lower costs or better differentiated products than industry incumbents.

Such a framework focuses on the five components of a business model that, according to Afuah, are: positions; activities; resources; industry factors; and costs.

According to this conceptualization, a firm can achieve profit only when customers keep buying its products rather than a competitor's products. This means firms need to offer their customers something their competitors cannot offer, or something able to create a superior customer value (*position*). In order to offer superior value and put itself in the right position to appropriate the value, a firm must perform the activities of its value configuration well (*connected activities*). This requires resources; where such resources are core to the firm's activities and difficult to imitate or substitute, they can give the firm in question a competitive advantage (*resources*). In gaining and maintaining the competitive advantage through the most valuable resources, it is important to take into consideration the cost drivers for determining the quantification of profit (*costs*).

The positions that a firm can attain and maintain, the activities that it can perform, the resources that it can acquire and exploit, and the costs that it can incur in offering superior value, are all a function of the industry and macro environment in which the firm operates (*industry factors*).

Another interesting perspective offered by holistic approaches is the consideration of organizations as organisms: "A way of viewing the world that emphasizes not the parts or units but the patterns, wholes, configurations that make the whole appear to be more than the sum of its parts" (Wren, 1972, p. 205). This assumption calls for a new way of interpreting management, and for the search of different scientific fields to investigate in which a new epistemology of the managerial mindset is developed.

In this regard, Wheatley (1999) links the understanding of the process of management and the activity in organizations to concepts developed in what she calls the "new sciences." She is referring to the pure and applied sciences as much as the social sciences that are usually aligned with the traditional approach to management. The new sciences are represented by physics, biology and chemistry, and all the developments in the fields of evolution and chaos.

Following this line of thought, Stacey (1992) states that businesses, as non-linear systems, are failing because they simply repeat their history once they reach what they consider a stable environment. He continues by saying that they could be most creative and innovative when they are allowed to work outside the confining boundaries of this stable equilibrium. All this is new for many of us: the idea of not having a plan to move forward with in the future is unthinkable, especially in a mechanistically structured organization.

Stacey's, Christensen's and Wheatley's messages are similar to that of Mintzberg (1994): to be effective, any organization has to couple analysis with intuition in its strategy making. His point is that as one tries to project a viable path for an organization into the future, linear thinking and formal statistical analyses need to be combined with a systems-thinking mentality that recognizes that organizations exist in a reality far from orderly and predictable.

The threats to theoretical frameworks and conventional practices in management, and the emerging of system thinking as a view to combine analysis, intuition and strategy to develop a systemic view of business and organizations tracks the challenge for today's managers and leaders. This means to "get beyond" the way that they may have been educated and behaviorally reinforced, to move into a mindset able to let them identify patterns of events that will promote a more creative view of the possibilities for their organization.

Under this perspective, an important contribution comes from the work of the biologist von Bertanlaffy (1968): he tried to develop a theoretical framework able to describe relationships in the real world, theorizing that "disciplines had similarities that could be developed into a General Systems Model" (Wren, 1972, p. 483).

He noted that each organizational system he investigated presented some common features, independently from the field in which it relied:

a. presented itself as a whole or organism;
b. performed continuous movements to stabilize itself; and
c. was open-ended, so that it was affected by its environment but reciprocally affected its environment (von Bertanlaffy, 1968).

He was able to put in correlation the behavior of biological organisms with the features of organizations, proposing a new way of regarding them, a new approach that would have been evolved to the systems-thinking approach.

2.4.2 The biological metaphor of organization

Looking back to Smith and Malthus in the 18th century, the concepts of natural selection and self-organization in organizational theory are not new and well represented in the notion of "invisible hand" of the market capitalism. When markets are ruled only by the laws of supply and demand, and not by a central authority, they behave in the most efficient way, thanks to a natural mechanism of effective allocation of resources. The novelty of that concept in the current age relies on its application to the area of management, and no more only to economy and market.

As Clippinger argues (1999), classical management theory and practice, lead by the systematization of Chandler (1977), was founded on the premise that, despite the existence of invisible forces able to govern effectively the markets, organizations had a different nature. They were also able to act following the "visible" power of their management, through the application of deliberate policies, reasoned decisions and active handling of businesses. The interventions of a management inspired by the rational principles of decision theories, financial analysis, operation research and planning were the only path to the effective allocation of the organizational resources. The 1980s managers were able to recognize that the business environment of that epoch was complex. But they tried to interpret complexity under the principles of the rational analysis, searching for a detailed decomposition of the complex world into a series of multiple simple problems to afford following the scientific legitimacy of the visible power of intervention.

The paradigm shift we experienced during the last years revealed a new perspective in management theory: it substantially pointed some similarities in market and organizational behavior, and provided a new view on complexity related both to market and organizations. The contributions of Stark and Arrow focus on the critical aspects of the contrast between the invisible hand of market and the visible hand of management, overcoming the differences between market and organization behavior. They also propose an application to organizations and enterprises of the same premises that guaranteed a bottom-up efficiency natural mechanisms in the Smith's theory. They move from the traditional limitations of the scientific reductionism to embrace complex phenomena in their full variety. They count on the conceptualization of Complex Adapting Systems (Coleman, 1999) as the starting point for the interpretation, explanation and guide toward the emerging business reality.

Accordingly, the principles of *Self-organization, Fitness and Co-evolution* become the elements of a triad representing the new lens by which a new perspective on organization and business can be developed; the three dimensions of the new management.

Complexity Theory views organizations as *"complex adaptive systems"*: they co-evolve with the environment thanks to a self-organizing behavior of the agents, which navigate "fitness landscape" (Kauffman, 1993) of market opportunities and competitive dynamics (Coleman, 1999).

Complexity Theory and Organization Studies find their common ground in the issue of the adaptation to change. The complexity of political, regulatory and technological changes that organizations are facing today asks for an urgency to adapt and to change the organizational structure. Behavior is defined as self-organizing when people are free and able to connect with others, to network with them and act to achieve their goals. Today the level of interconnectedness among people is helping the acceleration of change on a global scale. It allows communicating faster new changing customer's demands; enables organizations to provide innovative offer through the collaboration facilitated by new communication and information technology; but it is also boosting the natural attitude of actors to self-organize (Miles, Snow, Matthews, Miles and Coleman, 1997).

Complexity approach and organization science differ in the application of the concepts of adaptation and self-organization (Coleman, 1999).

In contrast with linear or mechanistic systems, complex systems cannot be extricated from their settings or easily differentiated in sub-units. Their shape is the result and the embodiment of the way of their interactions within their changing dimensions.

The Complex Adaptive System approach to management embraces a market perspective and introduces a wide set of concepts, methods and measures. This perspective is far from the reductionist view of classical approaches. Dismantling the assumptions that events are predictable and decomposable, now outcomes are the results of cause-effect relationships, while rational actors operating in the market are able to know complex situations.

In the current business environment, a wide variety of new opportunities is continuously created by the emergence of new knowledge and scientific findings. New market opportunities gain the role of *"attractors,"* allowing entrepreneurs and their teams to innovate within existing firms or creating new ones. These actors co-evolve with the environment in a *"fitness landscape"* (Clippinger, 1999) through a process of self-organization activated to achieve survival and growth.

The concept of *fitness* that informs the Complexity Theory represents in organization studies a perspective on the capabilities and the state of a company at a given time. It is consistent with the paradigmatic shift in managerial mindsets, contrasting with the classical sense of competition.

From a Complex Adaptive System perspective, self-organization poses systems between an excess of disorder and order, between order and chaos. The place between the two extremes is called "sweet spot" (Kauffman, 1993) and represents just the "edge of chaos" that is for Brown and Eisenhardt (1998) the metaphor of the new managerial mindset. It is the place in which the system is in a position of high sensitivity to the variation in the market, but where it relies in a sufficient equilibrium to perpetuate itself. Under a managerial view, the goal of an organization becomes the search for a large space of options, where some alternatives are available: enough to guarantee the survival of the organization but not so excessive that they could compromise the capability of the firm to identify and exploit them.

The affirmation of the *self-organization* principle in organizations, as well as the dimension of *fitness landscape* as the proximal environment of the organization, and the *co-evolution* process of organizations and environment, points the drivers of the Cultural Revolution in the role of manager and in the shaping of the emerging forms of organizations.

2.4.3 The centrality of people: the "Coaching" in management

The rising of self-organized organizations opens new challenges to the role of manager. In particular, the following question needs to be investigated:

How is the Manager's role changed over time, according to the new organizational features?

A step toward the draw of a new profile of manager consistent with non-linear systems can be done by identifying the attributes of a self-organized behavior. Following the contribution of Holland (1995), there are four main properties that could be associated with any self-organized system that will allow us to better delineate the merging new managerial profile; they are:

1. Aggregation: The dimension by which the behavior of self-organizing entities, acting in conjunction with others, creates a group behavior distinct from that of each individual. This vision of behavior contrasts with that of hierarchy: it is not top-down and emerges spontaneously through the evolving interactions. While the classical approach to management focused on the creation of hierarchical structures in which the top level made the rule that the low level had to follow, here one of the primary roles of a manager is the aggregation of workers and resources to form task forces, teams, groups or communities. This function is easily recognizable as the Clark's "*soft assembly*" (Clark, 1997), pointing the capability to combine different components to respond to local contexts and to exploit intrinsic dynamics. Consistent and complementary to this concept is that of "*scaffolding*": the practice of using environmental factors to face complex problems in order to develop a more flexible mechanism of adaptation to changing external conditions and market demand. The open source approach offers a set of real applications of *soft assembly* and *scaffolding*, leveraging the levers of a new organization's success.

2. *Non-linearity:* In classical theories, each analytical method for scanning markets, studying economies and positioning enterprises are based on some assumptions of linear paradigm, mainly in the perspective that future could be the linear consequence of the past. The focus on non-linear behaviors that occur naturally in commerce, business and economy, points the attention toward unexpected changes. Under a managerial view, companies positioned in a "rugged landscape" (Kauffman, 1993) face continuous, new and unpredictable challenges, without the capability of planning strategically any movement toward a codified goal.

3. *Flows:* Despite the classical vision of organizations as composed of functional units causally related, this complex perspective looks at organizations as networks of potential non-linear relationships able to continuously recognize and reconfigure themselves. The flow of assets like people, resources, capital, orders and goods, which move throughout the organization, become the major source of value for the company. The organization itself can be viewed as a bundle of channels along which the flow of resources can be redirected each time a failure or a radical change provokes a massive rethinking of the way the organization's behavior.

4. *Diversity:* Is the measure of the variety of system's components that grows as the number of agents and interactions increase. The diversity of a system enhances the fitting of "a rugged landscape." In a complex world, the number and variety of actors in the organization become the

measure of its wealth. A diverse system of complex interactions drives economic and social richness, boosting the emergence of new market niches and opportunities; it also acts as an antidote for non-linearity and volatility of the rugged landscapes. The manager in this context has the role of preventing a tight alignment of the company to a niche or to rigid processes, maintaining the capability of the organization to self-renew, to increase the repertoire of adaptive responses, to redefine in each moment the flow of resources.

Our overview of the main characteristics of the new management has highlighted the fact that new managerial practices are constantly in change and not stable, virtually integrated, organized around networks and not yet hierarchically. More than in the past, they also result in built-on partnerships and alliances, supported by great technological assets, and focused on a strategy of "mass customization" more than "mass production." The new management philosophy is embracing innovation as an ingredient of success and increased competitiveness, while the creative potential of the organization is a function of its capability to foster new ideas, grasping the creativity and enthusiasm of people across the organization.

In this new perspective, people are at all levels the most significant resources and valuable capital assets of the organization.

Managers have to be able to conduct the organization toward the expected results, tapping the innovative potentiality of employees and encouraging the proliferation of autonomy and entrepreneurship.

This represents in essence the new role of coaches to which managers are called. The new managers must learn to be team players, facilitators, process managers, human resources executives, visionary leaders and entrepreneurs. In doing their daily jobs, they have to assume the role of knowledge integrating boundaries, stimulators of creativity, innovation muses and promoters of a continuous process of learning (Jamali, 2005).

The challenge for competitiveness calls for an organizational environment able to develop, leverage and diffuse these valuable new competitive knowledge assets. The new managerial philosophy focused on the role of manger as coach of the organization can be resumed in the shift in management philosophy presented in Figure 2.4.

The Strategy-Structure-Systems management approach was the generator of an effective corporate model where the manager's primary goals were to allocate scarce resources to competing opportunities, and to monitor performance through sophisticated control systems. The process by which knowledge replaced capital as the critical scarce resource, brought the concept of organization into turn its focus from the "Structure" to the "People" dimension, as the locus of knowledge production. Accordingly, the management task turned to the creation of an organizational environment conducive to the development of the new valuable asset. The attention shifted from the formal rigid structure to the effective management processes; and from the planning of a fixed strategy to the building of an energizing corporate purpose.

In performing their new roles, managers have to change their priorities and become builders of the organization. They have also addressed their efforts in creating a sense of meaning within the company that members can clearly identify and in which they will feel free to share ideas and commitment (Ghoshal and Bartlett, 1997).

In facilitating firms' mission of being creators of the great amount of social capital, managers are in a privileged position to make a difference in the organizational external and internal environment. In defining the meaning of *Individualized Corporation*, Ghoshal and Bartlett (1997) argue that the results that managers will reach are a consequence of their capability of attracting, motivating, developing and retaining individuals.

As highlighted by Baets and Van der Linden (2003), the 21st century firms are constantly breaking boundaries as internal networks overflow external networks, configuring themselves more and more as networked organizations. Resulting as complicated, turbulent, chaotic, antagonistic, complex and ambiguous realities, the new organizations call for managers who do not present a unique position or role, and that live the leadership as a strategic assets much more distributed than before. As proposed by Baets and Van der Linden (2003), this means to be concentrated on managing complexities rather than to manage over

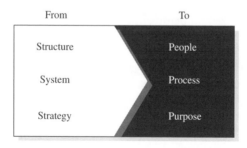

Figure 2.4   From "3S" to "3P" approach to management.
Source: Adapted from Ghoshal and Bartlett (1997).

complexity. In assuming the role of coaches, managers have to realize that they are part of the environment and have to be careful. They have to be engaged in promoting the creation of a working environment where people should be able to have fun in their jobs, to share experiences easily and create knowledge. Furthermore, they also have to demonstrate an eye for detail, an ability to listen and a capacity for critical distance and reflection.

The main challenges for the new management can be synthesized in: (Baets and Van der Linden, 2003):

- the promotion of a process of continuous innovation;
- a process of management and allocation of resources not only oriented at the profit;
- promoting the collective work toward shared goals and values; and
- the creation of excitement and satisfaction based on a honest and trusted integration.

2.4.4 A new strategy of competition: The "Edge of Chaos"

In 1998 Brown and Eisenhardt performed a field study of 12 global businesses in Europe, Asia and North America, starting from the research on complex adaptive behavior, evolutionary theory and the nature of change. Their goal was to highlight some insights on strategy and organizational design in high velocity settings where change is pervasive (Brown and Eisenhardt, 1998).

The specific setting of the analysis was characterized by emergent transformational and hypercompetitive markets, affected by unclear inter-industries or intra-industries boundaries, unstable business models, unclear competition, and pervasively impacted by new technological breakthroughs and shifts in regulation.

Such settings, cutting across the basic assumptions of traditional managerial approaches, like the stability of markets, the predictability of incremental changes and the sustainability of competitive advantage, outlined the unprecedented managerial problems these companies were facing. They also recognize that the nature of change in the business environment was making industrial economists unable to count on the time necessary to gather required data, and that the analysis of data and position the organization would take. By interviewing more than one hundred managers, it emerged that the main impact of the new reality on strategy in such a context was that advantages are temporary, and not actually sustainable, and that strategy was likely to shift.

For Brown and Eisenhardt, since change became the only certain element of the new scenario, the key challenge for managers is the ability to strategize and manage it.

Three levels of change entail three different managerial behaviors:

a. *react* to it, following a defensive behavior to contrast the competitors new moves, or unexpected customers demand, without creating really new opportunities;
b. *anticipate* it, predicting where possible its path and preparing for the exploitation of the early developed and lined resources or competences;
c. *lead* it, creating it by imposing the pace of change, like launching a new market, redefining the customer expectations and finally changing the rules of game.

These perspectives suggest a path toward the conceptualization of a paradigm shift in the managerial mindset. It doesn't state that they reject all preceding schools, and the sense of design, planning and positioning, but they show an ability to incorporate some of their concepts in its overall framework.

The model proposed by Brown and Eisenhardt describes synthetically a shift in the view of management facing a changing reality. Starting from the Porter's focus on Industry as the unit of analysis of competition, their model moves toward a new sense of competition "On the Edge"as shown in Figure 2.5.

The *"Competing on the Edge"* approach moves far from the linear approaches to management that assumed clear industry boundaries, predictable competition or a knowable future.

Far from developing a consistent and strong theory about tight rules of competition, the approach aims at guiding organizations to change constantly and develop a "semicoherent strategic direction" emerging

Figure 2.5 Decreasing linearity in strategic approaches.
Source: Adapted from Brown and Eisenhardt (1998).

from the organization itself. The attributes of the new vision of management become (Brown and Eisenhardt, 1998):

- *Unpredictable*: Unpredictability of change drives a pervasive uncertainty that dampens accuracy and the search for complete and perfect information about phenomena; it is not possible to forecast future conditions of the market; past experiences could be misleading in front of current challenges.
- *Uncontrolled*: Since planning activities are losing relevance and the time dimension is assuming different features compared to the past, it doesn't make sense to concentrate strategy and decision-making activities at corporate headquarters in a fast changing industry.
- *Inefficient*: Short-term efficiency is no more the primary goal of an organization; the features of the changing environment add randomness and indeterminacy to the managerial activity, so a "trial and error" culture could provide organizations with the required flexibility to use change to relentlessly reinvent the business by discovering opportunities for growth.
- *Proactive*: Reaction is no longer sufficient to ensure the survival and success of organizations; so competing on the edge moves toward the anticipation and leadership of change, developing a proactive strategy, looking ahead to the needs of the global market, lining up the right resources, and finally creating the change itself, forcing other firms to follow and changing the rules of game.
- *Continuous*: The rhythm of change leaves no chance to large moves, like big corporate transformations; it forces organizations to go along continuous change that becomes endemic to the organization itself.
- *Diverse*: Survival in a fast-changing environment is associated with diversification of risks; a combination of different strategies could ensure the balancing of good and bad results, letting the identification of a strategic path of diverse steps.

The authors strive to clarify this exotic concept by presenting what they name the five building blocks for this approach: *improvisation, co-adaptation, regeneration, experimentation and time pacing*.

1. Managing by *improvisation* ensures an adaptive culture where change is the norm and temporary advantages are identified and realized. A balance is needed between too much structure and not too much structure: a semi-structure. In such a semi-structure, few key issues are

identified and set as priorities; specific and strict rules are attached to the structure and deadlines and responsibilities are well identified.

2. *Co-adaptation* is the ability of diversified firms to balance the needs and constraints, and collaboration and individual success within the system, to focus efforts and synergies on high profit areas rather than any opportunity of a payoff. The goal is not only the maximum profit per group but the maximum profit for the entire firm.

3. *Regeneration* deals with the notion of time as a continuous flow that the firm has to navigate through. The key to success is to be able to exploit the past successes, failures and experiences and to explore the future. The goal to reach is to generate constant competitive advantage while emphasizing that it is the present that matters most. It is critical to retain experienced people to prevent existing knowledge from being lost and to develop an ability to recombine elements in new ways to create the future from the past today.

4. Similarly to the thought of Mintzberg (1994), the concept of *experimentation* strongly advocates the *learning by doing approach*. This approach considers the failures as constructive parts of the process since they are opportunities to learn and correct behaviors, decisions or strategies. For this, the firm needs a clear and powerful vision that could bring all groups together while not overly describing the future for fear of setting limits of directions and wrong expectations.

5. *Time-pacing* holds a special meaning within the theory, helps managers focus on two often-forgotten questions that are crucial in rapidly changing markets: how often to change and how to negotiate transition between activities. Instead of waiting for events, as other schools recommend, to act or react, time pacing prescribes a time-based approach to action where new products are introduced or new stores are opened at a certain frequency. This helps set an internal rhythm that could provide a much differentiated advantage over competitors.

A steady drive toward more knowledge-based firms is emerging, where the main source of competitive advantage is increasingly becoming the human factor and is pushing a growing number of industries toward high-velocity markets. This could allow this interesting (even if it is still a marginal perspective of strategy) to become more mainstream.

2.4.5   Toward the catalytic networks

In a social and economic scenario characterized by hypercompetitive dynamics and growing relevance of networks, the discussion about new organizational structures and forms is extremely pertinent. In particular, one relevant question to answer would be:

Which are the emerging organizational forms that could expect to survive and succeed; in a word to fit the variously "rugged landscape"?

The contribution of the complexity and evolutionary theories (Clippinger, 1999) to organizational studies provided a further shift in the focus on organizational forms: from the design of task-oriented structures thought to achieve determined long-planned goals, to the identification of the naturally emerging organizational forms more capable of surviving in an increasing complex environment. Under this perspective, the basic dimension of the company survival and success becomes the company's "fitness," that is a function of its ability to respond and anticipate the changes in the business environment. The challenge to contemporary business is to match business strategy and investment to the fitness landscape.

The range of variability of the competitive landscape makes the management role that of aligning the structure and function of the organization to the current and anticipated changes. The identification of the fitness landscape in which an organization is positioned is the key for the recognition of the right organizational form, and for the implementation of the right strategy.

In the work of Clippinger (1999) four different fitness landscapes are identified, as functions of:

a. the *"external ruggedness"* of the environment, representing the degree of interconnectedness among natural resources, suppliers, competitors, technology, customers and different social and economic factors; and

b. the *"internal complexity"* of the organization, representing the degree of interconnectedness among its internal components, individuals, business units, teams, functions, processes.

According to this analysis, the first challenge the manager should face is the accurate characterization of the degree of internal and external complexity of the landscape, as well as the identification of the pure model of organization closer to the company.

The logic behind this model presents four different situations corresponding to four categories of organizations:

- Classical Stereotypes;
- Byzantine Monoliths;

- Endangered Deniers; and
- Catalytic Network.

Stable environments, made of low level of ruggedness, are suitable for classical organizations. Named as *Classical Stereotypes*, these contexts are those that fit well the external conditions of relatively slow change. The main risk for this kind of business actor is facing their evolution into different entities, when changing the internal conditions in the phase of development or transformation their complexity could increase, forcing the rigid banks of the previous organizational boundaries.

More difficult is the survival of organizations shaped just on the needs and features of their environment. This kind of *Byzantine Monoliths,* like the inflexible bureaucracies or the systems based on patronage models, are often not ready to face the challenges of the free markets, or of new external conditions.

Where the landscape is characterized by a high rate of complexity, the organizations which are too strictly regulated to face the challenge of a continuous adaptation are also exposed to the risk of extinction. They tend to become *Endangered Deniers.* The pressure that the environment would exert on the company is such that any attempt to achieve a path of equilibrium is too hard to be accomplished with a linear strategy.

But when the complexity of the environment is counterbalanced by a high rate of complexity of the organization itself, a peculiar system emerges: the *Catalytic Network.* It is the kind of organization that stems in the right landscape area, at the edge of chaos, where classical managerial standards and top-down control cannot work. The role of managers in this organization is the fastening of fitness criteria. The interaction with the environment and internal recombination become the rules to benefit of increasing returns and network externalities. The classical organization leaves the place to new systems different permeable boundaries, where the *Self-organization, Fitness* and *Co-evolution* principles express freely their potentialities.

2.4.6   A non-linear dynamic approach to business management

The growing importance of knowledge and information as key competitive factors, as well as the rising of new and complex market dynamics, calls for firms to be more and more rapid in response to customer needs and to identify the emergence of new niche market.

In doing this, firms are called to reconfigure their structures adopting a more flexible, distributed (and not hierarchical) structures. For all these reasons, companies and various forms of business organizations assume more and more the form of Complex Adaptive Systems (CAS).

The *paradox* that organizations experience in this scenario is that most of the factors that contribute to their efficiency can undermine adaptability and compromise their self-organizing capability.

Labor division and *tasks standardization* contribute to improve the firms' effectiveness in terms of rationalization of the signals coming from the internal and external environment, but they could compromise the vision of enterprise as a whole as well as its flexibility.

Organizations can overcome this tendency to break down through some solutions:

a. *The Engineering Solution*: If the idea of reengineering the business processes (BPR) represented a great change in the managerial practices, it soon lost its luster because it was often associated with extensive software creation that always results in delay, the over-extension of the budget and was full of bugs. ERP is presented as the culmination of the BPR movement.

b. *The Evolutionary Solution*: *Adaptability arises naturally in complex systems*. The *Complexity Theory* suggests that order arises spontaneously all the time from complex, irregular and chaotic states of matter; the *second law of thermodynamics* suggests that closed systems that receive energy from the outside tend to produce order; the *Biology* highlights that notion that patterns arise spontaneously when a large number of components interact in a nonlinear way.

The self-organizing enterprise moves from the premise that effective organization is *evolved* and not designed. The aim of a self-organizing enterprise is to create an environment in which successful divisions of labor and routines not only emerge but also self-adjust in response to the environment. Self-organizing means that a new *behavioral* pattern emerges from the interaction of separate agents, who adapt their activities according to what they believe to be the consequences of their actions.

Another interpretation about evolution of organizations and their self-organizing capabilities is offered by theory on evolutionary systems (Donald Campbell, 1965; Murray Gell-Mann, 1996), which defines the *process of evolution* as based on three elements: *variation, selection, retention*.

New behaviors emerge spontaneously from the interaction of agents or organizational changes. The behaviors associated with the agent's definition of success are reinforced; the repeated ones are retained and become routines.

Some organizations are configured to evolve faster and more effectively than others. Interesting behaviors arise between the several parts of the organizations that result in being interconnected. *The structure of a network constrains how fast it can evolve and in what directions.* Managers can guide the evolution of a self-organizing enterprise more effectively if they learn to analyze the firm's network structure.

Four guidelines for diagnosing self-organizing systems based on complex adaptive systems allow managers to visualize the organization in new ways and diagnose whether the enterprise is configured to evolve rapidly and flexibly:

1. *Evolution proceeds more rapidly when networks are partitioned*: Complex systems evolve from simple ones much more rapidly if they are "nearly decomposable" (Simon, 1996). Systems assembled from such stable intermediate building blocks evolve much more rapidly.
2. *Chaos may signal that a network is too richly interconnected*: Networks are chaotic when every agent's output is influenced by the actions of many other agents (Kauffman, 1993).
3. *A slow rate of evolutionary improvement may reflect too much interdependence*: When the performance of an agent depends on the performance of many other agents, it is for individuals to become trapped in suboptimal performance. Abernathy (1979) called this trap the "productivity dilemma."
4. *It is more important to identify the worst-performing*: Element in a network than the best-performing one.

2.5   The new manager's profile

The paradigm shift that points to the rise of a new Managerial Mindset creates the profile of a new manager. The new environmental conditions no longer make them *"cardinal rational actors"* able to collect sound information, weigh alternatives and make decisions by which they can translate the strategy into action. In this new perspective, the manager becomes a sensitive operator able to face uncertainty, instability and unpredictability, dealing with people and knowledge as the primary drivers of organizations survival and success.

Today managers help structure the context within which self-organization takes place. They provide governance, not control, and

Functions / Processes	Planning	Leading	Organizing	Controlling
Selecting the external environment	X	X		
Defining performance	X	X		X
Managing meaning		X		
Choosing people		X	X	
Reconfiguring network		X	X	
Evolving vicarious selection systems		X		X
Energizing system		X		

Figure 2.6 The new managerial profile: A process/function matrix.

operate an indirect selection system devoted to create in the internal model the organization's external environment (Drucker, 1994).

The traditional manager profile, made up of the four functions of *leading, planning, organizing* and *controlling,* is no longer suitable to represent the set of competencies required to ensure the organization's performance. Adaptation, self-organization and fitness entail for him new roles, and a shift in perspective from the managerial "functions" to the managerial "processes," and that will guide the identification of the manager competences.

As stewards of networks that evolve effective behaviors, managers carry out a series of critical actions that can be grouped according to the *Seven Levers for Guiding Evolving Enterprise* (Anderson, 1999) as shown in Figure 2.6.

Comparing them with the traditional managerial functions in a process/function matrix, it will be possible to derive the characteristics of a new Leader, pointing the dramatic weight of the "leading" function against that of planning, organizing and controlling attitudes. The processes that the New Manager is intended to lead are:

1. *Selecting the external environment*: Set strategy, choose what markets to serve and how to win in them, define the firms' positioning, as well as the context for self-organizing, the rate and the evolutional directions.

2. *Defining Performance*: Define the firm's performance; shape the networks' behavior by emphasizing or not the indicators that will lead to long-term profitability; limit the risk-return's frontier; support political candidates; contribute to the growth of social value and public education.

3. *Managing Meaning*: Propagate culture that shapes competing interpretations into a consensus; they get more done by managing symbols than by managing things; in CAS language they manage by tagging and retagging flows through a network.

4. *Choosing People*: Attract the most capable agents to the enterprise; they have to guarantee the diversity; stimulate variation hiring external people but also to guarantee the exploitation of the veteran ones and the diffusion of their ideas.

5. *Reconfiguring Network*: Guarantee the continuous reconfiguration and reengineering of networks; change the existing network by creating new positions, or establish strategic alliances, sponsorships; they frequently adjust to change by reconfiguring instead of telling agents how to adapt; they add and subtract nodes, make and break connections.

6. *Evolving Vicarious Selection Systems*: Obtain good predictions when functional tests are representative of the environmental feedback. They use it to simulate the voice of the market; they develop theories about the best working systems. Managers have to consider that there are some signals that the system cannot predict; they have to avoid the institutionalization of the process and not be used as the tool of the competition.

7. *Energizing System*: Motivate employees, energize agents by providing inspiration and challenges; set aggressive goals and create the perceived mismatch between performance achieved and required; pump energy through vision and leadership; not controllers but inspirations.

The seven levers for guiding the evolving enterprise proposed by Anderson (1999) identify the competency areas of the new manager profile. The development of this radically new and complex set of competences requires a similarly radical innovation, in both the "product" and the "process" of creating such a Leader.

2.6   Conclusion

Several metaphors and conceptual frameworks have been presented in this chapter to come up with an interpretation of the (changing) business reality and managerial mindset that emerged during the

20th century. The rise of the new century draws the attention of organizations and presents new challenges to address, related to the complexity of managing these new paradigms.

In particular, a new managerial mindset has been described as the consequence of the evolutionary path that sees people and organizations engaged in the challenge of creating the most favorable conditions to be successful. A new profile of the manager is the expression of a transition from a linear to a non-linear way of thinking.

The strategies to enabling this transition will be investigated in the following chapters, with a specific focus on the relevant competencies for today's managers and the emerging trends in learning strategies and approaches adopted in the process of developing human and social capital.

References

W. Abernathy (1979) *The Productivity Dilemma* (Baltimore, MD: Johns Hopkins University Press).

A. Afuah (2003) *Business Models: A Strategic Management Approach* (New York, NY: McGraw-Hill).

R. Amit and C. Zott (2001) "Value Creation in E-Business," *Strategic Management Journal*, 22(6/7), pp. 493–520.

P. Anderson (1999) "Seven Levers for Guiding the Evolving Enterprise," in J. H. Clippinger III (1999) *Order from the Bottom Up. The Biology of Business, Decoding the Natural Laws of Enterprise* (San Francisco, CA: Jossey-Bass Publishers).

K. R. Andrews (1971) *The Concept of Corporate Strategy* (Homewood, IL: Irwin).

H. I. Ansoff (1965) *Corporate Strategy* (New York, NY: McGraw-Hill).

W. Baets and G. Van der Linden (2003) *Virtual Corporate Universities: A Matrix of Knowledge and Learning for the New Digital Dawn* (Norwell, MA: Kluwer).

J. B. Barney (1991) "Firm Resources Sustained Competitive Advantage," *Journal of Management*, 17(1), pp. 99–120.

T. Barnett and D. Hofler (2006) "Contingency Approach to Management," retrieved from www.referenceforbusiness.com/management/Comp-De/Contingency-Approach-to-Management.html.

P. M. Blau (1970) "The Formal Theory of Differentiation in Organizations," *American Sociological Review*, 35, pp. 201–18.

S. P. Borgatti (1996) "Organizational Theory: Determinants of Structure," Boston College: Analytic Tech retrieved from http://www.analytictech.com/mb021/orgtheory.htm.

L. M. Bravo-Castillo (1998) "Globalization: Strategic Options for Developing Economies," available at http://orpheus.ucsd.edu/las/studies/pdfs/bravo.pdf.

S. L. Brown and M. Eisenhardt (1998) *Competing on Edge: Strategy as Structured Chaos* (Boston, MA: HBS Press).

D. Buchanan and A. Huczynski (2004) *Organizational Behavior. An Introductory Text* (Harlow, UK: Prentice Hall Financial Times).

T. Burns and G. M. Stalker (1961) *The Management of Innovation* (London, UK: Tavistock).

D. T. Campbell (1965) "Variation and Selective Retention in Sociocultural Evolution" in Barringer, Blanksten, Mack, *Social Change in Developing Areas*, pp. 19–49 (Boston, MA: Schenkman Publishing Company).

A. D. Chandler (1962) *Strategy and Structure: Chapters in the History of the Industrial Enterprise* (Boston, MA: MIT Press).

A. D. Chandler (1977) *The Visible Hand* (Boston, MA: The Belknap Press).

J. Chen and A. Wang (2001) "Challenge of Innovation to Classic Business Management Theories," in *Proceedings of Change Management and the New Industrial Revolution*, IEMC '01.

C. M. Christensen (1992) "Exploring the Limits of the Technology S-Curve, Part 1: Component Technologies," *Production and Operations Management Journal*, 1(fall 1992), pp. 334–57.

A. Clark (1997) *Being There: Putting Brain, Body, and World Together Again* (Boston, MA: MIT Press).

J. H. Clippinger III (1999) *Order from the Bottom Up. The Biology of Business, Decoding the Natural Laws of Enterprise* (San Francisco, CA: Jossey-Bass Publishers).

D. Coleman (1999) "Groupware: Collaboration and Knowledge Sharing. Knowledge Management Handbook," in J. Liebowitz (eds) *Knowledge Management Handbook* (New York, NY: CRC Press), vol. 12(1), pp. 12–15.

D. Collis (1991) "A Resource-Based Analysis of Global Competition: The Case of the Bearings Industry," *Strategic Management Journal* (12), pp. 49–68.

D. W. Cravens, N. F. Piercy and S. H. Shipp (2005) "New Organizational Forms for Competing in Highly Dynamic Environments: The Network Paradigm," *British Journal of Management*, 7(3), pp. 203–18.

R. A. D'Aveni (1994) *Hypercompetition: Managing the Dynamics of Strategic Maneuvering* (New York, NY: Free Press).

J. Davis and K. Eisenhardt (2004) " Complexity, Market Dynamism, and Strategy of Simple Rules", Working paper, October 18, retrieved from www.london. edu/assets/documents/PDF/KEisenhardtpaper2.pdf.

G. G. Dess and D. W. Beard (1984) "Dimensions of Organizational Task Environments," *Administrative Science Quarterly*, 29(1), pp. 52–73.

G. Dosi (1988) "Sources, Procedures, and Microeconomic Effects of Innovation," *Journal of Economic Literature*, 26, pp. 1120–171.

P. Drucker (1994) "The Theory of the Business," *Harvard Business Review*, September–October.

J. Dunning (1997) *Governments, Globalization and International Business* (Oxford, UK: University Press).

W. J. Duncan and J. G. Van Matre (1990) "The Gospel According to Deming: Is It Really New?" *Business Horizons*, 14(3), pp. 3–9.

J. Elmeskov (2008) "World Economy at the Crossroads—Open Markets Versus Protectionism," *OECD*, retrieved from www.oecd.org/dataoecd/34/53/40917804.pdf.

H. Fayol (1949) *General and Industrial Management*. Translated from C. Storrs (London, UK: Pitman).

K. Galanopoulos (2008) "How Contemporary Are Charlie Chaplin's Modern Times? The Fordist and Post-Fordist Production Model," *Intellectum*, 3, pp. 117–30.

M. Gell-Mann (1996) "Fundamental Sources of Unpredictability," SFI Conference, available at www.santafe.edu/research/publications/workingpapers/97-09-079. pdf.

C. S. J. George (1972) *The History of Management Thought* (Englewood Cliffs, NJ: Prentice-Hall).

S. Ghoshal and C. A. Bartlett (1997) *The Individualized Corporation* (New York, NY: Harper Collins).

R. Grant (1991) "The Resource-Based Theory of Competitive Advantage: Implications for Strategy Formulation," *California Management Review* (Spring), pp. 119–35.

J. Hage and M. Aiken (1967) "Relationship of Centralization to Other Structural Properties," *Administrative Science Quarterly*, 12, pp. 72–92.

G. Hamel and C. K. Prahalad (1994) *Competing for the Future* (Boston, MA: HBS Press).

G. Hamel (2000) *Leading the Revolution* (Boston, MA: HBS Press).

C. Helfat (1994) "Firm Specificity in Corporate Applied R&D," *Organization Science*, 5, pp. 173–84.

F. Heylighen (1990) *Representation and Change. A Metarepresentational Framework for the Foundations of Physical and Cognitive Science* (Belgium, Gent: Communication & Cognition).

F. Heylighen and C. Joslyn (2001) "Cybernetics and Second Order Cybernetics" in R. A. Meyers (ed.) *Encyclopedia of Physical Science and Technology* (New York, NY: Academic Press).

F. Heylighen, P. Cilliers and C. Gershenson (2006) "Complexity and Philosophy" in J. Bogg and R. Geyer (eds) *Complexity, Science and Society* (Oxford, UK: Radcliffe Publishing).

J. H. Holland (1995) *Hidden Order* (Reading, MA: Addison-Wesley).

D. Jamali (2005) "Changing Management Paradigms: Implications for Educational Institutions," *Journal of Management Development*, 24, pp. 104–15.

S. A. Kauffman (1993) *The Origin of Order: Self-Organization and Selection in Evolution* (New York: Oxford University Press).

S. J. Kobrin (1997) "The Architecture of Globalization: State Sovereignty in a Networked Global Economy" in J. H. Dunning (ed.) *Governments, Globalization, and International Business* (London, UK: Oxford University Press).

A. Kruger (2003) "Sovereign Debt Restructuring: Messy or Messier?" *International Monetary Fund, Annual Meeting of the American Economic Association*, Annual Meeting of the American Economic Association, January 4, Washington.

R. N. Langlois (2003) "The Vanishing Hand: The Changing Dynamics of Industrial Capitalism," *Industrial and Corporate Change*, 351(85), pp. 376.

P. R. Lawrence and J. W. Lorsch (1967) "Differentiation and Integration in Complex Organizations," *Administrative Science Quarterly*, 12, pp. 1–47.

U. Lechner and J. Hummel (2002) "Social Profiles of Virtual Communities," *Proceedings of the 35th Annual Hawaii International Conference on System Sciences* (HICSS'02), pp. 2245–54.

D. Leonard-Barton (1992) "Core Capabilities and Core Rigidities: A Paradox in Managing New Product Development," *Strategic Management Journal*, 13(Special Issue Summer), pp. 111–25.

C. Litter (1982) *The Development of the Labour Process in Capitalist Societies* (London, UK: Heinemann Educational Books).

J. Linder and S. Cantrell (2000) "Changing Business Models: Surveying the Landscape," White Paper, Institute for Strategic Change, Accenture, available at www.accenture.com/xd/xd.asp?it=enweb&xd=_ins%5Cprojectmore_4.xml.

P. Mandelson (2008) "Globalization Needs a Global New Deal," *European Commission Trade and Competitiveness* available at http://ec.europa.eu/trade/issues/sectoral/competitiveness/pr090608_en.html.

B. Mascarenhas, A. Baveja and M. Jamil (1998) "Dynamics of Core Competencies in Leading Multinational Companies," *California Management Review*, 40(4), pp. 117–32.

E. J. McCarthy (1960) *Basic Marketing: A Managerial Approach* (Homewood, IL: Irwin).

R. E. Miles, C. C. Snow, J. A. Matthews, G. Miles and H. J. Coleman (1997) "Organizing in the Knowledge Age: Anticipating the Cellular Form," *Academy of Management Executive*, 11, pp. 7–24.

H. Mintzberg (1994) *The Rise and Fall of Strategic Management* (New York, NY: The Free Press).

R. M. Murphy (2003) "Managing Strategic Change: An Executive Overview," available at http://www.calumcoburn.co.uk/articles/articles-management-paradigm.html.

A. Osterwalder, Y. Pigneur and C. L. Tucci (2005) "Clarifying Business Models: Origins, Present, and Future of the Concept," *Communications of the Association for Information Systems* (16), pp. 1–25.

E. T. Penrose (1959) *The Theory of the Growth of the Firm* (Oxford, UK: University Press).

M. E. Porter (1980) *Competitive Strategy* (New York, NY: The Free Press).

C. K. Prahalad and G. Hamel (1990) "The Core Competence of the Corporation," *Harvard Business Review* (May–June), pp. 79–91.

S. P. Robbins and M. Coulter (2003) *Management: 2003 Update 7E* (New Jersey, NJ: Prentice Hall)

A. Romano, G. Passiante and C. Petti (2003) "Recent Approaches to Strategic Entrepreneurship," Proceedings of the *3rd International Conference on Entrepreneurial Innovation*, Bangalore, India, 6–8 March.

G. Salaman (1985) "Factory work," in: R. Deem and G. Salaman, G. (eds) *Work, Culture and Society*, Open University Press, pp. 1–21.

W. R. Scott (1987) *Organizations—Rational, Natural, and Open Systems* (New Jersey: Prentice-Hall, Englewood Cliffs).

P. Selznick (1957) *Leadership in Administration* (New York, NY: Harper & Row).

H. A. Simon (1996) *The Sciences of Artificial* (Boston, MA: MIT Press).

A. Smith (1776) *The Wealth of Nations* (London, UK: W. Strahan and T. Cadell).

J. C. Smuts (1926) *Holism and Evolution* (New York, NY: The Macmillan Company).

R. D. Stacey (1992) *Managing the Unknowable: Strategic Boundaries Between Chaos and Order in Organizations* (San Francisco, CA: Jossey-Bass).

P. Stähler (2002) *"Business Models as an Unit of Analysis for Strategizing,"* International Workshop on Business Models, Lausanne, Switzerland.

F. F. Suarez and R. Oliva (2005) "Environmental Change and Organizational Transformation," *Industrial and Corporate Change*, 14(6), pp. 1017–41.

M. Tushman and L. Rosenkopf (1992) "Organizational Determinants of Technological Change: Toward a Sociology of Technological Evolution" in

L. Cummings and B. Staw (eds) *Research in Organizational Behavior* (Greenwich, CT, JAI Press).

L. von Bertanlaffy (1968) *General System Theory: Foundations, Development, and Applications* (New York, NY: George Braziller).

E. von Hippel (2005) *Democratizing Innovation* (Boston, MA: MIT Press).

J. von Neumann and O. Morgenstern (1947) *Theory of Games and Economic Behavior* (Princeton, NJ: Princeton University Press).

R. Waldersee, A. Griffiths and J. Lai (2003) "Predicting Organizational Change Success: Matching Organization Type, Change Type and Capabilities," *Journal of Applied Management and Entrepreneurship*, 9(1), pp. 66–81.

Y. Wang, H. P. Lo and Y. Yang (2004) "The Constituents of Core Competencies and Firm Performance: Evidence from High-Technology Firms in China," *Journal of Engineering and Technology Management*, 21(4), pp. 249–80.

M. Weber (1947) *The Theory of Social and Economic Organization*. Translated by A. M. Henderson and T. Parsons (New York, NY: The Free Press).

B. Wernerfelt (1984) "A Resource-Based View of the Firm," *Strategic Management Journal* (5), pp. 171–80.

M. J. Wheatley (1999) *Leadership and the New Science: Discovering Order in a Chaotic World* (San Francisco, CA: Berrett-Koehler Publishers).

D. R. Wholey and J. Brittain (1989) "Characterizing Environmental Variation," *The Academy of Management Journal*, 32(4), pp. 867–82.

J. P. Womack, D. T. Jones and D. Roos (1990) *The Machine that Changed the World* (New York, NY: Rawson Associates).

J. Woodward (1965) *Industrial Organization: Theory and Practice* (London, UK: Oxford University Press).

D. A. Wren (1972) *The Evolution of Management Thought* (New York, NY: The Ronald Press).

3
Networked Learning for Human Capital Development

Giustina Secundo, Alessandro Margherita and Gianluca Elia

3.1   Introduction

In Chapter 1 we moved from major transformations in economy and business to raise the need for a new framework, the *Open Business Innovation Leadership* that should inform the practice of management at a threefold level: (a) the need to develop a new mindset that incorporates the changing competitive paradigms, strategic levers and drivers of success; (b) the need for a new perspective about human capital development in terms of people, learning processes and strategic purpose; and (c) the centrality to develop social capital and stakeholder value by adopting an integrated organizational learning and innovation model. From this perspective, Chapter 2 has investigated the emergence of a competitive mindset suitable for the new scenery; whereas this chapter focuses on the centrality of intangible resources, and in particular on human resources, in leading organizations that create value.

The growing contribution of intangible or non-financial value to the total wealth of organizations is confirmed by some estimates that rate the intangible value of several firms as being three, four and sometimes 16 times higher than their material value (Heisig, Vorbeck and Niebuhr, 2001). From the first report, published in 1994 by the insurance company Skandia, several studies have appeared that use case examples to investigate the most up-to-date ideas and methods for perceiving and measuring the value of intangibles (Morey, Maybury and Thuraisingham, 2000).

The mission of the firm in the New Economy is the ability to create, transfer, assemble, integrate, protect and exploit knowledge assets for non-financial value creation (Teece, 2000). These knowledge assets represent the "intellectual capital" of an organization, which can be described as three interdependent components (Seemann et al., 2000): *human capital*, the tacit and explicit knowledge, skills and experience possessed by individuals; *structural capital*, including the explicit knowledge embedded in work processes and systems, or encoded in written policies, documentation, databases and intellectual property such as patents and copyrights; and the *social capital*, which is the overall set of relationships that make the organization work effectively (Prusak and Cohen, 2001). Human capital has a central role in that it allows the other components to be continually in motion, enhanced, shared, sold or used to deliver superior business results (Seemann et al., 2000). The ongoing development and organization-wide integration of human capital effectively creates and deploys the intangible assets (especially the knowledge) within an organization.

This vision is based on a new managerial mindset (see Chapter 2) that recognizes the importance of human capital as being one of the distinctive features of the meaning and practice of today's management. The approach to human resource appropriate in the face of the transforming business scenery is the one that sees people as the most relevant organizational asset rather than a cost to minimize. A firms' success is indeed the result of the capabilities of human capital to continuously renew and emphasize the knowledge available, facilitate the development of relationships, and integrate distributed initiative and expertise.

In parallel with their strategic objectives and actions, leading organizations are also transforming the way in which human capital is perceived and managed. This chapter focuses on the emerging trends in human capital development, with an emphasis on the transformations related to peoples' competencies and roles, learning approaches and processes, and the strategic purpose of organizations that recognize that human capital growth is a driver of stakeholder value. In particular, the following questions are here addressed:

1. *In what ways are learning and human capital development processes being impacted by the new business and management paradigms?*
2. *What are the key dimensions characterizing human capital development and how they are being transformed?*
3. *What networked learning view and model can be developed to enhance the value creation potential of human capital?*

The answers to these questions are contained in the following chapter outline: Section 3.2 introduces the centrality of learning and human development in leading companies; next, the main forces impacting human capital development are investigated in 3.3. Section 3.4 introduces the key trajectories of change as related to people (3.5), processes (3.6) and strategic purpose (3.7) dimensions of human capital development. In Section 3.8, an organizational and technological model of networked learning is presented. Finally, some conclusions are drawn in 3.9.

3.2 The company as university: Why does learning matter?

> People are innately curious and, as social animals, naturally motivated to interact and learn from one another. Over thousand of years, families, clans and communities have evolved as teaching and learning groups, with individuals sharing information and synthesizing knowledge as central part of their social interchange and as a key engine of their collective progress . . . to create an organisation that is able to learn, a company must develop people who are hungry of knowledge, stimulating them through an education and development agenda that is built on the business goals.
>
> (Ghoshal and Bartlett, 1997, p. 69)

When we first began writing this chapter, we wanted answers to our questions based on the observation of leading companies showing fundamental *organizational capabilities*. We thus investigated how these companies create value based on a successful approach to managing knowledge, people and learning. The analysis of cases belonging to different industries has been very important. Whereas sectors such as banking and consulting have for a long time been aware of the importance of individual expertise and learning processes in creating a distinguishing competitive advantage, in recent years this awareness has spread to companies in a variety of other industries.

For instance, among steel companies, who, historically, have been reliant on the economies of scale, the power of knowledge-based competition has been demonstrated by the case of *Nucor* as shown by Ghoshal and Bartlett (1997). Indeed, managers once forced only to focus on defining a product-market position have been asked strategically to develop individual and organizational capabilities to sense and respond rapidly and flexibly to change.

Intel, the world's largest and most profitable semiconductor company, is characterized by a relatively young workforce. Most of the technologies used in Intel's *Pentium* chip did not exist when the scientists and engineers who developed it finished their graduate studies. Without recruiting the best brains worldwide and without large investments in training to keep them at the forefront of the rapidly evolving technologies, Intel could not survive in its business. Considering people as a value and not just a cost, and continuously upgrading their skills and expertise, becomes a requisite for the survival of organizations (Meister, 1998). The half-life of any employee's base expertise today covers a few years rather than a few decades. Companies like Intel understand this and create their own university, offering courses where employees can self-enrol, as well as a large variety of external courses delivered by universities and consultants.

General Electric and *Motorola* represent other important examples of companies very involved in the ongoing development of their human capital. Building employee development into the ongoing routines of corporate life contributes to learning in ways companies cannot anticipate (Ghoshal and Bartlett, 1997).

The case of *ABB* is interesting for similar reasons. The executive vice president of ABB and his top management team spent a lot of time representing a management approach focused on the reinforcement of individuals' initiative and personal responsibility. This was translated to peoples' empowerment and open communication, in top-down and bottom up processes of engaging managers in a dialogue about how to defend a position of competitive long-term and sustainable advantage.

When *McKinsey* decided to dramatically increase its commitment to the training of its associates in the 1970s, it found that forcing partners to take the role of professors allowed them to articulate and document knowledge that had been long tacit. Equally important was the impact on the participants; they learned about new tools, models and frameworks but also developed the contacts and the relationships that became a vital part of the firm's ability to develop and diffuse knowledge rapidly around the world. The more the company competes on the basis of superior knowledge and expertise, the more it overcomes the view of itself as a portfolio of purely financial resources to be distributed in the most efficient manner (Bartlett, 2000).

This concept is evident in *KAO*, the Japanese consumer packaged-goods company that sees itself not just as a detergent and soap company but, above all, as an educational institution. The responsibilities of managers are to teach and to learn and this powerful concept allowed KAO to became one of the most innovative and creative Japanese companies (Quelch, 1994).

3M is the best example of a company relying on people initiative. McKnight, the president of the company, referred to the vital role of his managers in creating "an organizational climate that stimulates ordinary people to produce extraordinary results" (Ghoshal and Bartlett, 1997). At the core of 3M management approach there are a series of policies sustaining the innovative potentiality of people and their entrepreneurial initiatives.

Skandia has been one of the first companies recognizing not only the importance of knowledge assets compared to the traditional financial assets, but also developing a system to incorporate the intellectual capital with the adjusted equity financial capital to measure the company's market value.

What is it that all these organizations have in common? Are there any "family resemblances" or similar organizational features that allowed them to be successful in their respective industries? A first answer could be that these companies have in common the centrality of people and learning, and the dynamic capabilities (Teece, 2000; Teece, Pisano and Shuen, 1997). These characteristics enable them to create, deploy and protect knowledge assets, competence and complementary assets to achieve a sustainable competitive advantage. The foundations of these capabilities are the distinct processes, organizational structures, decision rules, and people competencies and skills. Besides, these organizations have a distinctive capacity to initiate and sustain significant changes based on a concept of leadership as collective capacity rather than individual attitude. In boundary-less and knowledge-based organizations, leadership is diffused and concerns executives, line managers and all the people who spread and connect innovative ideas working behind the scenes to support new initiatives (Senge, 2000).

In Table 3.1 we try to synthesize some critical organizational capabilities that are shown by successful companies considered.

Put simply, the companies showing these capabilities are particularly skilled at: (a) recruiting the best human resources while creating mechanisms that allow their employees to continuously enhance, upgrade and broaden their competencies; and (b) developing tools, processes and relationships necessary to support information and knowledge-sharing that is at the foundation of innovation. In fact, these organizations are intensely "entrepreneurial" and focused on peoples' development and autonomy. Their organizational model is not based on hierarchical lines but rather on networks of interdependences at intra and inter-organizational levels. From this perspective, these companies are managed more like living organisms than machines and their capabilities are constantly developed through processes of organizational learning, the

Table 3.1   Success cases and organizational capabilities

Case	Organizational Capabilities
3M ABB	• belief in individuals • centrality of the right environment and culture • enhanced knowledge sharing based on trust, equity and shared values • facilitated flows of information to support productivity and innovation
3M McKinsey Skandia	• collaborative problem solving and cooperative resource sharing • development of frontline entrepreneurship • integrated networks to sustain collective intelligence • trust-based culture
3M Intel Kao	• continuous value creation through innovation and collaboration • dynamic disequilibrium • organization flexibility • sense of stretch and self-renewal • shared ambition
ABB	• company as a portfolio of processes • refining management roles and relationships
General Electric	• company integration as a key determinant of performance • importance of company "software" (values, motivation, etc.)
Motorola	• enhanced relationships between employers and employees • good relations with customers, employees, suppliers • importance of investing in people • smart collection of human resources • view of companies as "universities"

aggregation of diversified communities and networks, and the capitalization of idiosyncrasies and diversity.

The presence of such distinguishing features is not a purely theoretical fact without an impact on company results. This is indeed confirmed by the higher performance that these companies achieve in terms of revenues and overall value created for their shareholders. Table 3.2 shows the position of General Electric, Nucor, Intel and Motorola as ranked by Fortune 500 (http://money.cnn.com) in the years 1985 and 2005.

Table 3.2   Ranking of "Fortune 500" in 1985 and 2005

Company	1985	2005
General Electric	9	5
Intel	226	50
Motorola	67	49
Nucor	396	189

Besides commercial and market reasons, these and other companies improved their overall performance because they viewed organizational learning as a key success factor. What is the ultimate meaning of organizational learning and how this is translated into practice in a company's processes?

Although an extensive analysis of the organizational learning field is contained in Chapter 4, some definitions are useful to be mentioned here. One of the first contributions came from Argyris and Schön (1978, p. 2), who defined organizational learning as the process of *"detection and correction of errors"* whereas Senge (1990) talked of the process whereby organizations enhance their capacity for *effective action*. Marengo (1992) describes process as creating new competencies and increasing the existing ones. Kim and Mauborgne (1993) highlighted the ability of an organization to transfer and integrate the information and expertise developed in various parts of the network to all other parts so it is broadly available and can be generalized. Nevis, Di Bella and Gould (1995) referred to the capacity or processes within an organization to maintain or improve performance based on experience.

Knowledge, competencies, expertise, actions, system, performance: these are the main keywords presented in theory. From this perspective, success in companies can in some ways be assimilated to educational entities, like universities involved in a continuous and systematic development of individual and organizational learning capabilities with the ultimate purpose of improving the performance of business. A research study conducted on 100 learning departments and organizations (Meister et al., 2005) found that companies with high-performance learning processes return better results compared to their competitors and industry peers in terms of productivity measured by sales per employee (27% greater), revenue growth (40% higher) and net income growth (50% higher).

There are different causes for these outstanding results. The *alignment of learning initiative to business goals* is a primary, fundamental feature.

For many learning executives, measuring the effectiveness of learning and its impact on business is one of the first challenges. Specific measures should be used for this purpose, such as resource leverage, productivity, quality and risk management.

A second relevant aspect is the *extension of learning processes outside a company's boundaries*. About 50 percent of the organizations in the study expand training to customers and channel partners to increase satisfaction and build loyalty, and, by extension, to increase revenue and shareholder value.

Third, the *integration of learning and knowledge management* is a distinguishing trait of high performers. Traditional boundaries between learning and other related functions such as knowledge management, performance support and talent management are blurring. High percentages of learning organizations are incorporating learning with knowledge management (61%), performance support (59%) and talent management (56%). Learning organizations gather the knowledge created through experience and collaboration and distribute it through forms usable to everyone to optimize the performance of the company as a whole.

Ultimately, successful companies are organizations that promote intra and inter-organizational knowledge management and learning processes with the goal of enhancing peoples' potential. However, human capital development processes are impacted by the increasing complexity of the competitive environment and this is a concern for both public education institutions and corporations. In particular, what are the major forces affecting human capital development today? The following section tries to provide an answer to this question.

3.3 Major forces affecting human capital development

In our attempt to define a new managerial mindset, we moved from the first chapter's analysis of relevant *time, space, density* and then to *diversity*-related transformations in the economic and business world. We pointed out the *contraction of time* in economic and business transactions enabled by the Information and Communication Technology (ICT), coupled with a reduced life cycle of technology and innovation that results in reduced life cycles of products, markets and peoples' competencies. We also highlighted the widening scope and geographical distribution of economic and human activities, leading to the emergence of a truly global business environment in which a *virtual space* and a concept of organizational proximity gradually takes the place of physical proximity of agents and organizations. The increased inter-connection of organizations determines the appearance of integrated networks in which the *density* of relationships is a stimulus for innovation. Finally, we commented the widening *diversity* and *complexity* of business scenarios as a result of the proliferation of autonomous agents and organizations. In what way are these changes impacting on our unit of analysis, which is human capital development?

Jim Moore of Sun Microsystems stated that the shelf life of knowledge in his company is as short as one to two years. To illustrate the point, Moore estimated that over 75 percent of Sun revenues in 1996 were generated from products existing in the market for fewer than two years (Meister, 1998). The increased speed and frequency of changes in business and technology, and the resulting reduction of the competency life cycle, drives the need for organizations to adopt *on-demand learning* strategies and to facilitate a constant development and dynamic exchange of new knowledge and expertise. The use of ICT is a fundamental enabler in this process. Dell uses the Electronic Performance Support System (EPSS) as a support tool that allows sales staff to find on-line specifications about product components, prices, competitor's information and other critical knowledge to be successful on the job. This is a clear example of addressing the needs of employees to learn as they emerge in the workplace, by moving toward just-in-time and learner-centered competency development.

As borders disappear, business becomes more and more global and this amplifies the potential of organizations to learn on a global scale. *Open learning* communities emerge in which many actors belonging to the organization's value network can participate to develop competencies and experiment with new methods and technologies.

The increased density of economic and business connections is particularly relevant in the context of learning processes. Indeed, networks of actors interacting internally and externally in companies facilitate the *collaborative learning* processes. Companies believe that this is vitally important to sustain their competitive advantage. The Annual Survey of *Corporate University Future Directions* (www.corpu.com) found a definite trend toward leading corporate learning initiatives that involve suppliers and key members of the value chain in the development of specific skills in the area of quality, reliability, cycle time-reduction and customer service. Successful companies realize that everyone involved in bringing a product or a service to market must understand the company's shared vision and, most importantly, how to realize this vision in the marketplace. Harley Davidson has among its goals to train company's dealers in how to manage and sell all the new lines of business entered in the market.

More than previously, the proliferation of economic actors determines the need for organizations to manage aspects such as diversity and complexity. In terms of learning and management development, this asks the ability to develop a holistic view of business phenomena and problems through a *cross-disciplinary learning* and hypertextual approach to knowledge development. Organizations need to realize that they cannot predict anything with certainty, and that chaos is part of reality. In this sense, the company can be conceived as a complex system whose behavior is non-linear and not based on rigorous scientific approaches. Successful organizations lead the market since they are managed by people who make a difference because they are able to capitalize diversity and idiosyncrasies while creating a virtuous mix of individuals' personalities, leadership and creativity.

On-demand, open, collaborative and cross-disciplinary: these are some of the new challenges of concern for the practice of learning and human capital development in the future. The following section shows the trajectories of change in the journey toward a new approach of developing people within organizations.

3.4 Trajectories of change in human capital development

The transformations previously described affect different dimensions of human capital development: the main "actor" involved (the individual employee or manager); the approaches and mechanisms implemented in practice; and the ultimate purpose that human capital development should pursue. Based on the management framework of the *Individualized Corporation* (Ghoshal and Bartlett, 1997), we adopt the people-process-purpose paradigm to describe three trajectories of change in human capital development: (a) the evolution from the view of people as a cost to a value-creating asset; (b) the shift from a narrow training to a continuous learning perspective; and (c) the renewed purpose from the development of individual competencies to the creation of stakeholder value. Figure 3.1 represents these changes that are explored in detail afterwards.

People have been traditionally considered as a cost to monitor and control rather than an asset that creates value for the organization. Focused on maximizing short-term static efficiency, most companies have been designed to extract the most from all their assets, including people. In that process, however, they have sacrificed the long-term dynamic

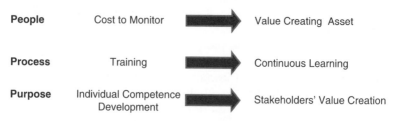

People	Cost to Monitor	→	Value Creating Asset
Process	Training	→	Continuous Learning
Purpose	Individual Competence Development	→	Stakeholders' Value Creation

Figure 3.1   Trajectories of change in human capital development.

efficiencies that come from continuously enhancing and upgrading the capabilities of individuals to enable them to create new value. The most renewed example of an organization adopting this philosophy is 3M, the company that had become the benchmark standard for those who rejected the notion that corporate entrepreneurship is an oxymoron by encouraging individual initiative. Rising to the top of the company in the 1920s, McKnight developed a management philosophy that was in many ways contrary to the principles of the leading practices emerging at the time by considering people as the most valuable asset in an organization. By the 1990s, the entrepreneurial initiative of generations of people in 3M created a portfolio of over 100 core technologies that had been used in 60,000 products and managed in 3,900 profit centers. The secret of this success lies in inspiring individual initiative that is supported by a sense of "ownership" in what the employees do. The new management philosophy embraces innovation as a key ingredient of success and increased competitiveness (Liyanage and Poon, 2002; Khalil, 2000) and this entails developing the creative potential of the organization by fostering peoples' ideas and enthusiasm, by tapping the innovative potential of employees and encouraging the proliferation of autonomy and entrepreneurship (Black and Porter, 2000; Boyett and Boyett, 2000; Blanchard, 1996; Kuczmarski, 1996).

The *process* of developing individual and organizational capabilities can hardly be based on periodic, narrow and isolated training initiatives. Rather, it needs a continuous, broad, integrated learning process. Learning is the foundation of professional development and human capital growth, which enables companies to drive innovation. Employees learn from each other and share innovations and best practices for solving real business issues (Meister, 1998). Learning speeds workers' readiness to do their new jobs and fit the roles needed, thus supporting better deployment of human capital (Marquardt, 2002). Moreover, human capital development should pay more attention to the managerial process than to theoretical knowledge by creating links between theory and practice.

A third trajectory relates to the *purpose* of human capital development that evolves from developing specific competencies of individual employees to preparing the right conditions for creating value for a network of internal and external stakeholders. The company of the 21st century should be able to link dispersed knowledge, initiative and expertise in a continuous process of action and learning. The new management paradigm revolves around teamwork, participation, learning and leadership (Lubitz and Wickramasinghe, 2006). It also revolves around improved communication, integration, collaboration and closer interactions and partnering with customers, suppliers and a wider range of stakeholders. These values are increasingly regarded as key features of a new idea of human capital development that addresses value creation rather than value allocation objectives as guiding management principles.

The next three sections explore these areas by investigating what new managerial roles and competency frameworks emerge (people), what new learning practices are being developed and adopted (processes), and how companies move to an extended value-creating paradigm (purpose). These paragraphs prepare the groundwork for introducing the paradigm of *networked learning* as a holistic model that integrates the strategic, organizational and technology aspects of human capital development.

3.5   People: New managerial roles and competency frameworks

The complexity of changes in the competitive landscape has had an impact on two aspects that are central in our analysis: (a) the evolution of traditional management roles at different levels and (b) the new competencies that are critical for success. Companies are faced with more competition and more varied forms of competitive pressure from international, knowledge-rich and unconventional rivals (Baets and van der Linden, 2003). Even organizations in relatively stable markets are threatened by more active and internet-based competitors. Rapid movements in markets, flexibility and leveraged competitors are the key aspects. Companies try to maximize their core competencies, strategic resources and capabilities by seeking and relying on partners to perform activities within their value chain. At the same time, firms are looking for new sources of competitive advantage beyond just their core competencies and strategic resources.

A survey of the *Economist's Intelligent Unit* (www.eiu.com) shows that the factors that will drive competition in the future are: relationships with suppliers and customers; human capital, capabilities and strategic resources; flexible organizational structures; high productivity; technology and low cost production. Renewed bases for competing have an impact on the role that operating, middle and top managers should have in their organizations.

3.5.1 The transformation of managerial roles

When capital was a scarce resource, the organizations were designed around organizational roles focused on the task of identifying and allocating financial resources. The core responsibility of *top management* in classic hierarchical models was to be the strategic allocator of resources and the evaluator of strategic plans and capital budgets. *Middle management* played the role of administrative controller, consolidating and filtering the plants and investment requests within the organization, and interpreting and controlling strategy. Finally, frontline or *operating managers* were asked to be the operational implementers, translating the directions and priorities received from above into actions and results (Ghoshal and Bartlett, 1997).

Knowledge replaced physical capital as the company's most valuable strategic asset, thus the strategies, structures and systems designed to distribute and control the use of financial assets have been replaced by a corporate model focused on the development and exploitation of strategic knowledge. Facing these changes, companies need business leaders capable of learning, while being coaches, team players, facilitators, process managers, human resources executives, visionary leaders and entrepreneurs (Longenecker and Ariss, 2002). The business leaders must be more bottom-line driven, more innovative, and more focused on the human dynamics of the organization (Chapman, 2001). They need multifaceted knowledge, intelligence and competencies necessary to create a flexible strategic vision facilitating the organization's continuous renewal.

Front line managers are asked to become *innovative entrepreneurs* taking the responsibility for continued growth through innovation. They develop into key actors of *entrepreneurial processes* in the organization and are asked to manage continuous performance improvement within units and to face an external environment with which they build strong relationships, rather than upward into a hierarchy from which they expect direction and control. *Middle managers* evolve into the role of *developmental coaches,* spending time and energy to enhance

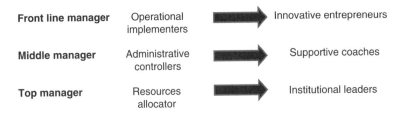

Figure 3.2 Changing roles of operating, middle and top managers.

the individual members of their organization and to link dispersed resources into a continuous *integration process*. They are asked to balance the tension between the pressure for short-term performance and the challenge of long-term vision. Finally, *top level managers* evolve into the role of *institutional leaders* who inspire and energize the organization. They create an over-arching corporate purpose while challenging existing assumptions, and play the crucial role of capability developers and provide a source of organizational disequilibrium and *renewal* (Ghoshal and Bartlett, 1997). Figure 3.2 synthesises the evolution of roles for the three levels of management.

3.5.2   A new competency framework

Changes in roles also have an impact on the competencies that are critical in order to be successful. Companies need to develop a richer understanding of their portfolio of managerial competencies that should be linked to actionable decisions. This task is complicated by the fact that the new flexible and decentralized organizational structures push responsibility and authority downward in the organization and more employees are thus required to think, decide and act as a manager. As the workplace flattens and the gap narrows between those in leadership positions and those responsible for producing and delivering the product or service, the role of individual employees becomes increasingly managerial in nature (Meister, 1998).

Managerial competencies have been related to the ability of bundling strategic resources and technologies underlying practices and process to understand, connect and use them in a uniquely competitive manner (Baets and van der Linden, 2003). Different classifications have been provided for critical management competencies. According to Mintzberg (2004), four different categories can be identified: (a) *personal competencies*; (b) *interpersonal competencies*; (c) *informational competencies*; and (d) *actionable competencies*. Table 3.3 shows the competencies related to each category.

Table 3.3   A classification of managerial competencies

Category	Managerial Competencies
Personal competencies	• Managing reflection and strategic thinking • Managing time, information and stress
Interpersonal competencies	• Leading individuals (selecting, mentoring, teaching, inspiring) • Leading groups (team building, mediating, resolving conflicts) • Leading the organization/unit (organizing, merging, managing change) • Linking the organization/unit (networking, representing, collaborating, promoting, lobbying, buffering)
Informational competencies	• Communicating verbally (listening, interviewing, speaking, presenting, writing, disseminating information) • Communicating non-verbally (seeing, sensing) • Analyzing data (data processing, measuring, evaluating)
Actionable competencies	• Scheduling • Administering (allocating resources, delegating, authorizing, goal setting, appraising performance) • Designing (planning, crafting, visioning) • Mobilizing (managing projects)

Source: Adapted from Mintzberg, 2004.

Another taxonomy can be derived from research conducted by the London Business School in 2004 on more than 100 executives from global companies across a variety of industries and geographies. The research demonstrated that companies need people with *Global Business Capabilities* described according to three dimensions: knowledge, skills and attitude (Andrews and Tyson, 2004). Knowledge refers to the foundation of global business capabilities and is the base of information required by successful managers to operate at the lowest managerial level. Skills are the practiced ability, the learning acquired through the repeated application of knowledge. They are developed through practice as well as through an understanding of theory. Business has always been action-oriented, and skills have been fundamental to effective management. Attitudes are the individual qualities, characteristics, or behaviors focused on leadership (Andrews and Tyson, 2004). Table 3.4

Table 3.4 Global business capabilities

Knowledge	Skills	Attitudes
Business Performance	Collaboration	Adaptability and
Business Planning	Listening and observation	responsiveness
Accounting Management	Make complex simple	Capacity to learn
Operation Management	Managing diverse culture	Coachable
ICT management	Dealing with ambiguity	Demanding excellence
Change Mgmt & Lead.	Dealing with uncertainty	Perseverance and
Competitive macroenvi-	Decision making	tenacity Boundless
ronment.	Networking	energy Curiosity and
e-Business	Project Management	creativity
Global macroeconomics	Presentation skills	Intuition
Global business strategy	Talent assessment	Self Confidence
Innovation management	Interpersonal skills	
Internet marketing	Teambuilding and	
Intellectual Capital man-	teamwork	
agement		

Source: Adapted from Andrews and Tyson, 2004.

shows the Global Business Capabilities, detailed in terms of knowledge, skills and attitudes.

Jeanne Meister (1998) provided another interesting taxonomy of seven *workplace competencies*. We used the skill, knowledge and attitude criteria to classify them.

Knowledge-related competencies include:

- *Technological literacy*: Using the latest technologies to connect the team to the world, to network with professionals and research best practices inside and outside the company. A good example is Dell, where technological literacy is a necessity for all the employees at all levels. Dell has developed a course for new managers and employees with limited PC or Web browser experience to access to the company intranet. Sometimes, managers are required to go on line to find the appropriate information that needs to be codified in the company's manual.
- *Global Business Literacy*: Understanding the big picture of how the business operates through a core set of business skills such as finance, strategic planning and marketing, having a command over the capital allocation process and knowing how to evaluate a business's potential. PDVSA's Petroleos de Venezuela developed an integrated

program in business management and leadership skills aimed to train employees in accordance with the strategic goals of the company and fostering skills suitable for reaching the business objectives.

Competencies more *skills-related* include:

- *Learning to learn*: Being responsible for continuous understanding of the optimal way to learn new skills and competencies; knowing how to manipulate new information; and being able to handle ambiguity and chaos. An example is presented in Saturn corporation, a Tennessee automotive company, that has created the course "Introduction to the Learning Organization" available to all the team members, with the objective to understand the optimal way to learn and to seek out opportunities for continuous and self-paced learning. The course incorporates many ideas of researchers such as Peter Senge and Howard Gardner.
- *Communication and collaboration*: Knowing how to listen and communicate effectively with co-workers and with customers; knowing how to work and collaborate in group; solving conflicts and share best practices across the organization. An example is represented by National Semiconductor that has promoted communities of practice (such as the "Faculty Club" for senior managers) as a methodology to design new products.
- *Creative thinking and problem solving*: Knowing how to identify problems and see connections between solutions and possible approaches to coming problems; initiating new ideas; taking action; tracking and evaluating results; possessing the cognitive reasoning skills necessary to transcend sequential thinking; and coming to creative solutions. In its annual learning event for senior executives, Kodak brings together partner organizations such as Intel, IBM and Nokia to discuss a range of critical initiatives, such as emerging technologies, new markets and competitiveness.

Attitude-related competencies include:

- *Leadership development*: Having a vision for work that fits into the corporate mission and goals; defining a shared vision and leading the organization in achieving it. Motorola's innovative leadership development program, the "China Accelerated Management Program" (CAMP), is an example of cutting edge leadership development program where learning is connected to a real business issue. During the program, managers learn value creation, business process design, market economy and systems thinking, with a particular focus on presentation style, situational leadership and team facilitation skills.

- *Career self-management*: Having the ability to manage one's own career by identifying the skills and knowledge needed to be valuable in the workplace and then working to acquire them. Raychem launched a program for peoples' development to cultivate the specific competencies needed for their success. In particular, an important objective of the program is to guide employees in developing a list of competencies they need for their current or future jobs. By providing resources on industry skill standards, Raychem helps employees see what their skill level is in relation to what the market demands, or will demand in the future.

Besides workplace competencies, an integrated view of managerial competencies should allow people to develop in two other broad areas: *corporate citizenship* and the *contextual framework* (Meister, 1998). Corporate citizenship refers to the awareness and identification with one's company culture, values, traditions and vision. A good example is the Chicago Hospital (UCH) that created an orientation program aimed at transforming employees into good citizens, acting to satisfy the customers' needs, and continually improving their performance, as a strategic process to share with all the employees the company's mindset and commitment to the highest quality. Contextual framework relates to the appreciation of the company's business, products and services, its customers, competitors, and the best practices of others. The underlying assumption is that corporate performance can be improved when all the employees, and not just management, operate with a shared vision about the organization. In 1995, Fidelity Investments created the Service Delivery University (SDU) as a response to the explosive growth of the company that reinforced the need to share with all the employees the big picture of business, teaching how to assess the regulatory, financial, operational and reputation risks associated with the business.

Managerial competencies, global business capabilities, workplace competencies: there are many possible criteria for describing the basic portfolio that each manager should possess at all levels of the organization. In each case, this portfolio is composed of a mix of diversified knowledge and experience accumulated over time. In analogy with products and technologies which are characterized by a certain life cycle, also the knowledge and experience of people have a *life cycle* and can become obsolete. Figure 3.3 shows a metaphorical representation

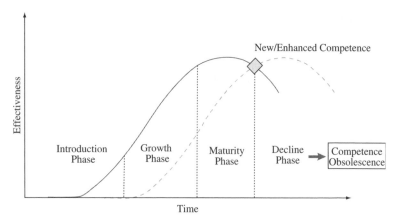

Figure 3.3   The life cycle of a competence.

of this lifecycle, in which the four phases of "introduction" (initial development of the competence), "growth" (further development and specialization), "maturity" (full application) and "decline" (competence obsolescence) are shown. When a competence is declining, meaning that its effectiveness when applied in the workplace is decreasing, the need arises to develop a new competence (or enhance/update the old one).

Today's business is characterized by a faster obsolescence rate of competencies (narrowing life cycles). The diffusion of information technology and related organizational changes are a major cause of skill shortages (Aubert, Caroli and Roger, 2004) and organizations are thus asked to continuously update the knowledge and experience of people. In fact, reducing the time it takes a new employee to attain a competent level of performance delivers financial value in two ways: it reduces the amount of training spent and the worker becomes more productive faster. The challenge today is not simply to train employees to learn more competencies but rather to introduce them to an entirely new way of thinking and working so they can perform broader roles in the workplace. Successful learning initiatives need to focus on developing competencies via real experience rather than through a purely theoretical knowledge transfer. This is only one of the challenges of developing peoples' competencies in a timely and effective manner. The next section will illustrate these challenges by providing an overview of the emerging practices in learning.

3.6 Process: Emerging practices in learning

Managerial roles are always changing, so the competencies relevant for success must also change. Human capital development needs to be closer to managerial processes and more focused on workplace competencies. This calls for a substantial rethinking in current management education practices and the need to innovate corporate learning processes that go beyond the organization's boundaries to include all the relevant stakeholders. Management education needs to reflect the changing times by overhauling not only its content and delivery modes, but also its overall approach and orientation (Liyanage and Poon, 2002). However, most of the current approaches are still linked to old paradigms of learning as the delivery of standardized curricula and content. In addition, knowledge may still be seen as a transferable commodity, with learning process localized within the company's departments.

In this section, we discuss the role of business education and business schools in developing human capital and the limits resulting from a misalignment with real management challenges. These limitations require a shift toward management development rather than a narrow management education perspective.

3.6.1 Does business education really develop human capital?

Business education has been traditionally involved in developing human capital. However, the dominant paradigm of business education is not entirely relevant to the needs of companies and hence does not prepare learners for managerial roles. A brief summary of how business schools have been historically engaged in "preparing" managers will explore these limitations.

The first MBA (Master of Business Administration) program appeared at the beginning of the 1900s. Harvard established its graduate business school as an experiment of five years, beginning a new era of education in the United States. The objective was to address the functional and hierarchical management inspired by the theories of *Scientific Management* of Taylor (1913), *Bureaucratic Management* by Weber (1922) and *Functional Management* by Fayol (1949), which viewed the management environment as stable enough to prescribe centralized decision-making processes and hierarchical communication channels.

However, despite the legitimacy conferred to business education by such a prestigious institution, the case of Harvard remained isolated because of the resistance based in two beliefs (Carter, 1998): (a) the skills required to run a business were considered low-class and ordinary, so no education was necessary; and (b) traditional colleges rejected the idea of including commercial subjects into the classical curriculum. Despite the criticism, the market demand for business education was growing and the people whose job it was to teach those subjects had to struggle with the fact that nobody knew exactly what "business" was or what a business curriculum should include.

Coming up with a curriculum was thus the challenge of the next three decades. Some theorists were convinced that the curriculum should be based in business activities. A different concept was provided by the Amos Tuck School of Business Administration that viewed business education as a pyramid becoming more specialized as it approached the top. An effective manager should have all the information and knowledge related to economics, psychology, social science, political science and philosophy that is necessary to undertake and understand a general business education. These proposals were criticized for not defining what a "*General Business Education*" should encompass (Carter, 1998).

Edward Jones, professor at the University of Michigan, summed up some principles and propositions for a typical business curriculum (Carter, 1998). These principles relate to the importance of defining the type of person to be trained in the business school and the patience needed to lay the foundation of instruction by systematic investigation of business. Concerning propositions, the purpose should be to train people in managerial functions with a focus on subjects like administration, corporate finance and theory of distribution, all grounded in the scientific method.

The emphasis on accounting, finance, distribution and the exclusion of both the "softest" and "hardest" subjects are typical features of that period. The concept of business was still pretty much mechanical. What happened between 1918 and 1922 was less qualitative than quantitative: the curricula of business colleges did not change much, but the number of institutions offering the opportunity for such study exploded. Still, however, "business" remained an undefined and mysterious subject, and the approach to teaching varied from one university to another. In 1916, the Association of Collegiate Schools of Business (today known as AACSB International) was founded as a professional association for college and university business educators. The first program standards were issued in the 1920s and, for the first time, the AACSB began to advocate management as a profession. Gradually, knowledge creation joined knowledge transfer as a core mission within business schools. It was also in this decade that the Harvard faculty adapted from their Law School colleagues the "case method" for teaching business.

By World War II, however, many things changed. Business schools became the largest division of most universities and came to occupy positions of great significance to the public in general. New production and management techniques experienced during the war took a prominent place in post-war curricula. These were expected to have an emphasis on small business, rather than on corporations exclusively, with a focus on marketing, more cooperation with industry, and more adult education programs.

The criticism grew after World War II when many businesses transformed into multidivisional enterprises trying to integrate functional specialism while striving to apply abstract and scientific knowledge to industrial technology (Locke, 1989). A new breed of managers was required to supervise multidimensional enterprise. Business schools, with their vocational and skills-based training programs, could hardly meet these new demands for scientific and integrated knowledge.

The landmark report of the Ford Foundation and the Carnegie Foundation, both published in 1959, were the causes of major MBA program transformations (Gordon and Howell, 1959; Pierson, 1959). The reports railed against the inadequacies of the MBA programs of the time. Business education was criticized as a "vague, shifting, rather formless subject." In those years, the business schools also initiated the research programs for which US schools are now well-known. The disciplines of finance, accounting, strategy and marketing became more rigorous, and management sought to become a science. It was also at this time that the classic two-year American MBA model was born, with the first year devoted to the core disciplines and the second year offering more specialized knowledge. While business schools were transforming themselves into "normal" scientific institutions, they gradually became disconnected from the real world of business. For this reason, Schlossman et al. (1987) identified the era 1959–85 as the *age of autonomy*, in which these schools were free to set their own education agendas. In the early 1990s, business schools were said to be once again out of touch with the real world of business. Schools responded by overhauling their curricula, this time by adding more practical skills to their MBA programs.

In *"Innovation in Professional Education: Steps on a Journey from Teaching to Learning"* Boyatzis et al. (1994) found that MBAs were too: analytical; not action-oriented; lacked interpersonal skills; were not global in thinking and values; had high expectations; were not oriented toward information resources and systems; and didn't apply well to groups. Linked to this, there was too much emphasis on knowledge transfer rather than on the transfer of learning.

In April 2002, the Management Education Task Force at the Association to Advance Collegiate Schools of Business (AACSB) issued a report titled *"Management Education at Risk"*, which questioned the relevance of business school courses. It recommended that American business schools focus more attention on basic management skills, such as communication, leadership development and change management, and *prepare managers for global adaptability*.

More recently, Mintzberg (2004) has argued that MBA programs offer "specialized training in the functions of business, not general education in the practice of managing", with an emphasis on the acquisition of knowledge rather than the development of skills and attitudes.

If business education is not always appropriate for preparing managers for their roles, what are the main challenges faced to enable real management development?

3.6.2   What are the challenges for management development today?

Today we are at a turning point in business education. The practice of business is not the same as the practice of management and it is thus necessary to shift from traditional business and management education and go against *management development* (Mintzberg, 2004). For this purpose, corporations, business schools, universities and education institutions should radically innovate the human capital creation process in terms of the "why" (vision), the "what" (curricula) and the "how" (learning strategy).

Business schools and management institutions control the majority of the human capital development market. Since the 1980s, some newer approaches have emerged, such as internal company programs called "corporate universities." Corporate Universities represent a growing trend in companies and will be explored in detail in Chapter 5. It is interesting to consider the explosion of these "in-house" corporate learning initiatives as a sign of the necessity for organizations to organize learning programs differently from the university, with more focus on the learner and on developing workplace managerial competencies rather than on narrow, functional knowledge. Companies still struggle to bring changes in the way that learning is conceived, curricula are designed, and knowledge is identified and created in management development. Table 3.5 illustrates some critical challenges that are relevant to the vision, the curricula and the strategy adopted in making learning the tool of peoples' growth within organizations.

Table 3.5 Future challenges in learning approach for management development

Aspect	Challenge
VISION	• enhance symbiotic corporate-academic links • involve key stakeholders in corporate learning process
CURRICULA	• break the isolation of disciplines and functional knowledge • design curricula based on business processes • offer interdisciplinary knowledge • provide contextual and experiential knowledge
STRATEGY	• develop action and on-demand learning • go beyond the passive transfer of theoretical knowledge • provide managers with knowledge and skills needed to create value

Vision

New management models have been created in the academy. Also, companies need new strategies that break down the barriers between theory and practice, like strategies based on co-production (Starkey and Madan, 2001; Jacob and Hellstrom, 2000). Relationships and collaboration among the company's key stakeholders should be enhanced to implement innovative approaches to human capital development and the creation of value. Corporate learning programs might be open to the external environment, with flexible infrastructures open to adopting technologies. From the other side, business schools have to be the center of a network that has enlarged its traditional boundaries through ICTs, to become "meta-planners," to support flexible teams coming together to develop and diffuse value in the different firms' network (Lorange, 2005). Ultimately, the collaboration between business "educators" and companies should develop new opportunities for learning, integrate know-how, recognize the different sets of competencies to be developed, and optimize costs as well.

Curricula

This is an area where little progress has been made, given the continuing inclination to compartmentalize education either in business or in engineering, to focus on specific business functions and limit the inter-disciplinary fertilization (Khalil, 2000). In the real world of business, managers are increasingly expected to contribute to multifunctional teams and work on projects that draw on a range of disciplines. Yet, the way managers are taught in business schools remains uni-dimensional; they are bound by functional disciplines rather than reflecting business reality. The isolation of basics such as marketing, operations, IT, finance, economics, accounting and strategy still endure. This aspect should be considered for designing curricula. In the 1970s and 1980s, the dominant philosophy guiding the design and delivery of business curricula was the aggregation of knowledge around isolated topics such as finance and marketing. The trend in the 1990s changed (Figure 3.4) to incorporate business competencies often independent from topics such as project management and leadership. In the future, a deeper understanding of core mechanisms underlying business will inform the design of curricula. In particular, key business processes such as new product development or value creation will inspire the logic of identifying, aggregating and using strategic knowledge for effective managerial action. Inside the logic of business processes, an interdisciplinary and multidisciplinary organization of content should be developed to offer programs as strategy for managerial development.

Another aspect to consider in designing curricula is the shift from linear to *hypertextual* programs, in which a dynamic approach to organizing and delivering curricula is adopted based on the targeted competencies. Learning patterns are thus interconnected according to the

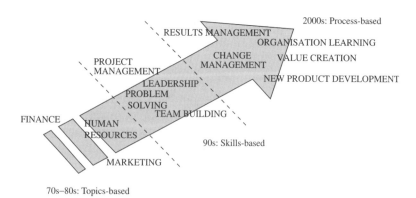

Figure 3.4   Toward interdisciplinary curricula.
Source: Adapted from Baets and van der Linden (2003).

knowledge, skills and attitudes required for the desired professional pro-files. Management development tries to create multidisciplinary profiles in which business and technology-related competencies are integrated and developed within the context of application. Both *contextual knowledge* (knowledge created and specifically referred to a case, a project, an industry, a market, a problem, etc.) and *experiential knowledge* (knowledge gained through experimentation and reflection in real situations) should be applied in multidimensional curricula.

Strategy

Business schools have traditionally provided a reflective learning space, which is a place to absorb information and knowledge. The new agenda of management development must be more practical and action-oriented rather than theory-driven and discipline-based (Secundo and Passiante, 2007). To enable people to move from the functional business organization to a value-creation perspective, corporate learning must develop a new approach to teaching and learning, also leveraging more ICT-enhanced learning. Everyday experience, not theory, helps people solve a problem or achieve a goal. The logic is thus reversed: application and experience are not a means to learning, but an end from which learning originates, in a process based on a series of trials/experiences, observation, reflection and systematization. Just-in-time and on-demand learning processes are appropriate for employees to develop competencies required in the workplace. Concerning the pedagogical approach, there's been an evolution from the idea of learning as a transferral of knowledge and a shaping of people to a new concept of learning as travelling and growing (Baets and van der Linden, 2003). In the transferral perspective, knowledge is viewed as a transferable commodity and the student is an empty vessel to be loaded. Courses are lecture-based and often provide students with duplicated concepts. The shaping concept refers to the idea that the student is considered as a piece of inert raw material, such as wood or metal, to be shaped with tools represented by the subject matter. From this perspective, the teacher is a craftsman who is able to work the wood or metal. Suitable teaching methods include workshops, practical instructions similar to recipes and exercises with predictable outcomes. A completely different perspective inspires the logic of travelling and growing. The metaphor of travel refers to the idea that the teacher guides the students through an unknown terrain that needs to be explored. The student is the explorer and the teacher is the experienced and expert companion and counselor who points out the way, but he/she also provides travelling maps and a compass. The methods are thus experiential and include simulations, projects, exercise with unpredictable outcomes, discussions and independent learning. The growing metaphor is an extension of the travelling; more focused on the idea of the student's own initiative; the student whose aim is to develop his/her own personality. The monitoring process addresses the personal development of the student and this is consistent with the fact that becoming a manager, in many respects, requires a working on one's own personality with the support of an experienced coach.

3.7 Purpose: Enhancing Stakeholders' value creation

In the previous sections we analyzed how human capital development is being impacted by radical changes related to the "people" dimension, with a specific focus on the emerging managerial roles and competencies, and the "process" dimension, focusing on the innovative approaches and mechanisms adopted to develop people and competencies. A third dimensional shift was introduced in Section 3.4: the idea that the ultimate "purpose" of human capital development is to shift from the focus on developing competencies of isolated individuals to one that contributes to the creation of value for a larger number of stakeholders.

In a pure market economy, companies are expected to maximize economic profitability. They must remain competitive and enhance the value of shares in order to attract investors available to support the company in the long term. Besides this idea of *shareholder value*, another perspective is becoming more and more important for companies operating according to a wider *multi-stakeholder* view of market and business. From this perspective, the concept of value is not simply referring to an idea of economic and financial performance but rather to emphasize responsibility besides profitability and see the success of the organization based on the satisfaction and development of the *stakeholder value*, which applies to many different actors.

Business is about how customers, suppliers, employees, financiers, communities, the media and managers interact and create value. Nurturing all the parties involved with the organization is the only strategy to ensure a sustainable competitive advantage. The stakeholder value becomes the expression of a management philosophy that maximizes the interests of all its stakeholders as its highest objective. Maximizing value requires policies that increase efficiency while improving the quality of its products and services, enhancing the employability and satisfaction of its employees, and contributing to the development of the overall community.

In his seminal work *Strategic Management: A Stakeholder Approach*, Professor Robert Edward Freeman (1984) laid the foundations for the stakeholder perspective in management, suggesting that businesses build their strategy around their relationships with key stakeholders. In *Managing for Stakeholders: Survival, Reputation and Success* (2007), Professor Freeman provided another key contribution to management thinking and practice by highlighting the need to move from a way of thinking about business and stakeholders based on a "value allocation" question (i.e. how to distribute the burdens and benefits of corporate activities among stakeholders?) to a new mindset guided by a "value creation" question (how to create as much value as possible for all of the stakeholders?).

In particular, ten key principles and seven techniques are presented by Professor Freeman for managing stakeholder relationships to ensure a firm's survival, reputation and success. Among the principles, one in particular is relevant to our discussion: the need for *intensive communication* and dialogue with all stakeholders. Two techniques should also be mentioned here: (a) the creation of *new modes of interaction* with stakeholders and (b) the development of *integrative value creation* strategies.

How do those principles and techniques impact on corporate learning and human capital development processes? What are the managerial implications of adopting those principles and applying those techniques? In what way is the concept of stakeholder value connected with the development of human capital?

Concerning this last question, the *Open Business Innovation Leadership* concept contains three fundamental aspects that can be used to describe the strategic priorities of organizations today: the centrality of developing social capital and enhancing the network of learning relationships; the importance of creating innovation-driven value for all stakeholders; and the founding role of human capital as a cause of organizational development. The role of innovation, learning and human capital as drivers of stakeholder value is a founding assumption of our analysis and has been illustrated throughout this book.

The following considerations can be made about the impact and the managerial implications:

a. The development of integrative value creation strategies requires involvement of all the stakeholders in critical decisions related to issues such as defining the ultimate organization purpose.

b. The need for intensive communication with stakeholders necessitates the strengthening of interconnections among people belonging to the organization's network.

c. The creation of new modes of interaction requires the definition of new processes and new enablers, also at a technological level, for supporting knowledge-sharing and collaboration among stakeholders.

The different impact on organizational performance and value created for stakeholders is a distinguishing trait of some human capital development initiatives. The next paragraph introduces networked learning as an integrated knowledge, process and technology model that addresses the challenges defined at (a), (b) and (c) (above), with the objective of enhancing the collective capacity of a community to boost stakeholders' value through learning.

3.8   A model of networked learning

Three trajectories of change have been investigated: the shift of human resources from costs to assets, the move from isolated training to a continuous learning view and the evolution from a focus of individual competence development to the creation of stakeholder value. Two questions at this point could be raised: (a) Which organizational model, in terms of managing knowledge and learning processes, can be implemented to address the "new" dimensions of human capital development? and (b) What could be the role of technology in supporting this model?

In our attempt to answer these questions, we moved from the basic consideration that, like any other human and business activity, learning becomes a networked and distributed process rather than an isolated and bounded one (Romano and Margherita, 2008). A concept of networked learning emerges therefore as a *collaborative, context-based and technology-enhanced learning process among networks of actors interacting to create value in different forms.* Networked learning is not primarily a technological concept but ICT today offers huge possibilities to support flexible, dynamic and interactive collaboration, knowledge management and learning processes in different contexts or scenarios, such as problems to solve, projects to carry out, etc.

Networked learning is thus a process that can drive human capital development since it addresses all three dimensions investigated so far. It addresses purpose through the idea of an extended involvement of diversified stakeholders inside and outside a single organization and a multi-faceted impact of life-long learning in creating long-term value, aligned with business goals. It addresses the process dimension by highlighting the centrality of inter-organizational learning and collaboration, the integration between learning and knowledge management, a more action-oriented approach to learning, and the interdisciplinary/ holistic approach to knowledge and learning. Finally, it also addresses the human (people) dimension through new managerial roles based on new competencies frameworks and mindsets inspired by principles such as the openness of organizational boundaries, peering, sharing of ideas and intellectual property, and global action (Tapscott and Williams, 2006).

From a conceptual point of view, networked learning is thus an appropriate framework to address the changing dimensions of human capital development. However, there's the need to put concepts into practice and define an integrated model that can actually support the processes of networked learning.

In the framework of our analysis, networked learning is not primarily a technology-oriented concept. However, Information and Communication Technologies (ICTs) in the past twenty years have had revolutionary effects on organizational structures, managerial practices and operational processes, changing the organizations both internally and externally. ICTs contributed significantly to supporting the new principles characterizing the emerging trends in management. Flat organizational structures, globally-integrated value chains, real time process monitoring, high internal and external coordination and interactivity, distributed leadership and dynamic synchronization of people/processes/tools represent multiple dimensions along which ICTs can express their potential.

Learning and knowledge management processes are also deeply influenced by technology that manages large knowledge bases and supports just-in-time and on-demand learning for a faster acquisition of competencies, and enhances interaction and collaboration through the emergence of virtual learning communities. Put simply, there are three complementary processes related to learning that are impacted by ICTs:

1. *Competence management;*
2. *Content management; and*
3. *Community management.*

Figure 3.5 frames these 3 "C-processes" in a model that (a) explains the relationships among networked learning and the critical issues related

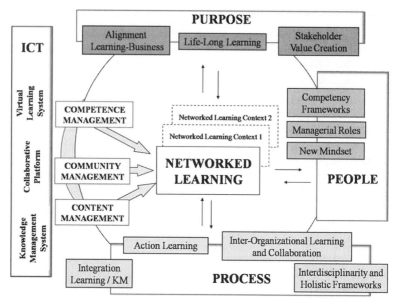

Figure 3.5 A model of networked learning.

to the people, purpose and process trends in human capital development; and (b) describes the role of technology in supporting competence, content and community management.

The effective *management of competencies* is fundamental to ensure the sustainability of an organization while continually enhancing its performance. In particular, managing the right mix between knowledge and experience, monitoring current competence profiles and identifying development plans at both individual and organizational levels represent key features. This implies the need to define an appropriate portfolio of skills, attitudes and knowledge required for the specific context in which those competencies have to be applied. Also, the policies to create project teams are impacted, such as trying to staff the people with the necessary profile and expertise requested to perform a specific task. An effective monitoring system is necessary that is able to indicate emergency situations and recommend actions to fill competence gaps. The competence management in our model is ensured by the design of an appropriate *virtual learning system* with the following components:

- *Competence taxonomy*: Identification and definition of which competencies are required for managers operating at different levels

- *Skills assessment*: Identification of the needed skills according the task
- *Profile management*: Management of all the information related to people using the system, their skills and competencies, learning experiences, assessment, etc.
- *Expert locator*: Service for identifying people according to their competencies and skills in solving specific business problems
- *Structured and unstructured learning curricula management*: Management of learning curricula based on a pre-defined catalog (structured) or a hypertextual and dynamic knowledge map (unstructured) and including sessions' time scheduling, browsing of learning bases, centralized or distributed tagging of learning material, creation of multimedia learning objects, and centralized or distributed enrollment. In general, these functionalities are managed by a LMS (Learning Management System) a web-based tool that allows access to learning resources, a LCMS (Learning Content Management System) used for the development, management and publishing of the content that will typically be delivered via an LMS, and by a set of authoring tools to realize the learning contents.
- *Assessment, monitoring and control*: Assessment/testing of participants, scores and transcripts display, integration with performance tracking and management systems.
- *Interface management*: Management with other external platforms such as e-business suites, project management tools, simulation engines, etc.

Figure 3.6 shows the main components of a *virtual learning system*.

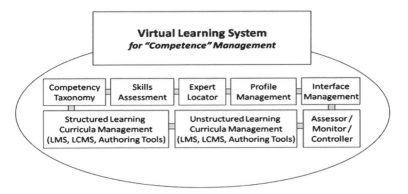

Figure 3.6 Virtual learning system.

The development of competencies has to be integrated with an effective *management of content* that is the 'food' of networked learning. Several types of content must be made available to learners. Multimedia format can increase the 'appeal' and accessibility of these contents. Distributed authoring, a high level of reusability, multiple sources of origin (internal and external to the organization) and user friendly interfaces guarantee a high level of productivity in knowledge publishing and content authoring processes. Moreover, having a single knowledge and learning base that feeds content management services can help avoid redundancy and mismatch problems. This would also allow subject matter experts to create complex learning objects starting from atomic documents and heterogeneous files, without having any specific technical competence in electronic authoring and advanced editing. Besides, the presence of a semantic layer to extract different pieces of knowledge from heterogeneous sources and to dynamically create a set of relations for a hypertext semantic navigation represents a value-added feature. In particular, applying semantic features to an electronic library containing case studies, scientific papers, e-books, technical reports, etc., would allow networked learners access to a contextual knowledge space of best practices and best principles that are potentially applicable to their tasks or problems. This combination of semantic web technologies, reasoning methods and artificial intelligence represents an efficient backbone for content management. As for access, interactive knowledge maps and customizable search engines can facilitate content retrieval. The ICT component for content management is the knowledge management system that supports the following tools:

- *Authoring*: Software tools for the creation of knowledge resources. These include office automation suites, multimedia processing tools, advanced editing technologies and "packaging" systems.
- *Spider*: Components to search within intranet, extranet and web-based sources.
- *Metadata repository*: Database of data about data (metadata) used to tag knowledge items.
- *Electronic library*: Collection of digital resources stored locally or accessible remotely.
- *Syntactic and semantic indexing and searching*: Tools for indexing knowledge resources through the association of metadata or semantic annotations that can facilitate the retrieval of specific and contextualized knowledge sources.

- *Recommendation engines*: Tools for personalizing access to knowledge bases according to user's needs and interests dynamically defined in the user's profile.
- *Knowledge maps*: Tools to access large knowledge repositories based on graphical multidimensional views of concepts and relationships.

Figure 3.7 shows the components of the *knowledge management system*.

Competencies are developed based on an effective management of critical knowledge and content. In networked learning, all this happens within an extended *community*. The community is the place in which learning processes occur, knowledge exchanges happen, new ideas arise, and individual and organizational growth can take place. Communities represent organizational forms that are more suitable to promote the innovation and experimentation of new ideas aimed at creating value. A community in this sense is like a 'space' of learning opportunities in which new concepts, ideas and projects are constantly developed. ICT can provide a big help in enhancing the dynamics of interaction, and in building the main collaboration infrastructure. Two other elements influence the value generation function of a community: the membership and the contents. With 'membership' we mean the different categories of actors interacting and their (heterogeneous) hierarchical or expertise level. The level of expertise represents the link to the second element mentioned: the content, which is the domain of interest characterizing learning processes and knowledge flows. Managing a

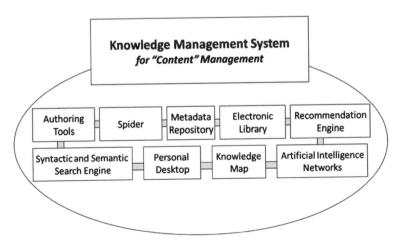

Figure 3.7 Knowledge management system.

community means balancing individual and organizational interests and needs, integrating knowledge domains, promoting exploitation and exploration of knowledge in a collaborative setting inspired to principles such as trust, collaboration, openness and peer recognition. The ICT component supporting community management in our model is the collaborative platform, which provides the following tools:

- *Cooperative working*: Suites that enable heterogeneous and geographically distributed groups of individuals to interact with each other for carrying out a common activity. Examples of tools in this category include e-meeting systems with audio-video conferences, e-mail, instant messaging, application sharing systems, shared tools for activities scheduling (calendars or virtual agendas), forums and whiteboard.
- *Project management*: These tools provide a set of functionalities to support process management by ensuring an efficient and effective management of resources, time, risks and quality. Advanced implications embed systems that manage individual and team competencies.
- *Social software*: Applications based on the emerging paradigm of Web 2.0 characterized by user-generated and peer-based knowledge creation through tools like blogs, wikis, RSS and folksonomies. This "social software" has the capacity to let users develop content in a collaborative manner (Tapscott and Williams, 2006) and places learners at the center of online co-creation, collaboration and consumption, creating new ways of interacting. Ultimately, Web 2.0 can be used to create platforms supporting a collaborative development of personal skills (Elia et al., 2008).

The Figure 3.8 shows the components of the *collaboration platform*.

Ultimately, networked learning refers to the creation of a context for integrating the management of peoples' knowledge, capabilities and relationships, with the ultimate goal of creating shared value. The model presented in this paragraph represents an attempt to systematize the different challenges posited by the creation of value beyond the financial context, and in the sense of growing the intellectual capital of organizations. The role of ICTs has been highlighted to optimize/enable the fundamental processes necessary to address those challenges successfully.

3.9 Conclusion

Leading organizations recognize human capital growth as a key value at the top of their strategic agenda. To this end, they behave like

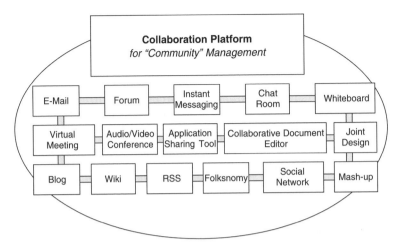

Figure 3.8 Collaboration platform.

universities and continually adapt the way individuals' talent and competencies are nurtured and developed, in a manner that is in line with their strategic objectives and actions. This assumption was at the basis of our investigation made of ideas of change related to mechanisms and approaches adopted to develop human capital, the role and the capabilities of "actors" involved and the ultimate purpose to pursue.

The ideological shift to stakeholder value rather than individual development can be assumed as a central point in our discussion, in that it involves radical changes in terms of people and processes. Like other human and business activities, learning and human capital development become distributed rather than isolated and bounded processes. As such, a networked learning model has been introduced as an integrated organizational and technology framework. The mission of creating value for stakeholders and the importance of networking, collaborating and federating represent two conceptual pillars and key assumptions that will be investigated in Chapter 5, where the stakeholder university is presented as a holistic model for business learning, innovation and leadership.

References

AACSB International (2002) *Management Education at Risk* (Tampa, FL: AACSB International).

N. Andrews and L. D. Tyson (2004) "The Upwardly Global MBA," *Strategy + Business*, fall 2004, pp. 1–10.

C. Argyris and D. Schön (1978) *Organizational Learning: A Theory of Action Perspective* (Reading, MA: Addison Wesley).

P. Aubert, E. Caroli and M. Roger (2004) "New Technologies, Workplace Organization and the Age Structure of the Workforce: Firm-Level Evidence," *MERIT Workshop on Information Technology and New Industry and Labor Market Dynamics*, Maastricht.

W. Baets and G. van der Linden (2003) *Virtual Corporate Universities: A Matrix of Knowledge and Learning for the New Digital Dawn* (Norwell, MA: Kluwer).

C. A. Bartlett (2000) "McKinsey & Company: Managing Knowledge and Learning," *Harvard Business School Teaching Note*, 398–065.

S. Black and L. Porter (2000) *Management: Meeting New Meeting* (New York, NY: Prentice-Hall Publishers).

K. Blanchard (1996) *Turning the Organization Pyramid Upside Down* (San Francisco, CA: Jossey-Bass Publishers).

R. E. Boyatzis, S. Scott, S. Cowen and D. A. Kolb (1994) *Innovation in Professional Education: Steps on a Journey from Teaching to Learning* (San Francisco, CA: Jossey-Bass).

J. Boyett, and J. Boyett (2000) *The Guru Guide: The Best Ideas of Top Management Thinkers* (New York, NY: Wiley).

D. Carter (1998) *MBA: The First Century* (Lewisburg: Bucknell University Press).

J. A. Chapman (2001) "The Work of Managers in New Organizational Context," *Journal of Management Development*, 20(1), pp. 56–68.

G. Elia, A. Margherita, C. Taurino and E. Damiani (2008) "A Web 2.0 Platform Supporting Collaborative Development of Personal Skills", Proceedings of *DEXA08 Workshop ELSYS08 International Workshop on E-Learning Systems*, Turin 5th.

R. E. Freeman, J. S. Harrison and A. C. Wicks (1984) *Strategic Management: A Stakeholder Approach* (London, UK: Pitman Publishing).

R. E. Freeman, J. S. Harrison and A. C. Wicks (2007) *Managing for Stakeholders: Survival, Reputation, and Success* (London, UK: Yale University Press).

S. Ghoshal and C. A. Bartlett (1997) *The Individualized Corporation* (New York, NY: Harper Collins).

R. A. Gordon and J. E. Howell (1959) *Higher Education in Business* (New York, NY: Columbia University Press).

P. Heisig, J. Vorbeck and J. Niebuhr (2001) "Intellectual Capital: Measuring Knowledge Management" in K. Mertins, P. Heisig and J. Vorbeck (eds) *Knowledge Management: Best Practices in Europe* (London, UK: Springer) pp. 151–78.

M. Jacob and T. Hellstrom (2000) *The Future of Knowledge Production in the Academy, Buckingham*, The Society for Research into Higher Education & Open University Press.

T. M. Khalil (2000) *Management of Technology: The Key to Competitiveness and Wealth Creation* (New York, NY: McGraw-Hill).

W. C. Kim and R. A. Mauborgne (1993) "Making Global Strategies Work," *Sloan Management Review*, 34.

P. D. Kuczmarski (1996) "What is Innovation? The Art of Welcoming Risk," *Journal of Consumer Marketing*, 5, pp. 7–11.

S. Liyanage and P. Poon (2002) "Technology and Innovation Management Learning in the Knowledge Economy," *The Journal of Management Development*, 22(7), pp. 579–602.

R. R. Locke (1989) *Management and Higher Education Since 1940: The Influence of America and Japan on West Germany, Great Britain, and France* (Cambridge, MA: Cambridge University Press).

C. O. Longenecker and S. S. Ariss (2002) "Creating Competitive Advantage through Effective Management Education," *The Journal of Management Development*, 21(9), pp. 650–54.

P. Lorange (2005) "Strategy Means Choice: Also for Today's Business School!," *Journal of Management Development*, 24(9), pp. 783–90.

D. V. Lubitz and N. Wickramasinghe (2006) "Dynamic Leadership in Unstable and Unpredictable Environments," *Int. J. Management and Enterprise Development*, 3, pp. 339–50.

L. Marengo (1992) "Coordination and Organizational Learning in the Firm," *Journal of Evolutionary Economics*, 2(4) pp. 313–26.

M. J. Marquardt (2002) *Building the Learning Organization* (Palo Alto, CA: Davies Black Publishing).

J. C. Meister (1998) *Corporate Universities: Lessons in Building a World-Class Work Force* (New York, NY: McGraw-Hill).

J. C. Meister, J. Andrews and T. Kraack (2005) "Increasing the Business Impact of Learning: Lessons from High-Performance Learning Organizations" in R. Paton, G. Peters, J. Storey and S. Taylor (eds) *Handbook of Corporate University Development* (Aldershot: Gower Publishing Limited) pp. 269–80.

H. Mintzberg (2004) *Managers not MBAs: A Hard Look at the Soft Practice of Managing and Management Development* (San Francisco, CA: Berrett-Koehler).

D. Morey, M. Maybury, B. Thuraisingham (2000) *Knowledge Management: Classic and Contemporary Works* (Boston, MA: The MIT Press).

E. C. Nevis, A. J. Dibella and J. M. Gould (1995) "Understanding Organizations as Learning Systems," *Sloan Management Review*, 36(2), pp. 73–85.

F. C. Pierson (1959) *The Education of American Businessmen* (New York, NY: McGraw Hill).

L. Prusak and D. Cohen (2001) "How to Invest in Social Capital", *Harvard Business Review*, June: pp. 86–93.

J. A. Quelch (1994) "Kao Corp., Teaching Note." *Harvard Business School Teaching Note* 591–138.

A. Romano and A. Margherita (2008) "Towards Networked Learning Processes for Organizational Development," Working paper accepted for the *Academy of Human Resource Development International Research Conference*, Panama City, FL, February 20th/24th.

S. Schlossman, M. Sedlak and H. Wechsler (1987) "The New Look, the Ford Foundation and the Revolution in Business Education," *Selections*, 14(3), pp. 8–28.

G. Secundo and G. Passiante (2007) "An innovative Approach to Creating Business Leaders: Evidence from a Case Study," *International Journal of Management in Education*, 1(3), pp. 214–30.

P. Seemann, D DeLong, S. Stukey and E. Guthrie (2000) "Building Intangible Assets: A Strategic Framework for Investing in Intellectual Capital" in D. Morey, M. Maybury and B. Thuraisingham (eds) *Knowledge Management: Classic and Contemporary Works* (Boston, MA: The MIT Press) pp. 85–98.

P. Senge (2000) "Reflection on a Leader's New Work: Building Learning Organizations" in D. Morey, M. Maybury and B. Thuraisingham (eds)

Knowledge Management: Classic and Contemporary Works (Boston, MA: The MIT Press) pp. 53–59.

K. Starkey and P. Madan (2001) "Bridging the Relevance Gap: Aligning Stakeholders in the Future of Management Research," *British Journal of Management*, 12(1), pp. S3–S26.

D. Tapscott and A. D. Williams (2006) *Wikinomics. How Mass Collaboration Changes Everything* (London, UK: Portfolio).

D. J. Teece (2000) *Managing Intellectual Capital* (Oxford, UK: Oxford University Press).

D. J. Teece, G. Pisano and A. Shuen (1997) "Dynamic Capabilities and Strategic Management," *Strategic Management Journal*, 18(7), pp. 509–33.

4
Fostering Innovation by Nurturing Value-Creating Communities

Francesca Grippa, Attilio Di Giovanni and Giuseppina Passiante

4.1 Introduction

In a rapidly changing environment, the success of any firm depends increasingly on the ability to continuously reinvent the sources of value creation, adapting rapidly to change to reach a continuous flow of competitive advantage (Teece, 2007; Brown and Eisenhardt, 1998). This ability is based on the organization's capacity to continuously learn from past experience and to be willing to unlearn and experiment with new ways of solving problems.

Within a complex environment, change is endemic to survival and the dynamic capability to continuously learn becomes a critical success factor. Organizations need to evolve from the era of strategic planning toward the era of organizational learning, through interdependent activities, collaborative problem solving, specialized and integrated network configuration, resource sharing and implementation.

New organizational forms—such as communities of practice, communities of innovation, industry consortia, knowledge-sharing networks—are now emerging in response to new environmental forces that call for new organizational and managerial capabilities (Dyer, 2000; Hamel, 2007). Among those socio-technical forces there are the:

- doubling of knowledge every 2–3 years;
- shortening product lifecycle and rapidly changing market needs;
- digital convergence and expansion of ICT competitive landscape; and
- disintermediation, co-development projects and industry consortia.

In the last two decades, a common perspective in business management literature has emerged, according to which "change equals learning," and survival in a self-organizing company needs to be based on a process of constant learning (Morrison, 2002). It is no longer possible to rely on linear models of management, and hierarchical organizations based on the command-and-control managerial mindset have to be replaced with networked, specialized, nonlinear, emergent and self-organizing groups.

Innovative organizations are recognizing the importance of shifting from a traditional to a more adaptive management approach. To innovate and reinvent the sources of value creation, the challenge for firms is to become learning organizations, acquiring the skills to learn from others and from past experience at individual, team, organizational and inter-organizational level. To pursue innovation in an open and systemic way, new organizational forms—such as communities of practice or communities of innovation—have been shown to be successful in creating and sustaining the level of flexibility and responsiveness required to continuously reinvent business and lead change. To act as a learning organization, innovative communities should behave as integrated networks and implement a model of knowledge creation emphasizing the role of socialization, externalization, combination and internalization processes.

Table 4.1 summarizes the main characteristics of this organizational transformation.

Our contribution in this chapter is based on a key research question: what are the emerging organizational forms that are fostering innovation

Table 4.1   Paradigm shift in the organizational dimensions

Dimensions	Traditional	Emerging
Organization	Closed systems	Open systems
Value creation	Internally-based	Community and network-based
Organization	Hierarchical	Network of partnerships & alliances
Culture	Compliance	Commitments and results
Leadership	Autocratic	Inspirational
Focus	Focus on tangible assets	Intangible assets
Structures	Functional	Based on multidisciplinary teams
Relationships	Hierarchical	Peer-to-peer
Knowledge	Explicit	Tacit
Strategy focus	Efficiency	Innovation

and value creation? We present the concept of community as the organizational answer to the challenges described in this section.

We combine field and desk research to test the validity of a conceptual framework for explaining how the dynamic capability to continuously learn and share knowledge is at the basis of today's ability to succeed.

We take examples from case studies like GE, 3M and Toyota to illustrate how individual, team, organizational and inter-organizational learning represent the key strategic factors for leading the change in a complex environment. We also introduce in more detail the case of Finmeccanica, and, in particular, a corporate-wide project—Mindsh@re—launched in 2003 with the goal of promoting technology sharing, network management and human capital development. It builds a "meta-organizational model" to generate competitive advantages for the group by supporting the cross-fertilization of ideas among different operating companies, clients, industrial and academic partners.

The chapter is organized in two parts. After presenting the conceptual framework for interpreting the relations between innovation, community and learning organization, Section 3 will explore the theoretical background of the topics of organizational and networked learning, by providing evidence from business case studies. The second part (Sections 4.4 and 4.5) contextualizes the framework to the Finmeccanica case, demonstrating how it is possible to foster *innovation* by activating processes of *organizational learning, knowledge creation* and building a *learning organization* with the support of *technology communities*.

4.2 The conceptual framework

In the discipline of organizational development, learning is a characteristic of *proactive* organizations, able to sense changes in signals from its internal and external environment and adapt accordingly. Both executives and academics have recognized organizational learning as *the* key factor in achieving continuous competitive advantage (Dyer, 2000).

In the "dynamic capability" approach to competitive advantage (Teece et al., 1997) a firm's ability to continuously learn, adapt and reconfigure is presented as its main capability to build competitive superiority. Others have proposed a "knowledge-based view" of the firm's success based on the ability to acquire, create, store and apply knowledge (Kogut and Zander, 1992).

From our perspective, innovation is not simply a technology-based process, but includes organizational change and market modifications, as well as structural transformations. It does not involve only R&D

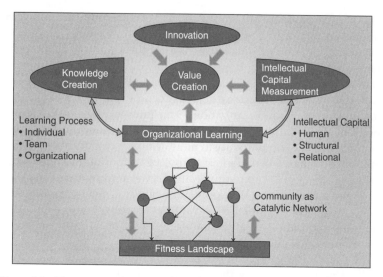

Figure 4.1   The conceptual framework.

but also production, customer needs evaluation (marketing), suppliers, users and regulations. In this systemic, non-linear and holistic view of innovation, value creation is the main goal of organizations who want to provide tangible and intangible results for all stakeholders. To achieve this objective, the challenge for firms is to become learning organizations, acquiring the skills to learn from others and from past experience at individual, team, organizational and inter-organizational levels.

The interdependence of these concepts to build value-creating organizations is represented in Figure 4.1.

As described in Chapter 2, "complexity theory" views organizations as "complex adaptive systems": they co-evolve with the environment because of the self-organizing behavior of the agents who determine *fitness landscape* of market opportunities and competitive dynamics. Since the focus of competition is moving from the firm to the network, and from rigid organizational structures to informal networks, innovative *communities* are presented as the governance model to build a value-creating organization that promotes individual and team entrepreneurship through the process of *organizational learning*. In the conceptual model, innovative communities are interpreted as *catalytic networks* that represent a viable adaptation to an unstable environment and the "most innovative and flexible organizational form" (Clippinger, 1999, p. 26).

In this landscape of challenges and opportunities, the process of organizational learning is what enables firms to constantly reinvent themselves, to recombine their knowledge assets co-evolving with competitors, customers, suppliers and, therefore, to *create value*. The firm's ability to generate value for stakeholders is now based on the capacity to continuously learn from past experience, and to be willing to unlearn and experiment new ways of solving problems. The *community* dimension is presented as a way to stimulate organizations to become "learning organizations." The process of *knowledge creation* that facilitates the processes of individual, group and organizational learning needs to be complemented by new ways of monitoring the performance of a learning organization. Managers need to use metrics derived from the field of *intellectual capital management* to capture innovation, people and community growth. This implies looking at the nature and evolution of human, structural and relational capital.

In the following sections, we describe in detail the theoretical background on which the conceptual model is grounded.

4.3 Fostering innovation through organizational learning

Examples of organizations that have been competing on the edge for many years demonstrate that a continuous self-renewal and the ability to foster continuous innovation require the capability of becoming a learning organization. General Electric, 3M, Microsoft, Toyota Motor Co. and Intel reveal how continuous learning is systemically built into the organization's DNA. In the Crotonville learning center at General Electric, the company created a program called "Best Practices Development" that drives learning by managers and other leaders. A dozen people from GE's businesses meet monthly in Crotonville to learn and teach, creating a collaborative environment based on cross-unit learning.

3M is the other emblematic success case of a company creating value by building a cultural environment able to "stimulate ordinary people to produce extraordinary performance" (Bartlett and Mohammed, 1995). 3M is almost universally recognized as one of the world's most innovative companies over time. Sharing knowledge was recognized by members of 3M research community as an important value to set the pace and scope of the company's development. This philosophy was supported by links of informal networks and by more formal mechanisms. One of the innovations introduced to facilitate knowledge transfer was the Technical Forum, a body created in the early 1950s and composed of scientists and technologists in each of 3M's U.S.-based laboratories. Among the events organized by this forum, the Annual Technology Fair was a three-day internal event in which 3M's scientists presented their latest findings to their colleagues.

Even if the focus of organizational learning in literature is the individual firm, scholars found that suppliers and customers can be the main source of innovation and that *inter*-organizational learning is critical to success (Dyer and Nobeoka, 2000). Toyota, widely recognized as a leader in continuous improvement and learning and as the biggest Asian company on the Global 500, bases its success on the multilateral knowledge-sharing routines with suppliers that result in higher inter-organizational learning.

Another example of a firm pursuing innovation by leveraging the learning process at different levels is McKinsey, which in the late 1990s committed 5 percent of its $1.8 billion annual revenue to the development of its four thousand professional staff (20.000 dollars per consultant per year). Skandia is widely recognized as the typical example of a firm developing an alternative measurement system, the Business Navigator, which includes the traditional financial focus but also the customer, the process and the "renewal and development" focus.

Cases of organizational success like McKinsey and Skandia tell us that "the most basic task in creating horizontal knowledge flows is [. . .] to create new channels of communication that encourage the rapid diffusion of strategic knowledge and expertise across the organization" (Ghoshal and Bartlett, 1997, p. 87). To build a cross-fertilization process among business units or operating companies, it is important to nurture leadership, creativity and individual entrepreneurship within an organizational context conducive to innovation.

For most of the 20th century, the dominant philosophy in many leading industrial organizations was a closed model of innovation, where a company generates, develops and commercializes its own ideas. Today, the boundaries between the firm and the environment are more porous, and a more open model of innovation is becoming accepted by many leading companies.

The most innovative companies are the ones pursuing what Eisenhardt and Brown called "competing on the edge strategy" (1998). This view on strategy calls for the ability to locate the constantly changing sources of advantage, considering as the "unit" of analysis the whole "business model" rather than a single product, technology or process. In a hypercompetitive and unpredictable environment, it is the innovation that takes place in some or all the business model components that creates a more competitive advantage (Hamel, 2000). Within a holistic view of business, we assume that "business concept innovation" is the key to creating new wealth (Romano et al., 2001). Business concept innovation is a meta-innovation; as it is non-linear, it goes beyond incremental innovation and takes the entire business concept as its starting point, being more comprehensive than product or technology innovation. This category of innovation is closer to what Teece (1994) calls "systemic innovation," which requires coordinated adjustment throughout the system. For Teece, different types of innovation (autonomous versus systemic) are associated with two factors: the specific "organization forms" and the extent to which the "capabilities" needed to exploit the innovation already exist within the firm or need to be acquired from the outside.

A lot of research has been done in the field of industrial innovation to recognize the evolution of five generations of innovation models, from the static views (1960s/early 1970s) to the more dynamic models starting in the early 1980s.

The first generation (technology push) is based on a simple linear sequential process with a heavy emphasis on R&D, and a perspective of the market as a container for the fruits of R&D. The second generation (need pull) considers innovation as a simple linear sequential process. Emphasis is given to marketing, and the market is seen as the source of ideas for directing R&D, whose role is reactive. The third generation models (coupling model) are still based on a sequential process, but with feedback loops and a combination of push/pull strategies. The activities of R&D and marketing are more balanced, as the emphasis is now on integrating the R&D and marketing interface. In the fourth generation models (integrated model), the new product development is a parallel process with integrated development teams and strong upstream supplier linkages. Other characteristics are: close coupling with leading-edge customers and the emphasis on integration between R&D and manufacturing, together with horizontal collaboration. Finally, the fifth generation models (systems integration and networking model), relies on fully-integrated parallel development with use of expert systems and simulation modeling in R&D. Further important properties of this new perspective on the innovation process are: strong linkages with leading edge customers; a strategic integration with primary suppliers, including co-development of new products and linked CAD systems; an emphasis on corporate flexibility and the speed of development; and an increased focus on quality and other non-price factors.

The open, systemic model of innovation is perfectly matched with the "fifth generation innovation process," which emphasizes horizontal linkages, joint ventures, collaborative research groupings, collaborative marketing arrangements and communities of practice (Rothwell, 1992).

In this section, we have illustrated the contributing literature to conceptualize the limitation of a firm-centric approach to innovation. The closed perspective on innovation is inadequate for creating value within an economy where processes of knowledge socialization are required to maximize the transactional value created by networks of firms (Sawhney and Prandelli, 2000). Recognizing the importance of an open, systemic view on the innovation process means supporting the notion that knowledge is not owned by individuals or firms, but can be distributed across a community of actors. The adoption of a model of "innovation governance" which is based on the *community* dimension represents a solution able to capture the value generated by the interdependence among exchange partners. In Section 3.4, we will describe how the community concept helps in shifting the focus of innovation toward more flexible organizational forms able to maintain balance between order and chaos.

4.3.1　The process of organizational learning

This section describes the process of organizational learning that represents in our conceptual model one of the underpinnings of innovation and value creation. Argyris (1977) defines organizational learning as the process of "detection and correction of errors." In his view, organizations learn through individuals acting as agents for them: "The individuals' learning activities, in turn, are facilitated or inhibited by an ecological system of factors that may be called an organizational learning system." The rate at which organizations learn is one—if not the only—sustainable source of competitive advantage.

Organizational learning has been defined as the process whereby organizations enhance their capacity for effective action (Senge, 1990). It also refers to the process by which the organizational knowledge base is developed and shaped, or the process of creating new competencies and increasing the existing ones. "Organizations do not have brains, but they have cognitive systems and memories" (Hedberg, 1981).

The process of organizational learning follows different stages of development (Kelly and Allison, 1999):

1. Recognition of unconscious self-organization: Self-organization is a hidden cultural mindset, and the command and control leadership is predominant;

2. Conscious self-organization: Presence of committed teams with open communication constantly assessing their performance by scanning the internal and external environment;
3. Guided self-organization: Disciplined teams disseminate successful lessons and communicate across the organization;
4. Quantitatively guided self-organization: Use of statistical models to predict and make decisions; and
5. Consciously competent autopoiesis: Co-evolution within and between environments as open systems.

Organizational learning involves different kinds of learning, defined as "the process within the organization by which knowledge about action-outcome relationships and the effect of the environment on these relationships is developed" (Duncan and Weiss, 1979, p. 84). As inter-organizational communities and teams become more and more important to deal with a complex fitness landscape, "team learning" rather "team training" needs to be fostered. While team learning emphasizes self-managed learning, creativity and a free flow of ideas, team training traditionally involves the mere acquisition of group skills, such as problem-solving techniques and team interaction skills. Team learning requires a change in the cultural mindset of people who share their experiences, both negative and positive, with other members and with external teams by promoting the corporate intellectual capital growth.

The focus on the learning process at individual, team and organizational level requires transformational changes. This brought other scholars to propose operative models to put the organizational learning into practice. The next section provides the main guidelines to build a learning organization. A final table will present a summary of the key drivers to build an environment based on organizational learning and conducive to innovation.

4.3.2 Toward a learning organization

The concept of a learning organization is increasingly relevant given the complexity and uncertainty of the organizational environment. The rapid pace of change in the business environment has undermined the relevance of strategic planning and forecasting methods, yielding to an interest in how to develop the organizational capabilities to sense and flexibly adapt to change.

Senge (1990) defines a learning organization as the organization in which you cannot *not* learn since learning is insinuated into the fabric of life. He also defines learning organization as "a group of people continually enhancing their capacity to create what they want to create" (Senge, 1990). It is the organizational form that offers the ability to anticipate, react and lead the change, complexity and uncertainty (Teece et al., 1997).

Being a learning organization provides a competitive advantage and builds dynamic capabilities defined as "the firm's ability to integrate, build, and reconfigure internal and external competencies to address rapidly changing environments" (Teece et al., 1997, p. 516).

A learning organization promotes open innovation, explores and exploits knowledge acquired from external sources (e.g. competitors, suppliers, universities, partners) and retains the best talent. The ability to become a learning organization is based on the following strategic building blocks:

- to promote teamwork for group problem solving;
- to experiment and reward risk taking behavior;
- to quickly share knowledge; and
- to learn from past experience, best practices and from others.

According to Senge (1990), learning organizations are organizations where people continually expand their capacity to create the results they truly desire, where new and expansive patterns of thinking are nurtured, where collective aspiration is set free, and where people are continually learning to see the whole together.

Senge (1990) notes that companies need to focus on Generative Learning or "double-loop learning" (Argyris, 1977). Generative learning emphasizes continuous experimentation and feedback in an ongoing examination of the way organizations define and solve problems. In Senge's perspective, generative learning, unlike adaptive learning, requires new ways of looking at reality. Senge defines five disciplines that represent a body of theory and method to be learned and put into practice by individuals within an organization:

1. Adopting a "System Thinking": Is the conceptual cornerstone ("The Fifth Discipline") of his approach. It is the discipline that integrates the others, fusing them into a coherent body of theory and practice.
2. Encouraging the "Personal Mastery": Personal mastery is the discipline of "continually clarifying and deepening our personal vision, of focusing our energies, of developing patience, and of seeing reality objectively." It goes beyond competence and skills, although it involves them.

3. Focusing on "Mental Models": These are "deeply ingrained assumptions, generalizations, or even pictures and images that influence how we understand the world and how we take action."
4. Building a "Shared Vision": When there is a genuine vision, people excel and learn, not because they are told to, but because they want to. Many managers and leaders have personal visions that never get translated into shared visions.
5. Facilitating "Team Learning": Such learning is viewed as the process of aligning and developing the capacities of a team to create the results its members truly desire.

In a learning organization, value is generated by nurturing informal relations and encouraging a free, horizontal flow of knowledge across organizational boundaries, by opening new channels of communication and sustaining a cross-pollination of new ideas. This characteristic derives from the property of "systems thinking," which involves seeing relationships rather than finding linear cause-effect chains (Senge, 1990; Morrison, 2002).

Miller (1997) builds on the classic perspective on learning organizations defined by Senge as an organization that must continuously adapt to its environment. The author considers the process of learning not merely as a matter of "adaptation as a chameleon, which changes itself externally but largely remains the same." The learning organization must go through a generative process of metamorphosis, transforming itself in butterfly from a caterpillar (Miller, 1997).

The organizational premises to build a learning organization are based on factors such as the creation of a collaborative climate against a hierarchical culture, supporting risk-taking, extended decision-making and professional development (Pedler et al., 1997).

The main way to manage knowledge is through a facilitation of relationships, flexible organizational structure and an open culture. The leaders' role in the learning organization is that of designers, facilitators of connections, stewards who can build shared vision and challenge prevailing mental models. They are responsible for building organizations where people are continually expanding their capabilities to shape their future (Senge, 1990). Leaders must recognize that long-term relationships are embedded in fluid social networks, either virtual or physical, and are the real bases of employees' commitment (Carley, 2000). The challenge to set up a model of open, networked innovation passes through leveraging ecological communities (Senge and Carstedt, 2001), to fostering hidden informal networks (Cross and Parker, 2002) within and across firm's boundaries and understanding the pathways where knowledge flows (Cohen and Prusak, 2001).

Michael J. Marquardt (2002, pp. 23–33) proposes a practical framework based on five sub-systems for facilitating corporate restructuring and building a learning organization. He considers the disciplines proposed by Peter Senge as required skills to become a learning organization.

1. *Learning* is the core subsystem of the learning organization. It refers to levels (individual, team, organizational) and types/approaches of learning: (a) *adaptive*, when people reflect on past experience and change their actions accordingly; (b) *anticipatory*, when the best future opportunity is searched for that achieves a desirable future; and (c) *action*, when people inquire about present knowledge to pursue individual, group or organizational goals.
2. *Organization* is the underlying structure of vision, values, culture and structure. The strategies to become a learning organization are: create structures that are community-like and facilitate relationships; act locally to cause change in large systems, since everything connected; and value mistakes and support structures with loose boundaries.
3. *Knowledge*—including acquisition, creation, storage, application and dissemination. The strategies for managing knowledge are: capture systematically relevant external knowledge and maximize knowledge transfer across boundaries; organize internal learning events; and build mechanisms for coding and storing learning that is accessible and makes sense to people.
4. *Technology* includes technologies for collaboration, coaching, coordination, simulation. Among the strategies for applying technology in a learning organization there are: develop multimedia learning centers; integrate web-learning in the overall action-learning strategy; identify technical experts; and capture their knowledge and transfer that knowledge to the site where it is required.
5. *People* are the drivers for continuous learning. Multiple strategies for empowering and enabling entrepreneurial spirit and creativity are: reward learning; encourage experimentation and reflection on acquired knowledge; avoid teaching and controlling; and create self-managed work teams. In a study on the capacity to build a learning organization, Silins et al. (2002) defined as key predictors of effective organizational learning the presence of an "active leadership" and "distributed leadership." Leadership in the current complex environment must be considered as a "collective self-leadership," not

concerned only with the power of senior and high ranked figures. Leaders can be found everywhere in the organization, and it is best conceived as a group quality because leadership is a process—and not a position—distributed between individuals in light of different circumstances and competencies. In the complexity theory, leaders do not evaporate, but become "quantum leaders" (Youngblood, 1997) disturbing and perturbing the system to stimulate change.

Other scholars offer some key features of a successful learning organization: scanning imperative; concern for measurement; experimentation mindsets; life-long education; open and multichannel communication; leader's support; and a systems perspective.

David Garvin (1993), after blaming scholars for adopting a "mystical terminology" to discuss learning organizations, proposes the "three Ms" (Meaning, Management and Measurement) to provide managers with a foundation for launching them. Citing cases like Boeing, which used lessons from earlier model development to produce the most successful launches in its history (Boeing 757 and 767), Garvin is one of the first authors to offer managerial suggestions on how to: create effective incentives to knowledge-sharing; cultivate the art of open, attentive learning; and avoid the "not invented here" syndrome.

In Table 4.2 we list the key drivers of a learning organization that are reported by many contributors.

In this section we have described the main characteristics and building blocks of a learning organization proposed by scholars and practitioners that are based on multiple dimensions. In summary, to build an environment conducive to continuous innovation, an organization needs to rely on life-long learning and a leadership style that enhances the culture of information-sharing and the democratization of the workplace.

The next section presents the theoretical background behind the assumption that "knowledge creation" is an important determinant of continuous innovation.

4.3.3 Knowledge creation: A key process for a learning organization

In a complex and unpredictable environment, where the outcome of knowledge creation is non-linear and predicting success is difficult, many companies are recognizing the importance of leveraging the collective knowledge embedded in communities. "Learning is the process whereby human beings build knowledge, enhancing their capacity for effective action" (Senge, 1990). This principle is stated in the McKinsey

Table 4.2   Key drivers for a learning organization

Key Drivers	Description
1. Foster Systemic Innovation	Open, networked or systemic innovation in the sourcing, integration and development of product and business system innovations through win-win external partnerships to capture maximum commercial value for R&D investment (Chesbrough, 2003).
2. Enable Democracy of Ideas	Decision-making process is based on aggregating collective wisdom and knowledge, building a democracy of ideas that are shared in formal and informal webs of relationships (Hamel, 2007; Tapscott and Williams, 2006; Ghoshal and Bartlett, 1997). In a learning organization, distributed knowledge is linked to distributed leadership, learning is rewarded and risk-taking is supported in a blame-free culture.
3. Nurture Individual Creativity	Companies need to amplify human imagination and creativity by turning ordinary employees into extraordinary innovators (Hamel, 2007). Organizational creativity has been defined as a subset of the domain of innovation, as "the creation of a valuable, useful new product, service, idea, procedure, or process by individuals working together in a complex social system" (Woodman et al., 1993, p. 293).
4. Promote Distributed Leadership	Leadership in a complex environment is conceived as a collective self-leadership, as a process, a group quality distributed between individuals in light of different circumstances and competencies. Managers have to abandon a transactional command-and-control and transformational perspective on leadership, moving toward a collective, democratic, and distributed or quantum leadership (Youngblood, 1997).
5. Sustain Life Long Learning	Investing in continuous learning means integrating organization development, change management, knowledge management, competency and leadership development. Learning strategy must enable dynamic and non-linear behaviors with a focus on community-based approaches and on Web 2.0 technologies (Hamel, 2007; Morrison, 2002).
6. Create New Measurement Systems	New metrics of performance are required to measure the learning process. Metrics able to capture innovation, people and community growth, and learning processes must be introduced (Kaplan and Norton, 1992; Iyer et al., 2006).

motto: "The most important knowledge is in our people." Companies like Xerox, IBM, Daimler Chrysler and McKinsey developed, supported and sometimes institutionalized new forms of interactions among workers, internal and external of the organization's boundaries (Clippinger, 1999).

Managers in several companies are discovering how business performance depends on the strength of each business component, as well as on the effectiveness of their integration.

As David Skyrme noticed (1998), the distinction between a knowledge-based organization and a learning organization is becoming less defined: a learning organization does not mean "more training," but, instead, developing higher levels of knowledge and skill. It is about innovation and creativity, and designing the future rather than merely adapting to it. In his view, individual, team and organizational learning occur "when assumptions are challenged and knowledge is reframed."

As Skyrme said (1998): "Knowledge and other forms of 'intellectual capital' are the 'hidden assets' in a company. They do not appear on the balance sheet in annual reports, yet they underpin value creation and future earnings potential." This is one of the reasons why many knowledge intensive companies, like Microsoft and Glaxo Wellcome, have market values at least ten times the value of their physical assets.

In their famous book *The Knowledge Creating Company* (1995), Nonaka and Takeuchi state that the most important asset for a firm is the capability to create, disseminate and embody knowledge in their products and services. According to the authors "knowledge is created and expanded through social interaction between tacit and explicit knowledge" (1995, p. 61).

Adopting the categorization introduced by Polanyi in the 1960s, they postulate four different modes of knowledge conversion: "socialization" (from tacit to tacit); "externalization" (from tacit to explicit); "combination" (from explicit to explicit); and "internalization" (from explicit to tacit). Nonaka and Takeuchi ground their theory on the learning theories of Argyris: "From our viewpoint, the creation of knowledge certainly involves interaction between these two kinds of learning, which forms a kind of dynamic spiral" (p. 44).

The SECI model emerging from this conceptualization (socialization, externalization, combination, internalization) suggests that the process of knowledge creation is represented by an *ongoing repeated spiral* based on an epistemological and ontological dimension. If the epistemological dimension refers to the process of conversion between tacit and explicit knowledge, the ontological dimension focuses on the individual, group, organization, or inter-organization level of knowledge creation. In this sense, the "extended, inter-organizational community" is the organizational structure that better reflects the concept of "hypertext organization" (Nonaka and Takeuchi, 1995).

The importance of the space, intended as the virtual and physical place where knowledge and learning occur, is suggested by Nonaka and Konno (1998) who propose a concept representing the background for the knowledge conversion process. Based on a concept that was originally introduced by the Japanese philosopher Kitaro Nishida, "Ba" is described as "the shared context in motion," a shared mental space, shared context for emerging relationships, physical, virtual, mental or any combination of them (Figure 4.2). Ba is conceived as "the platform for knowledge creation"; the space where the interaction takes place and the "knowledge assets" are activated as resources. Nonaka and Konno (1998) propose a model in which knowledge assets are the inputs and outputs of the SECI process. They are firm-specific resources that are indispensable to the creation of values for the firm. Among them, *social relations* represent a valuable resource, as the authors make clear when they refer to different types of Ba: *originating Ba* (sharing of feelings, emotions experiences and mental models); *interacting Ba* (selection of people with the right mix of knowledge and capabilities); *cyber Ba* (a virtual space of interaction, supported by ICT system); and *exercising Ba* (focused on training with mentors and colleagues). Ba exists at many ontological levels transcending the boundary between micro and macro and explaining the spatial and temporal context where knowledge is created dynamically.

Concepts like communities of practice or communities of creation (Wenger and Snyder, 2000; Sawhney and Prandelli, 2000) are grounded in the concept of Ba, where members learn through participating in a shared space. The principal difference is that the boundaries of the community are usually set based on the task, culture and history of the community, whereas the boundary of Ba can be easily and frequently changed. Whereas the membership of a community of practice is stable, the membership of Ba is not fixed, as participants come and go.

To build a truly integrated and interdependent organization able to develop and diffuse knowledge rapidly, it is vital to invest into the creation of flexible communities, where information, knowledge and expertise flow freely.

From this perspective, an important role for ensuring success to any knowledge creation and sharing process is played by the organizational *culture*, whose aspects can promote or hinder the handling of knowledge within and across organizations. To be successful in changing the cultural mindset of management, some lessons come from the case of General Electric. The powerful ideas of the CEO Jack Welch changed

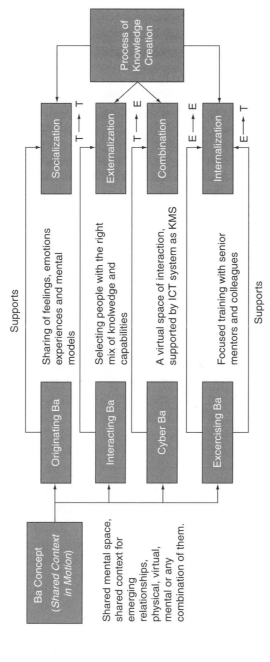

Figure 4.2 The concept of Ba and the SECI model.

the criteria for bonuses to reward idea-seeking and sharing, not only idea generation. There was no place at GE for the adherents of the old culture. As he said: "If you're self-centered, don't share with people and aren't searching for ideas, you don't belong here" (Bartlett and Wozny, 2005).

As the Chief Executive Officer of American Skandia Inc., Jan Carendi, said: "We must think of ourselves less as insurance specialists and more as specialists in collaboration." To reach this goal, partnership was offered only to those who developed a strong expertise and a network of colleagues who draw on that knowledge to help the customers. Skandia's CEO created "Strategic Competence Centers" out of Skandia's divisions whenever he noticed that strategic capabilities were developed in those divisions. What he created and nurtured was a kind of Ba; an institutionalized and specialized network, a community where no leader was permanent. Each competence center was aware that as soon as another Skandia's unit passed it on the learning curve, the prestigious designation would have to be ceded to the new "centers of excellence."

As noticed by David Skyrme (1998): "The difficulty comes, not through handling 'explicit' knowledge, but 'tacit' knowledge which is harder to express and codify. Very often the most valuable knowledge that an organization has is in the heads of its people." Skyrme proposes seven dimensions or levers through which knowledge should be managed (Table 4.3). This perspective on managing organizational knowledge provides insights for any business strategy that is based on creating value for all the stakeholders. Whereas Nonaka and Takeuchi suggested looking at the ontological dimension of knowledge creation to recognize the importance of crossing the firm's boundaries, Skyrme added the management consultant's point of view to the topic. The assumption of his model is to explore and exploit new sources of innovation by continuously scanning the business landscape.

The knowledge creation process that we have described here is based on knowledge networks: *communities of interaction* able to activate processes of knowledge generation through socialization processes (Nonaka and Takeuchi, 1995). More recently, Sawhney and Prandelli (2000) propose a similar concept, *communities of creation*, representing the governance mechanism particularly relevant when knowledge is the main source of economic rent. This and other concepts will be discussed in the next paragraph, where we investigate the importance of extended, collaborative communities to increase the innovation rate and create value for all stakeholders.

Table 4.3   Knowledge sources

Sources of Knowledge	Examples
Customer Knowledge	• Understanding customers' needs • Articulating unmet needs • Identifying new opportunities
Stakeholder Relationships	• Improving knowledge flows between suppliers, employees, shareholders, community using this knowledge to inform key strategies
Business Environment Insights	• Systematic environmental scanning, including political, economic, technology, social and environmental trends • Competitor Analysis
Organizational Memory	• Building best practice databases • Sharing online documents, procedures • Implementing forums, wiki, blog
Knowledge in Processes	• Embedding knowledge into business processes and management decision-making
Knowledge in Products and Services	• Knowledge embedded in products • Surround products with knowledge; e.g. in user guides and enhanced knowledge-intensive services
Knowledge in People	• Innovation workshops • Expert and learning networks • Communities of knowledge practice

Source: Adapted from Skyrme, 1998.

4.3.4   Building communities

As described by Ghoshal and Bartlett (1997), a value-creating organization "reverses the focus from value extraction to value creation by establishing continuous learning of individuals as a cornerstone of its organization." It is able to continuously renew itself by recognizing and nurturing the untapped ability of people and by building an integrated process of organizational learning.

To deal dynamically with their fitness landscape, organizations need to rely on new organizational forms based on networked communities. In our conceptual model, communities are considered as *"catalytic networks,"* which is an organizational form that best adapts to the highly volatile, interconnected global business environment (Clippinger, 1999). Since they are in the ideal zone of fitness—at the edge of chaos—they can only be managed by setting protocols, standards and rules able to define the processes of interaction and collaboration inside and outside the networks' boundaries (Brown and Eisenhardt, 1998). The traditional managerial approach based on "top-down control" must be replaced by a "directed co-evolution" among all stakeholders, as the cases from the open source movement illustrate. Amazon's decision to provide financial incentives to create a network of recommenders and the growth of the community of developers around the Linux operating system are both examples of how a self-organized network of customers can drive innovation (Rizova, 2006).

As several examples of successful companies like GE and ABB have demonstrated, the synergic integration of multiple units in cross-functional teams or communities is a key element to providing the company with that level of flexibility and responsiveness required to continuously reinvent the business and lead the change.

In what has been widely recognized as a knowledge-based economy, the rise of the "community dimension" as the natural locus of the learning processes is complemented by a view of the company's value as being based on human, structural and relational capital.

Assuming the concept of an extended, networked, catalytic community as the most flexible organizational form to adapt and quickly respond to change, the next question is about the characteristics of a community that is able to create value for all the stakeholders. The underpinnings of this question are in the community's ability to become a learning organization. This is done by constantly carrying out a process of organizational learning that enables a continuous self-renewal, and by reconfiguring their flow of knowledge assets in co-evolution with competitors, customers, suppliers. To act as a learning organization, communities should behave as integrated networks and use new metrics to define their performance.

It is widely recognized that pursuing innovation in a systemic manner flows from the development and application of new technology and the adoption of new organizational forms (Teece, 1994). Executives and academics have used different categories to describe these new forms, introducing the concepts of community of practice, community of interests, virtual teams, work groups, project teams and informal networks (Wenger and Snyder, 2000; Gloor, 2006; Ancona and Bresman, 2007). Despite differences in terms of goals, communication media used, use of volunteer participation or not, the common characteristic of these emergent social networks is the *facilitation of learning and knowledge-sharing* between individuals conducting practice-related tasks. Each member brings his or her special knowledge and capabilities, but also interpersonal relationships with the rest of the community, as well as with external members.

Nurturing intra- and inter-organizational communities helps to build an integrated network of interdependencies with clients, employees and other stakeholders (Dyer, 2000). Ghoshal and Bartlett (1997) stream-lined how to ensure a continuous renewal by supporting formal and informal connections, avoiding the traditional centralized hub and building a community-based organizational model that is able to create an entrepreneurial spirit and personal commitment.

The cross-pollination of ideas that emerges through this coopera-tive learning helps to support that level of creativity that characterizes organizations that are willing to allow for innovation. To let creativity guide the organizations, managers have to adopt a proactive approach to their fitness landscapes, the customers and the marketplace, rather than a reactive, passive approach. To manage a networked organization, with nodes both internal and external to the formal structure, commu-nities represent a flexible answer that allows for the freedom required for growth (Hite, 1999).

Organizations have recognized these informal communities as an important new engine of innovation, as their most versatile and dynamic "knowledge resource" at the basis of their ability to know and learn.

> Traditional knowledge management approaches attempt to cap-ture exiting knowledge within formal systems, such as databases. Yet systematically addressing the kind of dynamic "knowing" that makes a difference in practice requires the participation of people who are fully engaged in the process of creating, refining, com-municating, and using knowledge. We frequently say that people are an organization's most important resource. Yet we seldom understand this truism in terms of communities through which individuals develop and share the capacity to create and use knowl-edge. Even when people work for large organizations, they learn through their participation in more specific communities made up of people with whom they interact on a regular basis. These "Communities of Practice" are mostly informal and distinct from organizational units.
>
> (Wenger and Snyder, 2000, p. 1)

Recognizing the value generated by the informal social networks within and across the organization requires a continuous investment to support and nurture communities. Scholars found that less dynamic companies initiate new projects within a rigid mechanistic, framework and suffered accordingly (Rothwell, 1992; Chesbrough, 2003). On the other side, flexible and dynamically responsive organizations adopt an "organic style of management." Building a learning organization by supporting flexible, innovative communities has been chosen by a number of large companies to develop organizational structures and practices able to encourage in-house entrepreneurship and new product development. 3M is one of the most renowned cases of a company that is successful in developing a system of continuous innovation via the mechanism of "internal venturing."

The community perspective on value creation and innovation is associated with a horizontal management style that emphasizes participation and open communication rather than formal directives and a command-and-control style. Since the 1960s, studies have demonstrated how a style that emphasizes the flow of information not only upwards, but also downwards and outwards from the center, is more conducive to innovation (Burns and Stalker, 1961). The concept of "community" emerges as the organizational form most typical of the organic organization. Instead of little individual freedom of action, long decision chains and slow decision-making, the organic organization promotes interdisciplinary teams, breaking down departmental barriers. Building a learning organization by nurturing innovative, extended communities allows the firm to benefit from the creativity and diversity of its partners. In a business environment where knowledge is required to take advantage of distributed innovation, communities represent a "governance mechanism" able to balance order and chaos. As clearly stated by Sawhney and Prandelli (2000):

> The community functions as a complex adaptive system, [. . .]. It is neither closed nor completely open. Like the Ba, the community can be physical as well as virtual or mental. Such an emergent system has the ability to self-organize and evolve into higher levels of order that are both more complex and more stable.
>
> (p. 26)

Other scholars propose that organizational communities can be productive even when they are self-organized and self-sustaining. Peter Gloor (2006) introduced the concept of Collaborative Knowledge Networks (CKN), a virtual instance of communities of practice, defined as "groups of self-motivated individuals driven by the idea of something new and exciting, a way to greatly improve an existing business practice, or a new product or service for which they see a real need" (Gloor, 2006). These forms of communities create settings conducive to the development of new products, services, practice and methodologies. They are based on two mechanisms that are active in the CKN ecosystem: *innovation dissemination* and *innovation incubation*.

A new concept introduced to focus the attention on the real objective of such communities is "collaborative innovation networks." A collaborative innovation network (COIN) is a set of individuals and groups working together using various communication technologies to achieve a common vision (Gloor, 2006). It can be formed when like-minded, self-motivated peers become interested in a new idea and "swarm" around it, working together to informally develop the new concept. It can also be formed intentionally by companies who come together to create an innovative product when their talented developers happen to be living and working in different physical locations. Indeed, very often collaborative innovation networks include members from different companies, countries, cultures and time zones. The diffusion of the ICTs allowed communities to benefit from the virtual networking information advantage, delocalization and fast-paced processes (Cothrel and Williams, 1999). The technology-based interaction made them harder to be developed, but at the same time more able to deal with the challenges of the new business environment.

Besides informally and autonomously built innovation networks, organizations are also intentionally sustaining the development of collaborative innovation networks for several reasons. They represent an ideal forum for sharing and spreading best practices across a company. In situations of mergers and acquisitions, or in supporting new product development projects, combining knowledge from several companies or departments is facilitated by the identification of informal communities that share common interests, are willing to learn and interact and collaborate toward common goals.

Sawhney and Prandelli (2000) propose a new governance mechanism for managing systemic innovation: the concept of "community of creation." They present it as the answer to the increasing complexity of the business environment:

> The community of creation is a permeable system, with ever-changing boundaries. It lies between the closed hierarchical model of innovation and the open market-based model. Intellectual property rights are owned by the entire community. The community is governed by a central firm that acts as the sponsor and defines the ground rules for participation.
>
> (p. 25)

Other studies have distinguished communities according to their goals, as proposed in the following classification:

- Helping Communities: Provide a forum for community members to help each other solve everyday work problems.
- Best Practice Communities: Develop and disseminate best practices, guidelines and procedures for their members' use.
- Technology Sharing Communities: Organize, manage and share the technological information from which the community members can benefit.
- Innovation Communities: Create breakthrough ideas, knowledge and practice.

Given the importance of the knowledge creation process to promote open innovation inside and across the organizational communities, scholars started to investigate more tangible and manageable ways to measure knowledge flow.

The next section will describe how value and innovation are measured through innovative methodologies and tools able to capture the evolution of intellectual capital within learning organizations.

4.3.5   Measuring the value created by a community

Since knowledge represents an important asset for value creation, it is often conceptualized using the term "intellectual capital" to refer to the knowledge of a social collectivity, such as an organization, a business community, or a cluster of firms. It is often explained using the following classification (Bontis, 2001; Edvinsson and Malone, 1997):

- *Human Capital*: Refers to the know-how, capabilities, skills and expertise of the members of the organization. It is the knowledge generated by each individual.
- *Organizational or Structural Capital*: Includes the organizational capabilities developed to meet market requirements (i.e. patents). It is that knowledge that has been captured/institutionalized within the structure, processes and the culture of an organization.
- *Social or Relational Capital*: Includes connections outside the organization such as customer loyalty, goodwill and supplier relations. It is the perception of value obtained by a customer from doing business with a supplier of goods/services.

In our conceptual model, we adopt an approach to the definition of "communities" that assimilate them to "networks." Whether speaking about communities of practice, knowledge communities or knowledge networks, all these concepts have a common core that can be subsumed under the "social capital" construct.

In our view, social capital includes "relational capital," which is often used to stress the inclusion of customers in the organizational network. Burt (2000) suggests that the social capital concept is "a metaphor about advantage" (p. 2): the better the social connections between people, the higher the collective and individual returns for them. This conceptualization makes the concept of social capital inclusive of the relational one, since the former include relations developed among between organization's members and different stakeholders, not only between the company and its customers.

The literature on communities of practice, knowledge communities or innovative communities has long discussed natural and community life cycles (Wegner and Snyder, 2000), though there's a lot that remains to be said about the topic of *measuring value* and contribution of communities and their members.

In accordance with the intangibles perspective, value can be redefined more broadly as a tangible or intangible good or service, knowledge or benefit that is useful, so that the receivers are willing to return a fair exchange or price (Allee, 2000).

Although many researchers agree that knowledge is the key strategic asset for creating value in modern organizations (Penrose, 1959; Nonaka and Takeuchi, 1995), an effective system and set of tools with which to evaluate and manage knowledge flows does not yet exist. Because of the tacit nature of knowledge, the current accounting system cannot adequately capture the value generated (Edvinsson and Malone, 1997).

Material- and financially-oriented methods to assess value are recognized as antiquated when confronted by the demands of a knowledge-based economy, as they look essentially at the history of a firm without making a statement about its future capabilities (Heisig, Vorbeck and Niebuhr, 2001).

The growing awareness of the importance of intangible assets and intellectual capital has led to the need for managing companies and measuring their performance in a new way. Over the last ten years, several intellectual capital measurement methodologies have been developed: Balanced Scorecard (Kaplan and Norton, 1992); Skandia Navigator (Edvinsson and Malone, 1997); Intangible Assets Monitor

(Sveiby, 1997); Inclusive Value Methodology; IC Rating of Intellectual Capital Sweden; and VAICTM (Value Added Intellectual Coefficient).

The Balanced Scorecard was developed as a strategic approach and performance management system that enables organizations to translate a company's vision and strategy into implementation, working from four perspectives:

1. *Financial Perspective*: Includes the tangible outcomes of the strategy in traditional financial terms.
2. *Customer Perspective*: Measures the value delivered to customers (time, quality, cost and service) and the resulting outcomes (e.g. customer satisfaction, market share).
3. *Internal Process Perspective*: Measures all the key processes required to excel at creating value for all stakeholders.
4. *Innovation & Learning Perspective*: Measures the intangible assets of an organization. It is concerned with the human capital, the information capital, and the climate (organization capital) of the company.

The Skandia Navigator is a collection of intangible measurement methods, pioneered by Leif Edvinsson at Skandia (Edvinsson and Malone, 1997). Five focus perspectives capture different areas of interest, and each of them visualizes the value creation process. The authors report 90 measures in five groups:

1. *Financial Focus*: Captures the financial outcome of the activities through 20 measures, e.g. income per employee and market value per employee.
2. *Customer Focus*: Gives an indication on how well the organization meets the needs of its customers via services and products through 22 measures, e.g. number of customer visits, satisfied customer index and lost customers. It represents a view that looks from the outside toward the inside of the company and provides a view more similar to the concept of "social capital."
3. *Process Focus*: Captures the processes of creating the services and the products through 16 measures, e.g. administrative error rate and IT expense per employee.
4. *Renewal and Development Focus*: Aims at reassuring the organization's long-term renewal and in part its sustainability through 19 measures, e.g. training per employee, R&D expense/administrative expense and satisfied employee index.

5. *Human Measures Focus*: Is the heart of the organization and is essential in an organization that creates value. It refers to 13 measures, e.g. leadership index, employee turnover and IT literacy.

A selection of other methods suggested by scholars and practitioners to evaluate intellectual capital is presented as follows:

- The Intangible Assets Monitor (by Karl Erik Sveiby) divides intangible assets into external structure, internal structure and competence of people.
- The Inclusive Value Methodology combines financial and non-financial hierarchies of value.
- The Danish Template developed in a three-year project by the Danish Ministry of Industry.
- The VAICTM (Value-Added Intellectual Coefficient) method from the Intellectual Capital Research Center in Zagreb.

All the approaches used to deal with the challenges of measuring knowledge assets had the limitations to be made "ex-post." Methods like the Balanced Scorecard or the Skandia Navigator provide a static view of the quality of intellectual capital. They are tools able to offer a photograph of the knowledge assets with focus on human capital (i.e. education, skills, attitude) and structural capital (patents, licenses) without adding a dynamic perspective. While measuring human capital and structural capital may be less challenging and different methods have already been put in practice, measuring relational capital is more problematic, given that it's not as easy to explicitly define.

Around the 1980s, managers, academics and consultants slowly became aware that a firm's intangible assets, its intellectual capital, were often a determinant of the corporation's profits. In the same period, in Japan, Hiroyuki Itami (1987) attributed the difference in performance among Japanese companies to differences in the firm's intangible assets. He concluded that intangible assets are "unattainable with money alone, are capable of multiple, simultaneous use, and yield multiple simultaneous benefits." In 1991 and 1994, Thomas Stewart, a staff writer at *Fortune* magazine, wrote two articles on "Brainpower" in which he discussed the idea that the company's intellectual capital had much to do with its profitability or success.

The first example of a company organized to profit from intangible assets was Skandia AFS, who in 1991 created the first corporate intellectual capital office and appointed Leif Edvinsson its Vice-President.

By the mid-1990s, two separate but related streams of research about intellectual capital started to emerge.

The first path, the resource-based perspective or the "value extraction" movement, was focused on how to create profits from a firm's unique combinations of intellectual and tangible resources. The second path, the brainpower path or the "value creation" movement, was more focused on creating and expanding the firm's knowledge within and outside the organization's boundaries. Organization's intellectual capital has been described as "the economic value of the three categories of intangible assets" that we have previously described human, structural and relational.

According to Bontis (2001), intellectual capital is the pursuit of effective use of knowledge as opposed to information, whereas information is raw material, and knowledge is the finished product.

There are some variants on such a classification. One is to separate out those assets protected by law like intellectual property, to include trade-marks, patents, copyrights and licenses. Besides this traditional classification, a more recent classification considers also the concept of "social capital," defined as the resources available in and through personal and business networks (Baker, 2000). These resources include information, ideas, business opportunities, financial capital, power and influence, emotional support, trust and cooperation. This category of "intellectual capital" can be seen as a meta-category that goes beyond *what you know* (human capital) by including also *"who you know"* and *"what you get to know thanks to who you know."*

Most of the traditional methods proposed for measuring intellectual capital have been widely criticized for their static nature. There is a need to build a system for evaluating and managing the knowledge assets of a firm effectively and in a dynamic way. Innovation-driven organizations need to rely more and more on their ability to exploit social networks, to make fast decisions based on changing market needs.

In this way, a social network analysis (SNA) is considered "the disciplined inquiry into the patterning of relations among social actors, as well as the patterning of relationships among actors at different levels of analysis" (Breiger, 2004, p. 506). SNA is a set of methods and tools used to dynamically assess the growth of value derived by social interactions. It can be used to identify, visualize and analyze informal networks that exist within and between organizations according to structure, content and context of knowledge flows.

As shown by late studies among several communities of practice across a number of industries (Cross et al., 2006), SNA is a "warning system" that is particularly effective to measure social capital by connecting knowledge seekers and knowledge providers, by supporting and optimizing knowledge flows, and by discovering innovative networks. It allows managers and executives to visualize the myriad informal relationships that can facilitate or impede communities' effectiveness. Cross, Parker and Borgatti (2002) suggest a list of benefits deriving from the adoption of organizational network analysis, defined as the application of SNA to solve organizational problems:

- Improving a network's ability to sense and respond to opportunities;
- Supporting strategic partnerships (e.g. joint venture, alliances, consortia);
- Assessing strategy execution (e.g. core competencies or market strategies);
- Integrating networks across core processes (e.g. commercial lending or software development);
- Improving innovation (e.g. new product development, research and development);
- Finding and supporting communities of practice (e.g. promoting connectivity or finding opinion leaders); and
- Ensuring integration post-merger or large-scale change (e.g. targeting collaboration and correcting over time).

To measure the evolution of social capital (the knowledge embedded into relationships), a set of metrics have been proposed (Gloor et al., 2008) to identify a community's evolution, as well as the position of people in the network (e.g. individual and group degree and betweenness centrality, density, core/periphery structure).

In this first section of the chapter we introduced our model, based on the conceptual metaphor of "community as network." We illustrated the role that the process of organizational learning plays in supporting the ability of innovative communities to create value for all stakeholders. To do so, we used several examples from successful companies. In the following section of the chapter, we will introduce the case of Mindsh@re, a corporate project launched by Finmeccanica to boost the innovation process and shape the culture of all its members.

4.4   Innovation within Finmeccanica: The Mindsh@re project

In the previous section we described the components of our conceptual model that connect the role of organizational and inter-organizational communities with the process of organizational learning and the model of knowledge creation. We have seen how the firm's ability to create value for stakeholders is based on the capacity to continuously learn from past experience, and to be willing to unlearn and experiment with new ways of solving problems.

In this section we illustrate the Finmeccanica case through the lens of the framework presented in the previous section. We will explore the Mindsh@re mission, organization structure and the governance model to connect its results with the elements typical of a learning organization. The case will help us to demonstrate that successful, innovative organizations have the characteristics of a learning organization and are based on "community-based governance models."

Mindsh@re is a systematic process that supports the emergence and flow of information and knowledge through people and communities, generating value for the Finmeccanica Group. Mindsh@re is based on a process of knowledge-sharing and technology-transfer involving all the operating companies as well as different stakeholders, recognized as active co-innovators rather than passive recipients. We observe how the meta-organizational model created by Mindsh@re reflects the typical characteristics of a learning organization that we read also in other cases presented to support the framework.

Finmeccanica is an Italian and UK Industrial Group operating globally in the aerospace, defense, energy, transportation and security sectors.

It is composed of a workforce of more than 60 thousand people and a revenues volume of almost 13.5 billion Euros. Because of its international growth strategy and its multi-domestic approach to the market, the group is enriched by the culture and knowledge of almost 10,000 new employees in the UK, 3,500 in France, and 1,600 in the United States. The group's investment in R&D activities is more than 1.8 billion Euros a year (representing about 14% of revenues), making Finmeccanica the leading Italian investor in hi-tech sectors. To maintain its leadership in hi-tech sectors, Finmeccanica focuses on the value of its human resources, and the laboratories of its subsidiaries are staffed by around 3,000 highly specialized researchers. Research into new technologies and new solutions forms the core of Finmeccanica's mission, and the group applies its resources by employing about 9,100 people in engineering activities and 3,100 of its employees in research and development projects. Finmeccanica does not do research in isolation. The group participates in the activities of 19 institutions and universities in Italy and 29 academies and research centers worldwide. The result of these exchange arrangements is a growth in knowledge for all those taking part.

Innovation is acknowledged and enhanced in Finmeccanica through initiatives such as the Innovation Award, which identifies and annually rewards projects with the highest innovative potential presented by the group's employees. The total number of proposals presented in the four editions exceeds 2,000. The number of projects has more than doubled over the years (from 320 innovative projects presented in the first edition of 2004 to 758 projects in 2007). This means that in the past four years, more than 6,000 people have been involved in the prize. The participation of colleagues abroad has also increased greatly: from ten projects in 2004 to 203 in 2007, which makes the prize an international initiative.

The excellence of Finmeccanica in technology and research has been recognized by the MIT Technology Review in terms of "R&D Ranking," where the Finmeccanica Group was defined as the "Second Best Innovator in Aerospace and Defense in 2005."

Innovation is a top priority for Finmeccanica in order to increase the capacity of the group and confront the challenge of technology markets. The company recognizes the importance to accompany the evolution of technology with *cultural innovation*, which means being able to offer solutions that are increasingly personalized and customized, on a complex global market, and that are achieved by developing ideas and projects in collaboration with the customers and with all their stakeholders.

A leading element in Finmeccanica's innovation is the Mindsh@re project, which brings together the main "technological communities" of the group that constitute the backbone of Mindsh@re and allow Finmeccanica's research to be transferred into the production chain. The mission of the Mindsh@re project is to:

- develop and share technological know-how;
- identify and appreciate Company Best Practices;
- promote common goals; and
- manage the R&D networking between organizations within and outside the Finmeccanica Group.

The stated development goals include: fostering collaboration between operating companies as members of a team; sharing the outcomes of the product technology appraisal; promoting communities of practice across the companies; evaluating the opportunity of setting up common technology platforms; and facilitating exchange and interaction with the external stakeholders' system. Mindsh@re is a continuous process to manage and develop technology communities within Finmeccanica and to facilitate the re-utilization and exchange of information, experiences and capabilities within each company.

The next paragraph will describe how the Mindsh@re project and its communities, which are our unit of analysis, fit with our conceptual model. We will map its mission, governance model, improvement program and communities' results, with the model of knowledge creation and the process of organizational learning (Senge, 1990). We will see how the meta-organizational model created by Mindsh@re reflects the typical characteristics of a learning organization.

4.4.1 Mission of the Mindsh@re project

Designed as *an unconventional engine for value innovation*, the Mindsh@re project—and the currently developed seven communities—are the result of a path that started in 2003 and has witnessed the early experiences of knowledge-sharing among companies. Through the increasing interaction of people, technologies and skills, Mindsh@re is experimenting with an innovation governance capable of producing value due to a corporate-wide integration among research and development, marketing and strategy.

The seven technology communities are the real exchange junctions of shared knowledge. They have the objective to provide innovative ideas though distinctly transversal subjects:

1. Radar
2. Homeland Security
3. Software & Capability Maturity Model Integration
4. Materials
5. Simulation for training (SET2)
6. Integrated Environment for Design & Development (IED2)
7. Logistics & Services

As with other companies that are experimenting with open innovation models, Finmeccanica included in the communities' boundaries its different stakeholders to leverage one another's innovation assets, people, intellectual property and existing competencies. The case of P&G described in the "Connect and Develop" Harvard Business Review case study (Huston and Sakkab, 2006) described how most of P&G's best innovations had come from connecting ideas across internal business.

> For every P&G researcher there were 200 scientists or engineers elsewhere in the world who were just as good. [. . .] But tapping into

the creative thinking of inventors and others on the outside would require massive operational changes. We needed to move the company's attitude from resistance to innovations "not invented here" to enthusiasm for those proudly found elsewhere.

(Huston and Sakkab, 2006, pp. 2–3)

In this same path that avoids a brick-and-mortar R&D infrastructure (Huston and Sakkab, 2006), Finmeccanica is still supporting the Mindsh@re project to radically change the approach to R&D at a corporate level and within the individual operating companies. As Skandia institutionalized the "competence centers" to diffuse a culture of cross-pollination of ideas, Finmeccanica supports Mindsh@re communities as "permanent centers for processing business intelligence and knowledge."

Seven key elements have been defined as main components of the Mindsh@re mission, as shown in the external layer of the mission framework in Figure 4.3: Finmeccanica companies; teams; self (individual level); other business; product technologies; research centers; and market/competitors/partners.

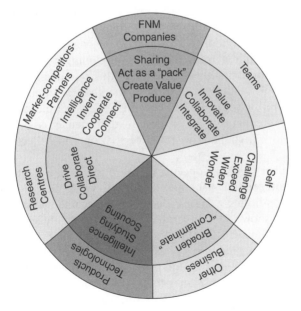

Figure 4.3 Mindsh@re mission and its components.
Source: Finmeccanica Mindsh@re Document (2007).

The external components (companies, teams, self, other business, product technologies, research centers and market/competitors partners) can be seen as the seven drivers through which the Mindsh@re mission and strategic intent are defined.

The mission has been defined according to a multiple perspective including actors external to Finmeccanica. This decision indicates how Mindsh@re is based on a view of strategic management that relies on effective inter-firm collaboration (Dyer, 2000). As pointed out by Michael Dell, CEO of Dell Computers: "Virtual integration means you basically stitch together a business with partners that are treated as if they're inside the company." The Mindsh@re communities operate to produce value innovation in a collaborative network involving operating companies, other businesses, competitors, partners, universities and research centers.

In the mission statement, there are explicit references to the creation of a new innovation model that considers the organization as an integrated network, in line with innovative companies like Skandia, McKinsey, ABB, 3M and P&G. Defining the mission using elements like "Sharing knowledge between companies," "Contaminate the usual business with new different fields, practices, sectors," "Cooperate in all possible way to create value," implies avoiding compartmentalized units, centralized knowledge flows, formalized relationships. To the contrary, it means building a specialized network configuration supportive of cross-unit learning that helps developing trust, rich horizontal flows of information, knowledge and other resources.

The mission is a clear expression of the goal to support the group and the operating companies to become leaders in innovation within a dynamic competitive environment that demands collaborative problem solving, cooperative resource sharing and collective implementation.

The frequency of key concepts in the mission statement—Sharing, Innovate, Integrate, Collaborate, Challenge, Cooperate, Connect (see Table 4.4)—indicates a strong decision to become *specialists in collaboration*. As shown in the Skandia case, to successfully leverage global knowledge, top management needs to convert a strong commitment to organizational learning into a powerful competitive tool.

Designed to be centers of intelligence and knowledge, Mindsh@re communities represent an expression of the nature of industrial holding that Finmeccanica intends to achieve. Innovation, meant as an underlying and continuative practice rather than as a temporary exercise, is the main feature of Finmeccanica's industrial action.

Table 4.4 Mission of the Mindsh@re project

Components	Value Creation Drivers
Finmeccanica companies	• Sharing knowledge between companies • Act as a pack about business possibilities • Create value through knowledge sharing, coordinated cost reductions, common development of projects, synergies in production, zeroing cost duplications • Produce new common ideas, practices, projects, products
Teams	• Innovate Processes, projects, products, mindsets, corporate cultural background • Integrate output between teams for maximum cost reduction and profit raising
Self	• Challenge individual believes and behavior • Exceed personal usual expected individual performance • Widen professional and personal horizons • Wonder about new possibilities, behaviors, paradigms, outcomes
Other Business	• Broaden Business Areas and possibilities to new unexplored fields • Contaminate the usual business with new different fields, practices, sectors
Product technologies	• Carry on intelligent data searching about competitors' projects/products • Studying new possible value innovations • Scouting existing ideas/projects
Research Centers	• Get all useful hints and drives from existing centers on a global scale • Collaborate directly with the most relevant centers to produce common value • Direct the research activities of centers to valuable innovation issues
Market Competitors Partners	• Exercise intelligence on ongoing current activities • Invest Invent new markets and new possible partnerships • Cooperate in all possible ways to create value • Connect to any possible reality that can bring new value

Source: Finmeccanica Mindsh@re Document (2007).

4.4.2 Governance and organizational model of the Mindsh@re project

In the Mindsh@re project, seven communities have been developed. These communities are embedded in a context of continuous knowledge and technology sharing, taking advantage of internal and external technology bases, and profiting from the involvement of external stakeholders working together with the operating companies to come up with innovative ideas.

Mindsh@re communities have primarily the characteristics of a community of practice, since their members "share a passion for something that they know how to do, and who interact regularly in order to learn how to do it better" (Lave and Wenger, 1991). This description matches the concept of Mindsh@re communities where people are encouraged to actively participate by creating new laboratories or focus groups around new challenging opportunities or new partnerships with stakeholders. Collaborative innovation networks, as well as Mindsh@re communities, are a type of informal network that originates from the interaction of like-minded and self-motivated individuals who share the same vision. People join not for immediate monetary reward, but because they share a common vision, and want to be part of a community that enables innovation.

In Section 4.3.4 we proposed some of the most frequently used taxonomies to describe organizational and inter-organizational communities (e.g. communities of creation, X-teams and collaborative innovation networks). Mindsh@re communities are "innovation communities" but with some elements of "technology sharing" and "best practice."

An interesting parallelism with the characteristics of Mindsh@re communities can be found in the conceptualization of the X-teams (Ancona and Bresman, 2007). With their flexible membership and leadership structure, X-teams reach outwards to foster the innovation process.

The governance model is based on a mechanism of supervision and co-ordination of the technological activities and the initiatives of process improvement that is centrally held by a technology Steering Committee at the corporate level (see Figure 4.4).

The Mindsh@re governance model is based on the following layers:

- The *Technology Steering Committee*: Has the role of supervising and coordinating the technological activities and the engineering processes' improvement initiatives.
- The *Technology Council*: Defines priorities and subject areas that Community Focus Groups will address. It is also in charge of identifying mentors and operating companies' experts (champions) who will lead Community Focus Groups jointly with younger professionals (prospects). Finally, the Council reviews the achievement of the targets and objectives at the Community and Community Focus Group level.
- The *Community Focus Groups*: Analyze the specific subject areas, within the relevant technology identified by the Council.

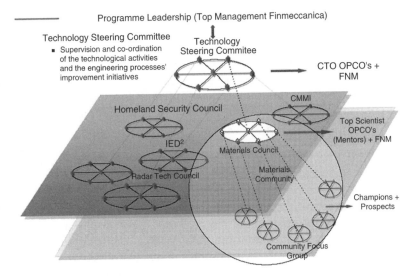

Figure 4.4 The Mindsh@re governance model.
Source: Finmeccanica Mindsh@re Document (2007).

- *Laboratories*: Develop innovative ideas within a Community. Over time, the ones with the highest impact on the operating companies may become either focus-groups or a first nucleus for other communities.

A principle of voluntary participation helps to maintain a self-motivating environment conducive to innovation. People with a role in their companies that would enhance the process of innovation are strongly recommended.

Within each community, people assume different flexible roles according to the technology plans and to the needs of the operating companies. The roles are so defined:

- The *Chairman*: Presides and coordinates the Community activities. He/she can come from one of the operating companies, from Finmeccanica or can be an external consultant.
- The *Mentor*: Coordinates the Community Focus Group's activities and is represented by a member of the Council. A mentor is an expert in the area assigned to the focus group.
- The *Deputy Mentor*: Is a highly recommended role, in order to secure full back up to the mentor to sustain the focus group activities.
- The *Champion*: Is a senior expert, in most cases "guru," in the different subject areas addressed by the community focus groups.

- The *Prospect*: Is a junior professionals with 2–3 years of experience, relevant technological know-how, and team-working skills.
- The *Specialist*: Is an outstanding expert in his/her area of expertise
- The *Community Performance Manager* :Is in charge of coordinating the process and liaise with the Project Office Team.
- The *Sponsor*: Is a Finmeccanica person who is in charge of reducing conflicts within the group/operating companies and promoting the communities' activities.
- The *Special Guest*: Is an individual without an active role in the communities' activities who attend a council/focus groups meetings to offer an outside perspective to the conversation.

The focus on people is meant to reach the objective to institutionalize entrepreneurship, decentralize responsibilities and inspire a creative tension that can ignite innovation. Providing decisional power to people at different levels increases the chances to connect to external actors (competitors, suppliers, customers), bringing information and strategic knowledge closer to the top management. An organization based on "command and control" is what Jack Welch, General Electric's CEO, colorfully reported as the "organization that has its face toward the CEO and its back toward the customer."

To harness the collective genius of its people and stimulate ordinary people to produce extraordinary performance, Mindsh@re works together with the operating companies to support the use and development of professional skills for the benefit of the Group. Mindsh@re invests in recognizing the potential of people and supports them while they share their time between their normal tasks and Mindsh@re involvement. This process is similar to what 3M institutionalized as the "15 percent rule," which allowed anyone to spend up to one-seventh of his or her time pursuing personal "bootleg projects" that could bring value to the whole organization.

Mindsh@re brings together interdisciplinary competencies and know-how to provide innovative solutions as reported by the Logistics and Services Community:

> Finmeccanica Companies operate with integrated Teams, built on skilled people such as ILS Project Managers, Logistic Engineers, Software Engineers, Analysts, Lawyers, Sales and Marketing Managers, in order to produce innovative solutions and to be able to work in the operational field with qualified engineers.
>
> (Brochure of the "Logistics and Services Community")

From 2004 to 2007, Mindsh@re involved more than 540 people, 39 active focus groups, four UK companies of the Finmeccanica Group, 26 Italian companies of the Finmeccanica Group and seven Active Communities.

The structure that supports the communities reflects the principles of successful team as defined by Ancona and Bresman (2007): *extensive ties, expandable tiers* and *exchangeable membership*. Mindsh@re communities go beyond their boundaries, adapting their structure over time to enable useful outsiders to contribute on common projects, requirements specifications. Examples of the *extensive ties principle* are the involvement of the Italian Army in round tables, as well as the "Big Event" organized every year by the Logistics and Services Community, where universities and institutional clients are invited to understand the state of the art in a specific topic and propose new areas of common agreements. Another example is the cross-pollination of ideas and know-how between focus groups inside a community or between different communities: Security and SET2 communities share a project on homeland security and organized together in 2007 the workshop "THz and mmW technology in Italy," where ten speakers from Academia, four from Finmeccanica Corporate and 60 attendees provided their contribution to define the Italian roadmap to THz and mmW technologies.

Exchangeable membership means the inclusion in the community of people who come in and out and rotate leadership. An example is the launch in the Security Community of Focus Groups about "Terrorism and Criminality," "Crisis Management" and "Critical Infrastructure," where the appointed coordinators are managers of partner companies (i.e. Università Cattolica, the Civil Protection and the Army.

The third principle of the extended community (X-teams) is *expandable tiers*. This means adopting a flexible structure with a core that coordinates the community (the Council in Mindsh@re), a group of other members who carry out the activities (e.g. Focus Group members, Champions) and others who drop in and out for short periods (i.e. Special Guests).

Mindsh@re Communities represent committed teams with open communication constantly assessing their performance by scanning the internal and external environment. Their goal is to be "guided self-organization," which are disciplined teams that disseminate successful lessons and communicate across the organization (Clippinger, 1999).

4.4.3   Nurturing human and social capital in Mindsh@re communities

In the Mindsh@re model, a great emphasis has been put on coaching people: "We have mentored all participants one by one since Mindsh@re launch. We have tracked their personality and invested in the most motivated individuals. Starting from the engagement phase, we support each community by identifying innovators, creative thinkers, performers," said one component of the Mindsh@re Project Team.

The Mindsh@re Improvement Program has been created to increase the effectiveness of the communities' activities, by designing a four-step maturity model, characterized by formalized steps. Table 4.5 presents the taxonomy of the Program's core tasks, which we matched with the classification proposed by Ancona and Bresman to define the tool for building X-teams (2007, pp. 165–93).

As part of the *selecting* phase, the members self-organize their activity in focus groups according to the individual skills and competencies.

Table 4.5   Tools to create and nurture communities

Mindsh@re Improvement Program		Tool for building X-teams	
Engage	In this initial step, either new members or new communities or new focus-groups are coached to be fully engaged in the objectives and values of Mindsh@re.	Selection	Select the members and set the stage. The initial phase goes from selecting and motivating members to encouraging team learning and knowledge sharing.
Align	Already existing communities are constantly aligned to the Mindsh@re principles.	Exploration	Explore internal and external possibilities. This is the time of intense sense-making, task coordination and relating.
Innovate	The Innovation phase is addressed to communities that are well positioned with respect to the Mindsh@re principles. They are particularly supported in their innovation efforts.	Exploitation	In this phase members must shift from brainstorming on different ideas to actually creating one reality.
Ambassador	The last step in the community's growth model has the objective to promote the Mindsh@re Model to the external stakeholders.	Exportation	This is the time to bring the community's work to other parts of the extended organization.

A dedicated team of "coaches" and the Council members support and energize the community in their path of leadership development and ability to work as a team. In this initial period, people need to know each other and to define the role within the team. Another important ingredient to complete the kick-off phase is looking at the social networks or ties that each member may bring to the future development of the community.

In the *alignment* or *exploration* phase, members "need to suspend their prior views of the situation and look at the world with new eyes—to explore their new terrain so that they're able to describe it, to find hidden opportunities" (Ancona and Bresman, 2007, p. 170). In Mindsh@re, this means changing people's mindsets, encouraging trust development between operating companies and setting the basis for collaboration and trust in the future. In this phase it is vital to strengthen the collaboration with other communities that might have been engaged in similar tasks and to learn from other experiences. To be aligned to Mindsh@re goals means also to explore customers, competitors and current trends, as shown by the example of the Logistics and Services Community: the "Strategic Self Assessment" identifies the operating companies' competencies gaps in the area of logistics. This activity was possible only because of the exploration process activated inside and outside Finmeccanica's boundaries. This process helped the Logistics community to plan investments and synergies at corporate level, with a strong impact also on the companies of the group.

In this phase, the Chairman is in charge of communicating with top managers—at corporate and operating companies' level—to determine whether the community is going in the right direction. Not surprisingly, a huge effort is put in developing leadership skills in Chairmen and Mentors, and tutoring Champions who might become the key individuals for future activities. This is aligned to what the mission's component "Self" says: "Exceed personal usual expected individual performance." With this decision expressed in this statement, Mindsh@re is helping the group to position itself as an organization based on generative learning, stimulating individual entrepreneurship and creating a "creative tension" between the vision and the current reality (Argyris, 1977; Senge, 1990). The most important output for Communities experiencing this phase is the definition of the Technology Plan that is shared with the other communities and aligned with the Technology Plans of the Operating Companies.

In the *exploitation or innovation phase*, the Community must shift the focus from the brainstorming of ideas and possibilities to a stage of implementation and execution. This is the phase when product prototypes are made and roles are re-allocated and re-defined to meet new stakeholders' expectations. The Communities test their ideas by scanning continuously the environment and facing the dilemma of building external relations with the need of being internally focused and respect the coordination mechanisms.

The Mindsh@re model is currently in a phase in which stakeholders have been included in the communities' activities: events, seminars, round-tables, requirements definition, focus-groups and council meetings.

This "ambassador step" is defined by Ancona and Bresman (2007) as *exportation*. Teams turn outward exporting the project to the rest of the organization and to the external stakeholders: other companies of the group, end users, suppliers, academic institutions and research centers. The goal of exportation is to transfer the excitement, the motivation, the know-how generated and the tacit knowledge of the community. The focus of the community is mainly external and the effort is in transforming the output in something that is recognized as "value creating" for the organization and not just something that the only community is excited about.

The Mindsh@re Communities are followed in their different phases of development at individual and team levels. The path that the communities follow to reach high performance is represented by the four stages of the model defined by Bruce Tuckman (1956): *forming* (initial enthusiasm and relationships establishing), *storming* (defining roles and responsibilities), *norming* (establishing rules and codes of behavior) and *performing* (successful team interactions with interdependent team members who act as knowledgeable decision makers). These phases that match the previously described classification are all necessary to allow the team to grow, deal with internal and external challenges, tackle problems, find solutions, plan work, and produce results.

The expected results for the Mindsh@re Communities vary according to the different phases. Table 4.6 puts together the models used by Mindsh@re to help communities in their path toward innovation and value creation. Contributions from the X-Teams classification (Ancona and Bresman, 2007) and the model of group development (Tuckman, 1965) are considered a complementary way to look at a community's results.

A knowledge management initiative, the Mindsh@re Event, is representative of the shift toward the exportation/ambassador phase that the Mindsh@re Communities are experiencing. Beside the increase of

Table 4.6 Phases of community development

Phases	Levels	Results
Engage (Selection/Forming)	• Knowledge Sharing • Knowledge Management	• Formative and Informative Sessions for aligning people and communities to Mindsh@re Mission and Values • Organization of 15 seminars with 1000 Finmeccanica Participants and 400 external participants (IED2 Community) • Use of the Technological Platform MindLink
Align (Exploration/Storming)	• Cross-Fertilization • Awareness	• Security Community magazine *"INSIDE Edition"* • Monthly magazine *"Open Connection"* (IED2 Community)
Innovate (Exploitation/Norming)	• Creating New Ideas • Organizational Learning • Performance Management	• Common Guidelines on Software r Re-use (CMMI Community) • Common Transmit/Receive Module (Radar Community) • Competencies appraisal (IED2 Community) • First Product Catalogue in the Simulation Area (SET2)
Ambassador (Exportation/Performing)	• Value creation (tangible and intangible) • Transformational Innovation	• seven web-based e-Learning modules now managed by ElsagDatamat and Telespazio (Logistics and Services) • Round Tables with the Italian Army and Article on Finmeccanica Corporate Magazine (Logistics and Services)

participants from 2006 to 2008 (from 649 to more than 1,000 people), the event represented the official declaration of the new phase in which the Communities and the Project itself currently are. To attend the 19 round tables, demo lives and seminars there were 180 representatives from military institutions and 150 from academia. Until then, 24 universities and research centers in Italy and in the world had been involved, and participation to international conferences including the Defense Technology Asia (Singapore) and IDL Bruxelles. The messages from the event can be summarized in three streams of activities aiming to activate the open, systemic innovation model:

1. *Building the Knowledge Marketplace*, which means searching for partners external to the Finmeccanica Group that could contribute to the transformation of Mindsh@re in "Marketplace for knowledge, competencies, experiences" to be exchanged both internal and external to the company's boundaries.
2. *Involving the Institutional Customers* in an innovative pattern of collaboration Defense/Industry, in the perspective of building together new ways to generate innovation through the joint contribution of know-how from different worlds.
3. *Exploiting the new Mindsh@re Portal*, through which Finmeccanica's activities of Technology Transfer and Intellectual Property Development can be developed.

By supporting the Knowledge Marketplace, Finmeccanica is pushing Mindsh@re to stress its initial vocation as virtual and physical space where all the stakeholders can acquire and provide knowledge at all levels of the integrated network, from the individual's competencies to patents. Within this scenario, already planned in the project's mission, the Communities have the key role to act as "advisors" in the activity of knowledge and technology transfer. This implies facilitating the creation of a continuous and strong connection between the market's requirements and the technical/engineering component.

This process of integration of the customers' voice into the community is a strong, necessary step, but not sufficient. As the P&G Connect and Develop case illustrates, "No amount of idea hunting on the outside will pay off if, internally, the organization isn't behind the program" (Huston and Sakkab, 2006, p. 7). This means that this new innovation model will need to be based on nurturing internal cultural change, while developing and sustaining systems for making connections. As Jack Welch said, "When the change outside is higher than inside, the end is in sight."

With the launch of the knowledge Marketplace, a new collaboration scenario has been promoted, that will result in the implementation of a "knowledge trading/exchange portal" available within and across Finmeccanica's boundaries. Examples of knowledge assets that will populate the Web Portal are the list of patents that partners may want to share with the groups operating companies, or all the ideas coming from the Innovation Awards.

In this paragraph we have highlighted the main characteristics of Mindsh@re that make Finmeccanica an organization skilled at creating, acquiring and transferring knowledge, and at modifying its behavior to reflect new knowledge and insights, that is how David Garvin defines a learning organization (Garvin, 1993).

4.5   Innovation and value creation in Mindsh@re project

The benefits created by a corporate-wide initiative like Mindsh@re are visible not only in the change management and people management dimensions. A great impact, in fact, is also visible in the way of managing corporate projects and developing innovative ideas for the whole organization. The new approach to Research and Development enabled the launch of projects in which different stakeholders were involved.

As a Top Manager in the Mindsh@re Project Office stated: "The strategy of Research and Development for the whole Group is now conducted in a totally different way. All the efforts and the investments are not mandated to single companies. For the first time, Finmeccanica acts as main player in the European and International context, increasing the visibility as Group."

This focus on treating innovation as a corporate wide task, involving all operating companies in the project from its earliest stages, represents the first important success factor of the initiative. This element is listed as one of the key factors that Rothwell (1992) describes as characteristics of an innovative company. From the results of several studies undertaken between the 1950s and the 1970s, the author presents other factors, among which we list the ones that we found as distinctive of the Mindsh@re project:

- The establishment of good internal and external communication; effective linkages with external sources of technological knowledge.
- The presence of key individuals: Product champions and technological gatekeepers.

- High quality of management: Dynamic, open-minded managers, committed to the human capital development.
- Strong market orientation: An emphasis on satisfying user-needs; efficient customer linkages; if possible, involving potential users in the development process.

Table 4.7 describes how the key drivers to foster innovation by building a learning organization are experienced in Mindsh@re (see Table 4.2 for a detailed description of these drivers).

Table 4.7 Drivers to build a learning organization: The Mindsh@re project

Key Drivers	in Mindsh@re
1. Foster Systemic Innovation	• The project to build a "knowledge marketplace" aims to nurture the ability to continuously learn from inside and outside the organization. • Stakeholders participate as active members to the Communities' activities. • Specialized workshops are open to academic and industrial partners, clients and suppliers who are invited to share the knowledge generated within the community.
2. Enable Democracy of Ideas	• The communication of mission and vision is made through workshops, big events organized by each community, and the Mindsh@re Event where all stakeholders meet to share the knowledge co-generated with partners, clients, suppliers.
3. Nurture Individual Creativity	• Communities' members are supported by a facilitator/ expert in social dynamics that energizes the council and the focus groups. • New communities, new focus groups and new laboratories spontaneously emerge from individual's suggestion. 80 percent of them are then supported by the operating companies.
4. Promote Distributed Leadership	• Chairman, Mentors and Council Members are the appointed leaders, but in each groups everybody is pushed to promote ideas and build Laboratories to cultivate and realize those ideas. • The MPM keeps track of "Level of Shared Leadership"
5. Sustain Life Long Learning	• Two examples are: the newly formed labs in the IED2 Communities and the new Community on Intellectual Property Management.
6. Create New Measurement Systems	• The MPM keeps track of dimensions of team working such as "Feeling as team member," "Ability to produce synergies."

The nature and purpose of the Mindsh@re communities make them very similar to the "virtual networks" defined as permeable structures without physical borders of separation from the environment, comprising a multiplicity of autonomous, adaptive, interdependent, and self-organizing actors that rely on the Internet infrastructure to integrate and exchange value. As the Chairman of the IED2 Community said:

> I do believe that the strong involvement of end users, partners and suppliers helps Finmeccanica to gain more bargaining power, an increased knowledge about new markets or new distribution channels. New competencies are emerging in particular for the adoption of integrated technologies, which will benefits different operating companies. The inclusion of customers and partners in the activity of the Communities is increasing the likelihood for the single companies to be heard by the market.

The objective of the next paragraph is to understand how an innovative learning organization—like the one created through Mindsh@re—relies on new tools to measure the performance results and to monitor the evolution over time and to discover areas of weaknesses and new opportunities.

4.5.1   A tool to measure the performance of Mindsh@re

This section explores the question of how to measure the results of the activity of a community showing the characteristics of a learning organization. Within the Mindsh@re Project, a tool to measure the value generated by each of the technological communities has been developed. This tool reflects the effort undertaken in many large companies of measuring knowledge assets in the perspective of Intellectual Capital Management (Bontis, 2001).

A tool used to support the Council of a specific Community, as well as the whole Community, is the Mindsh@re Performance Monitor (MPM). It helps each community to learn from past experiences, to capitalize on other communities' best practice and from their past experience (see Figure 4.5).

The MPM has been defined as a "Framework to Translate Strategy into Actions," a tool built in the process of monitoring and assessing communities' performance with respect to the core dimensions of Mindsh@re:

- People dimension: Measures the degree of alignment to Mindsh@re mission, the shift from operating to strategic perspective, the level of

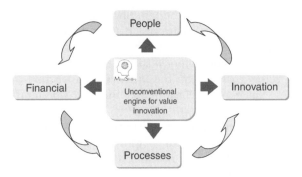

Figure 4.5   The Mindsh@re Performance Monitor.

shared leadership, ability to produce synergies, communicating with other teams.

- Financial dimension: It focuses on traditional financial aspects: additional revenues, cost savings, funds raised by the community.
- Processes dimension: It includes indicators able to capture the process of knowledge sharing (e.g. sharing of "best practices" among companies of the Group, improvement of professional skills), and the execution of activities (e.g. team's ability to generate ideas that become approved projects).
- Innovation dimension: Includes metrics of *Collaborative Innovation* (Competitive Intelligence, Innovation/Technology Scouting), *Innovative Mindset* (Team's ability to produce innovative ideas, Origination of Innovation, number of interfunctional workshops, Customer & Market perception of the Community as Innovation Provider).

Each of the four dimensions is assessed through a number of key items and metrics that are then compared to pre-assigned target scores. The data collection phase is expected to occur every six months. The output is a snapshot of the activities and level of growth of the community with reference to the Mindsh@re four core dimensions.

The use of the Mindsh@re Performance Monitor assesses the evolution of the community with reference to indicators useful to measure different dimensions such as:

- *Competitive Intelligence*: Information gathered on competitors through the Community and shared within the Repository;
- *Innovation/Technology Scouting*: Number of innovations/technologies externally identified by the Community;

- *Innovation Delivery*: Number of innovations/technologies transferred to the Operating Companies;
- *Number of Requests Received*: number of requests of "Advising" received (by Corporate, Operating Companies, Third Parties);
- *Number of Proposals Delivered*: Number of proposals generated by the Community (toward Corporate, Operating Companies, third parties);
- *Number of Proposals Accepted*: Number of accepted proposals generated by the Community (by Corporate, Operating Companies, third parties);
- *Team's ability to produce innovative ideas*: Number of innovative ideas originated by the Community (Origination of Innovation);
- *Inter-functional/Cross Innovation*: Number of interfunctional workshops; number of events participated by professionals external to the Community (e.g. from other functions such as marketing, strategy);
- *Customer & Market perception of the Community as Innovation Provider*: Number of acknowledgments obtained by the Community from the Customer & Market (i.e. prizes, articles, newspapers/magazines quotations, and so on).

Each Community is required to have target scores for each identified item and metric of the four dimensions. The assignment of target scores is completed beforehand by Finmeccanica/Steering/Council members with the support of the Team of Consultants.

Each Community nominates a Community Performance Manager among the Council members, who is in charge of coordinating the process and liaise with the Project Team. The Council is responsible to coordinate and manage the process by scheduling an appropriate allocation of time and resources for the distribution of the actual Mindsh@re Performance Monitor (hard copies or electronic format) and the assignment of the current scores to each metric.

The information gathered through MPM is used:

- to map the different life cycles of the communities with respect to where each community is in relation to Mindsh@re and in relation to the other communities;
- to identify the areas where a specific Community needs support the most;
- to identify elements of best practice that can be shared among communities;
- to assess the financial impact of Mindsh@re with reference to the activities carried out by each Community; and

- to assess the alignment of the activities and trends with reference to the Vision and Mission of Mindsh@re.

The advantages of the "balanced scorecard" methods (Kaplan and Norton, 1992) are that they can create a more comprehensive picture of an organization's health than financial metrics and that they can be easily applied at any level of an organization. Their disadvantages are that the indicators are contextual and have to be customized for each organization and each purpose, which makes comparisons very difficult.

In Section 3.5 we illustrated some of the most used methods to measure the growth of intellectual capital. We have seen the Balanced Scorecard, Skandia Navigator, Intangible Assets Monitor and Inclusive Value Methodology. Table 4.8 presents the perspectives proposed by the Balanced Scorecard, the Skandia Navigator and the Mindsh@re Performance Monitor (MPM).

The Mindsh@re performance monitor covers all the main dimensions that are present in the other scorecards, with the exception of the "customer" focus that is included in the "innovation" perspective. Indeed, the indicator "Customer & Market perception of the Community as Innovation Provider" captures the ability of the community to generate value for customers.

Besides using an *ad-hoc* category for monitoring the "people" dimension, in the MPM there are several other indicators that are used to measure the "improvement of professional skills" or the "ability to work in teams." This indicates that human capital, together with social capital, are considered strategic for the company's innovation process.

Table 4.8   MPM and methods for measuring Intellectual Capital

	Balanced Scorecard	Skandia Navigator	MPM
	1. Financial	1. Financial	1. Financial
	2. Customer	2. Human Measures	2. People
Dimensions	3. Internal Process	3. Customer	3. Processes
	4. Innovation and Learning	4. Process	4. Innovation
		5. Renewal and Development	

A positive aspect of the MPM is the focus on the processes of Knowledge Sharing, considered in the "process" dimension as key aspects of the community performance. This is a confirmation of the importance that innovation plays at all levels of the Group.

To better understand the evolution of the community over time and recognize the emergence of informal roles within and across Mindsh@re communities, we conducted a social network analysis through pilot studies on four of the seven communities.

A secondary objective was also to investigate how social network indicators could be integrated in the MPM to offer a better picture of the community's performance and evolution. Almost 400 community members have been asked to report over a period of two months the frequency of communication with members of their own community, other communities and external stakeholders, including suppliers, customers, research centers, academic and industry organizations. The visualization of those relationships in "*sociograms*" and the quantitative evidence coming from network metrics (e.g. betweenness centrality, degree centrality, density, core/periphery structure) provided insights on the informal roles within the community (boundary spanners, central connectors, ambassadors) and the degree of centralization of the community. This analysis discovered that community members had strong or weak ties to key individuals inside and outside the organization. With reference to the IED2 Community, seven external members were identified as being very prominent, as shown by their values of "actor betweenness centrality." This measure represents the total number of shortest paths between every possible pair of nodes in a graph that pass through the given node. The betweenness of a point measures the extent to which an actor can play the part of a "broker" or "gatekeeper" with a potential for control over others.

The survey participants had the chance to learn how to better collaborate and communicate to avoid excessive centralization and increase idea circulation. They recognized areas of improvement for themselves and for their focus-groups, as in the case of the Chairman whose high level of individual betweenness centrality (that measures the extent to which an actor can play the role of gatekeeper with a potential for control over others) indicated the possibility of an information bottleneck and overburdened member. In order to eliminate the information bottlenecks, other people should have assisted the Chairman in pulling in peripheral people who represented untapped expertise.

Besides providing managerial suggestions on the evolution of the communication patterns within and across the community, the Social

Network Analysis has been considered a useful set of methodologies and tools to complement the Mindsh@re Performance Monitor. In particular, it could be integrated:

- *In the People dimension*: Looking at the position of people within the network, it is possible to collect information on the hidden, informal role of each actor, their contribution index, their centrality or their total disconnectedness from the network. Roles such as gatekeeper and boundary spanner can be recognized and then supported to foster the innovation process.
- *In the Innovation dimension*: Studying the structure of the network, it is possible to understand the phase in which a community is. According to a series of studies conducted by Peter Gloor (2006), when the density is high and the group betweenness centrality is low, there is a good chance to assist at the generation of new ideas from the community.

The next paragraph will explore the results that Mindsh@re have obtained over time. Since it can be seen as a knowledge management initiative in addition to an innovation development project, it is important to remember that the results are visible over the long period. This is why we will stress in particular the changes in terms of cultural mindset that people experienced by participating in the communities' activities.

4.5.2   Tangible and intangible results in Mindsh@re

Mindsh@re has been defined by the Finmeccanica Chairman and CEO Pier Francesco Guarguaglini "A systematic and defined process that supports the emergence and flow of information and knowledge through the right people at the right time, generating value for the whole Group."

As reported by a Top Manager, the Finmeccanica's revenues deriving from the Logistics services—calculated over the global revenues in the industry—are now 15 percent, against 6 percent of Northrop Grumman and 23 percent of BAE: "This success is mostly due to the integration of all the competencies and technologies that before Mindsh@re were scattered all around the world within the individual operating companies." Learning how to share experiences, know-how, and ways to approach the market has been the first result of this project. Table 4.9 summarizes some of the results achieved by the Mindsh@re project.

Table 4.9 Tangible results from the Mindsh@re project

Knowledge Management Initiatives	
• Mindsh@re Event	Edition 2006 (649 participants) Edition 2008 (more than 1,000 participants) Finmeccanica Corporate, Operating Companies, Clients, Industrial and Academic Partners
• Dissemination Workshops	IED2 community (2005–8) (15 seminars with 1,000+ Finmeccanica Participants and 400+ external participants) to illustrate the new frontiers of product development engineering.
• Itinerant Council Meetings	The Council Meeting is done on average every 2 months and the location changes every time. This allows the Community to bring their results closer to the operating companies, increasing the level of motivation for top managers to invest in Mindsh@re.
• Event of the Extended Community	Every year each Community organizes an event where all the members, internal and external to the Community, gather together to share the latest results, the Technology Plans, the future challenge and opportunities.
• Specialized seminars	To facilitate context-specific learning processes, a cross-fertilization of ideas, and resolution of problems common to different operating companies. They are open to the participation of external stakeholders.
• Technology Appraisal	To share the technology plans and use the same reporting tools so that knowledge sharing and cross-monitoring of performance is easier.
• Newsletter and Brochure	Examples are: • IED2 Community's monthly "Open Connection" • Security Community's Monthly Newsletter
• Chairmen Meetings	To increase the sharing of knowledge across communities, the Technology Plan is prepared by the Council and then discussed during a meeting among all the chairmen.
Community Level Innovation	
• Logistics & Services	• e-Learning Solution: Seven web-based training modules • 15 percent of Finmeccanica's revenues from the Logistics services over the global revenues in the sector (BAE: 23%; Northrop Grumman: 6%) • Common Taxonomy of Competencies at group level • Strategic Self Assessment to identify companies' competencies gap in logistics and plan investments/synergies at corporate level. • Round Tables with Italian Army • Customer Satisfaction Model for the electronics companies

(continued)

Table 4.9   continued

Community Level Innovation	
• IED2	• Competencies appraisal • Technical Knowledge Library • Two Inter-Organizations Laboratories (SMD&DM, CSE) • 7 Position Papers
• Radar	• Common Transmit/Receive Module • Corporate projects GaN LNA and CELL Computing Node • PNRM Project financed by the Minister of Defense
• Materials	• Prototype of Nautical Bridge • Nanotechnology Multiscale Project assigned by Segredifesa • OPTOLINK Finmeccanica Corporate Project
• SET2	• Standards for the Distributed Simulation • Centers for Simulation Internetworking • First Product Catalogue in the Simulation Area
• Security	• Leadership for Finmeccanica in 2 European Projects (SOBCAH, TRIPS) • Budget of 3.2 Ml Euro (8% of the total)
• CMMI	• Guidelines Metrics and Re-use • Software Safety Critical: AS IS analysis and GAP Analysis

Mindsh@re Project Financial Results	
• External funds acquired and brought to operating companies	38 ML euro
• Corporate Projects Financed toward Companies (2006–7)	2.9 ML euro
• Expected External funds (2007–9)	52 ML euro
• Expected Savings (2007–9)	43 ML euro

Source: Finmeccanica Mindsh@re Key Data (2007).

Most of the indicators from which the previous data are identified are rated and make available each semester. Using the data generated through the Mindsh@re Performance Monitor, the Council of each community is able to periodically measure the value generated also in terms of cost savings. The Council is asked to calculate the Total Cost Savings generated at company level as a consequence of actions set by the Community (in particular by FGs). Cost savings, defined as the difference between acquisition cost and market cost, can come from:

- Acquisition of best practices from other operating companies;
- Sharing of resources and tools among different operating companies;
- Knowledge sharing (e.g. about suppliers, competitors, R&D);
- Common development of systems, sub-systems, components, capabilities;

- Joint search of suppliers; and
- Additional items to be defined by the Community.

As stated by all the chairmen and project officers interviewed, the base for the above mentioned results is always a radical change of mindset. As the Chairman of the Logistics Community referred:

> The Customer Satisfaction Project took us seven month only to select documents to share and a lot of coordination and trust between the electronics companies. A strong cultural change was required, but the companies reacted very well, as they had a clear objective in mind: increase efficiency by learning from other companies.

Another example of the important role of Mindsh@re in shaping the new corporate culture of the industrial group is provided by a member of the Homeland Security Community:

> During the early phase of the Project, our Community experienced a high level of conflicts and lack of trust among people belonging to different companies. The first meetings were done under a cloud of suspicion. You could feel that the atmosphere was not relaxed and most of them were unwilling to become a group. Today a lot of walls have been destroyed and the culture of integration permeates each of our activities.

The main result generated by the activity of the different communities is visible in nine corporate projects that have been launched in three years around innovative topics.

> We were used to work as separate units, avoiding any type of knowledge sharing with other operating companies. This was just part of our training. The Mindsh@re project radically changed our way of working together, as people and as companies. In our community the synergic collaboration among the fifteen Italian companies and the three British ones created the basis for presenting 5 corporate projects. That would have been totally impossible in the previous situation of companies' isolation.

Some of the results can be classified *lato sensu* as "product innovation" and "process innovation." But the main aspect that defines the value generated by Mindsh@re is the innovation of the corporate culture.

90 percent of the interviewed chairmen confirmed how Mindsh@re helped the organization to acquire a new managerial mindset.

The previous statements taken from interviews to members of the communities confirm the importance that in this initial phase of Mindsh@re has been given to developing soft skills. Workshops on leadership development and innovation management are held at all levels of the Mindsh@re organization structure, to stress how much the company values cultural changes as a means to foster business innovation.

4.6   Conclusion

In this chapter we have illustrated a conceptual framework where companies build their path toward a continuous self-renewal through the development of communities acting as learning organizations. To illustrate how to create the dynamic capability to un-learn old habits and learn how to share strategic knowledge for the whole corporation, we presented the Finmeccanica's Mindsh@re initiative, supported by references to other business cases of success.

As illustrated by the General Electric case, during the two-decade transformation driven by the Jack Welch's leadership, the decision to build integrated networks inside and outside the company's boundaries helped to develop "the soul of a small company within the body of a big one" (Ghoshal and Bartlett, 1997, p. 264). Finmeccanica is another example of large company that launched an important change through the Mindsh@re initiative, by challenging managerial mindsets dominated by engineering models built into their traditional hierarchies. As Welch developed a self-renewing organization by investing in the entrepreneurial and integration processes, so Finmeccanica launched a corporate-wide process that passed through the construction of technology communities, guided by the belief that no change occurs until people change. In both cases, the top management had to challenge the dominant managerial culture that prevented managers to focus on how to change individual motivations and social relationships.

As illustrated by the Toyota case, a continuous competitive advantage can be created through knowledge-sharing processes within the extended enterprise. This means that a community-based organization like Finmeccanica is able to survive only if it develops superior routines to transfer knowledge to and among suppliers, customers, and partners (Dyer, 2000).

A meta-organizational model like Mindsh@re is a case of corporate effort to build formalized horizontal linkages, develop horizontal knowledge flows, and create value by changing the corporate culture.

The decision to support a change management initiative like Mindsh@re and invest in creating communities acting like "catalytic networks" with highly interconnected companies (Clippinger, 1999) is the signal of a movement toward a process of corporate renewal as it has been described by Ghoshal and Bartlett (1997). The authors proposed a model starting from the empirical observation of several companies: Motorola, ABB, General Electric and AT&T. The "phased model of corporate renewal" suggests how to increase the quality of performance focusing on the effectiveness of the inter-organizational units' integration. The objective of the process is that "individually strong units work together to create competitive advantage none of them could achieve independently" (Ghoshal and Bartlett, 1997, p. 246).

Mindsh@re represents for Finmeccanica the opportunity to pursue a cultural change, by creating communities where hierarchy and bureaucracy is minimized, self-discipline is nurtured, and empowerment is pursued at all organizational levels. After a first *rationalization* phase, where behaviors are changed, management processes are redefined and structural changes are put in place, the *revitalization* phase supported by the Mindsh@re project helps to develop integrative synergies among companies. Coordination mechanisms are required to create a lean and agile organization, as it is shown by the process of sharing Technology Plans that is required to all the companies. In this phase of corporate renewal, Mindsh@re changes peoples' cultural attitude by investing in transferring values of collaboration, team learning, and distributed leadership. In this phase, decisions like "what type of managers the company wants to have" are crucial for dealing with complex decisions, as demonstrated by the case of Jack Welch. GE's CEO removed the "Type IV Manager" explaining that "they get results but they do so without sharing the values of openness and collaboration."

The third phase of *regeneration* facilitated by projects like Mindsh@re requires a change in the managerial role, a guided transformation of managers into leaders. As Jack Welch described: "Our goal is to build a GE that renews itself constantly, exhilarates itself with speed, and freshens itself through constant learning."

The continuous knowledge management initiatives promoted by the Mindsh@re communities (i.e. innovation workshops, knowledge marketplace) or the coaching/leadership programs built *ad-hoc* for chairmen and mentors are an expression of this effort for achieving continuous self-renewal.

Table 4.10   Research method and tools used

Research Strategy	Applications in this Study
Case study	Each of the seven technology communities was treated as a case study to observe the Mindsh@re Model
Interviews	*Seven* Semi-structured Interviews to the Communities Chairmen • Four Face-to-face Interviews, three Phone Interviews • *Four* Semi-structured Interviews to Managers at the Mindsh@re Project Office
Archival Analysis	• Documenation on Mindsh@re Performance Monitor • Newsletter of the IED2 and Security Community • Description of the Mindsh@re Project and Communities: mission, vision, structure, roles, working templates
Direct Observation	• Big Event "Logistics Community"—Roma, April 2008 • Two Council Meeting "IED2 Community." Torino and Roma (March and April 2008) • Mindsh@re Event 2006 and 2008

Appendix: Research strategy[*]

We collected data through a direct participation to meetings, events and seminars by looking at archival data, by administering semi-structured interviews to the communities' chairmen, mentors and to members of the Mindsh@re Project Office (see Table 4.10).

References

V. Allee (2000) "The Value Evolution. Addressing Larger Implications of an Intellectual Capital and Intangibles Perspectives," *Journal of Intellectual Capital*, 1(1), pp. 17–32.

D. Ancona and H. Bresman (2007) *X-Teams. How to Build Teams that Lead, Innovate, and Succeed* (Boston, MA: HBS Press).

D. Ancona, T. W. Malone, W. J. Orlikowski and M. P. Senge (2007) "In Praise of the Incomplete Leader," *Harvard Business Review*, 85(2), pp. 92–100.

C. Argyris (1977) "Double Loop Learning in Organizations," *Harvard Business Review*, September–October 55(5), pp. 115–24.

W. E. Baker (2000) *Achieving Success through Social Capital. Tapping the Hidden Resources in your Personal and Business Networks* (San Francisco, CA: Jossey Bass Wiley Imprint).

C. A. Bartlett and M. Wozny (2005) "GE's Two-Decade Transformation: Jack Welch's Leadership," *Harvard Business School Case*, 399–150.

[*] Mindsh@re is an Italian registered trademark owned by Finmeccanica company S.p.A.

C. A. Bartlett and A. Mohammed (1995) "3M: Profile of an Innovating Company," *Harvard Business School Case*, 395–016.

N. Bontis (2001) "Assessing Knowledge Assets: A Review of the Models used to Measure Intellectual Capital," *International Journal of Management Reviews*, 3(1), pp. 41–60.

R. L. Breiger (2004) "The Analysis of Social Networks" in M. Hardy and A. Bryman (eds) *Handbook of Data Analysis* (London, UK: Sage Publications) pp. 505–26.

S. L. Brown and K. M. Eisenhardt (1998) *Competing on Edge: Strategy as Structured Chaos* (Boston, MA: HBS Press).

T. Burns and G. N. Stalker (1961) *The Management of Innovation* (London, UK: Tavistock Publications).

R. S. Burt (2000) "The Network Structure of Social Capital" in R. Sutton and B. Staw (eds) *Research in Organizational Behavior* (New York, NY: JAI Press).

K. M. Carley (2000) "Organizational Change and the Digital Economy: A Computational Organization Science Perspective" in E. Brynjolfsson and B. Kahin (eds) *Understanding the Digital Economy: Data, Tools, and Research* (Boston, MA: The MIT Press).

H. W. Chesbrough (2003) "The Era of Open Innovation," *MIT Sloan Management Review*, 4(3), pp. 74–81.

J. H. III Clippinger (1999) *The biology of business. Decoding the natural laws of enterprise* (San Francisco, CA: Jossey-Bass Publishers).

D. Cohen and L. Prusak (2001) *In Good Company. How Social Capital Makes Organizations Work* (Boston, MA: HBS Press).

J. Cothrel and R. Williams (1999) "On-line Communities: Helping them Form and Grow," *Journal of Knowledge Management*, 3(1), pp. 54–65.

R. Cross, T. Laseter, A. Parker and G. Velasquez (2006) "Using Social Network Analysis to Improve Communities of Practice", *California Management Review*, 49(1), pp. 32–60.

R. Cross and A. Parker (2002) *The Hidden Power of Social Networks. Understanding how Work Really Gets Done in Organizations* (Boston, MA: HBS Press).

R. Cross, A. Parker and S. P. Borgatti (2002) "Making Invisible Work Visible: Using Social Network Analysis to Support Strategic Collaboration," *California Management Review*, 44(2), pp. 25–46.

R. B. Duncan and A. Weiss (1979) "Organizational Learning: Implications for Organizational Design" in Staw B. (ed.) *Research in Organizational Behavior* (Greenwich, CT: JAI Press) pp. 75–123.

H. J. Dyer (2000) *Collaborative Advantage: Winning through Extended Enterprise Supplier Networks* (Oxford, UK: Oxford University Press,).

H. J. Dyer and K. Nobeoka (2000) "Creating and Managing a High Performance Knowledge-Sharing Network: The Toyota Case," *Strategic Management Journal*, 21(3), pp. 345–67.

L. Edvinsson and M. S. Malone (1997) *Intellectual Capital: The Proven Way to Establish Your Company's Real Value by Measuring its Hidden Values* (London, UK: Piatkus).

Finmeccanica Mindsh@re Document (2007) "Technology Innovation & IP Management," Piazza Monte Grappa, 4, 00195 Roma.

D. A. Garvin (1993) "Building a Learning Organization," *Harvard Business Review*, 71(4), pp. 78–92.

S. Ghoshal and C. A. Bartlett (1997) *The Individualized Corporation* (New York, NY: Harper Collins Publishers).

P. A. Gloor, F. Grippa, Y. H. Kidane, P. Marmier and C. Von Arb (2008) "Location Matters—Measuring the Efficiency of Business Social NetworKing," *International Journal Foresight and Innovation Policy*, 4(3/4), pp. 230–45.

P. A. Gloor (2006) *Swarm Creativity. Competitive Advantage through Collaborative Innovation Networks* (New York, NY: Oxford University Press).

G. Hamel (2007) *The Future of Management* (Boston, MA: HBS Press).

G. Hamel (2000) *Leading the Revolution* (Boston, MA: HBS Press).

B. Hedberg (1981) "How Organizations Learn and Unlearn?" in P. C. Nystrom and W. H. Starbuck (eds) *Handbook of Organizational Design* (London, UK: Oxford University Press) pp. 8–27.

P. Heisig, J. Vorbeck and J. Niebuhr (2001) "Intellectual Capital" in K. Mertins, P. Heisig and J. Vorbeck (eds) *Knowledge Management—Best Practices in Europe* (Berlin: Springer) pp. 57–73.

J. H. Hite (1999) *Learning in Chaos* (Houston, TX: Gulf Publishing).

L. Huston and N. Sakkab (2006) "Connect and Develop. Inside Procter & Gamble's new Model for Innovation," *Harvard Business Review*, 84(3), pp. 58–66.

B. Iyer, C.-H. Lee and N. Venkatraman (2006) "Managing in a Small World Ecosystem: Some Lessons from the Software Sector," *California Management Review*, 48(3), pp. 27–47.

R. S. Kaplan and D. P. Norton (1992) "The Balanced Scorecard Measures that Drive Performance," *Harvard Business Review*, January–February, pp. 71–79.

S. Kelly and M. A. Allison (1999) *The Complexity Advantage: How the Science of Complexity can Help your Business Achieve Peak Performance* (New York, NY: McGraw-Hill).

B. Kogut and U. Zander (1992) "Knowledge of the Firm, Combinative Capabilities, and the Replication of Technology," *Organization Science*, 3(3), pp. 383–97.

J. Lave and E. Wenger (1991) *Situated Learning: Legitimate Peripheral Participation* (Cambridge. MA: Cambridge University Press).

M. J. Marquardt (2002) *Building the Learning Organization: Mastering the five elements for corporate learning* (Palo Alto, CA: Davies-Black Publishing).

D. Miller (1997) "The Future Organization: A Chameleon in all its Glory" in F. Hesselbeing, M. Goldsmith and R. Beckhard (eds) *The Organization of the Future* (San Francisco, CA: Jossey-Bass) pp. 119–25.

K. Morrison (2002) *School Leadership and Complexity Theory* (London, UK and New York, NY: RoutledgeFalmer).

I. Nonaka and N. Konno (1998) "The Concept of Ba: Building a Foundation for Knowledge Creation," *California Management Review*, 40(3), pp. 40–54.

I. Nonaka and K. Takeuchi (1995) *The Knowledge-Creating Company* (New York, NY: Oxford University Press).

M. Pedler, J. Burgoyne and T. Boydell (1997) *The Learning Company: A Strategy for Sustainable Development* (Maidenhead, UK: McGraw-Hill).

E. T. Penrose (1959) *The Theory of the Growth of the Firm* (New York, NY: Wiley).

P. Rizova (2006) "Are you Networked for Successful Innovation?," *MIT Sloan Management Review*, 47(3), pp. 49–55.

A. Romano, V. Elia and G. Passiante (2001) *Creating Business Innovation Leadership: An Ongoing Experiment. The e-Business Management School at ISUFI* (Napoli: Edizioni Scientifiche Italiane).

R. Rothwell (1992) "Successful Industrial Innovation: Critical Factors for the 1990s," *R&D Management*, 22(3), pp. 221–40.

M. Sawhney and E. Prandelli (2000) "Communities of Creation: Managing Distributed Innovation in Turbulent Markets," *California Management Review* 42(4), pp. 24–54.

P. M. Senge and G. Carstedt (2001) "Innovating our Way to the Next Industrial Revolution," *MIT Sloan Management Review*, 42(2) 24–38.

P. Senge (1990) *The Fifth Discipline: The Art and Practice of the Learning Organization* (New York, NY: Doubleday Business).

H. Silins, S. Zarins and B. Mulford (2002) "What Characteristics and Processes Define a School as a Learning Organization? Is this a Useful Concept to Apply to Schools?," *International Education Journal*, 3(1), pp. 24–32.

D. J. Skyrme (1998) *Measuring the Value of Knowledge: Metrics for the Knowledge-Based Business* (London, UK: Business Intelligence Limited).

K. E. Sveiby (1997) *The New Organizational Wealth: Managing & Measuring Knowledge-Based Assets* (San Francisco, CA: Berrett-Koehler Publisher).

D. Tapscott and A. D. Williams (2006) *Wikinomics. How Mass Collaboration Changes Everything* (New York, NY: Portfolio-Penguin).

D. J. Teece (1994) "Firm Organization, Industrial Structure, and Technological Innovation," *Journal of Economic Behavior and Organization*, 31(2), pp. 193–224.

D. J. Teece, G. Pisano and A. Shuen (1997) "Dynamic Capabilities and Strategic Management," *Strategic Management Journal* (18)7, pp. 509–33.

D. J. Teece (2007) "Explicating Dynamic Capabilities: The Nature and Microfoundations of (Sustainable) Enterprise Performance," *Strategic Management Journal*, 28(13), pp. 1319–50.

B. Tuckman (1965) "Developmental Sequence in Small Groups," *Psychological Bulletin*, 63(6), pp. 384–99.

E. C. Wenger and W. M. Snyder (2000) "Communities of Practice: The Organizational Frontier," *Harvard Business Review*, 78(1), pp. 139–45.

R. W. Woodman, J. E. Sawyer and R. W. Griffin (1993) "Toward a Theory of Organizational Creativity," *Academy of Management Review*, 18(2), pp. 293–321.

M. Youngblood (1997) *Life at the Edge of Chaos* (Dallas, TX: Perceval Publishing).

5
The Emergence of the Stakeholder University

Alessandro Margherita and Giustina Secundo

5.1   Introduction

In the previous chapters we moved from major transformations in the economic and business scene (Chapter 1) to address the need for a new managerial mindset (Chapter 2), to offer a different perspective on human capital development in companies behaving as universities (Chapter 3), and to posit new organizational models to drive innovation (Chapter 4).

The framework in which the analysis has been conducted is the *Open Business Innovation Leadership* (Chapter 1), a concept in which we embedded three fundamental strategic priorities of organizations today: (a) the centrality of developing social capital and enhancing the network of learning relationships; (b) the importance of creating innovation-driven value for stakeholders; and (c) the founding role of human capital as a cause for organizational development. Following these assumptions, the previous parts of this book have presented a threefold investigation based on literature and cases from which the following key considerations can be extracted:

Emergence of a new managerial mindset:

- a new cultural model emerges in management as the result of the evolution from a linear/mechanistic to a non-linear/emergent way of thinking;
- the ultimate purpose of companies moves from efficiency and profitability to searching a larger space of value creation options;
- the interrelatedness of processes and people challenges managers to adopt a holistic and more dynamic view of business and management, in the perspective of "strategic entrepreneurship";

- *self-organization, fitness* and *co-evolution* are adopted as metaphors describing the dimensions of a new perspective about organizations and business;
- as complex systems, organizations tend to position at the border between order and chaos because this is somehow the most flexible and evolvable position and thus a source of continuous competitive advantage; and
- new organizational forms emerge like *catalytic networks* that take full advantage of intra and inter-organizational connections.

Emergence of new paradigms in human capital development:

- leading companies behave like educational institutions, putting learning and human capital development at the top of their strategic agenda;
- the meaning and practice of human capital development is impacted by key dimensional changes related to people (who), processes (how) and strategic purpose (why);
- new management roles emerge at operating, middle and top levels, resulting in the need to develop different competency frameworks;
- innovative learning strategies and practices are needed to develop in a shorter time frame a set of integrated competencies and skills applicable in the workplace; and
- a wider perspective arises in corporate learning processes in terms of strategic focus and links with the business strategy, scope of stakeholders involved and the degree of interconnections among them.

Emergence of new innovation-oriented organization models:

- within a complex and fast-changing environment governed by innovation, the dynamic capability to continuously learn and share knowledge is a critical success factor;
- the main concern of organizations evolves from long-term and strategic planning toward organizational learning;
- flexible and responsive organizational forms, such as virtual communities, are needed to pursue open and systemic innovation;
- individual, team, organizational and inter-organizational learning processes represent the main driver of continuous innovation; and
- a meta-organizational model is needed to support cross-fertilization of ideas, systematic knowledge flows and continuous interaction among stakeholders acting as co-innovators.

Building on these key facts, this last chapter addresses strategic priorities of organizations today, enclosed in the *Open Business Innovation Leadership* concept, with the evolution of mindset, human capital practices and organization/innovation models. Moving from the transformation of corporate learning and corporate university initiatives as the strategic response of companies to fast change and hypercompetition, the emergence of the Stakeholder University is shown as a new "archetype" characterized by very large focus, scope and interconnections. In particular, the following questions describe the focus of this chapter:

- *What are the key facts characterizing the evolution of corporate learning strategies and initiatives?*
- *In particular, how have corporate university models evolved over time to address the changing needs and challenges of organizations?*
- *What are the distinguishing features and components characterizing the Stakeholder University model?*
- *What design and implementation roadmap can be defined to build a Stakeholder University?*
- *In what sense can the Stakeholder University be a driver of Open Business Innovation Leadership?*

To provide answers to these questions, this chapter is structured as follows: Section 5.2 introduces the scope, focus and interconnection dimensions of corporate learning to describe four different "archetypes"; Section 5.3 provides an analysis of the corporate university, based on research investigating seven areas; Section 5.4 synthesizes the most innovative trends emerging from the observation to support the definition of a model of the Stakeholder University that is also applied to three cases described; and finally, Section 5.5 provides a design and implementation roadmap while Section 5.6 summarizes conclusions.

5.2   The evolution of corporate learning archetypes

Besides the evolution of management roles and competency frameworks, a transformational change in the meaning and practice of human capital development is related to the ultimate purpose that companies pursue. In particular, the changing impact on business performance and value created for stakeholders is a distinguishing trait of some corporate learning and human capital development approaches.

We identify three variables that we believe are directly connected to the value-creation potential of a human capital development initiative: the *focus*, the *scope* and the level of *interconnection*.

The *focus* refers to the *strategic width* of the initiative, which ranges from a narrow training purpose (e.g. developing specific skills), through broader forms of professional development—including the diffusion of organizational values, and initiatives incorporating research and human resource management by integrating learning, knowledge management and organizational development.

The *scope* refers to the *physical width*, that is the level of involvement of internal and external stakeholders that can range from purely employee-oriented actions to learning processes that address the entire value network of the organization, including customers, suppliers, partners and other actors.

Finally, the level of *interconnection* refers to the degree of *mutual interactions* among actors involved. This is related to the amplitude of scope, since the more actors are involved, the more their potential interactions. As a consequence, the degree of interconnection is also dependent on the location of people, ranging from a site-specific initiative (only employees) to a highly distributed program (many external actors involved). In the latter case, the use of Information and Communication Technology (ICT) can be a fundamental enabler of distributed and collaborative learning processes, as illustrated in Chapter 3.

It is possible to identify four *illustrative archetypes* of learning initiatives (Figure 5.1) characterized by a different degree of focus, scope and interconnection:

1. initiatives characterized by low focus and scope width and low degree of interconnection → archetype: *"training department"*;
2. initiatives characterized by medium/low focus and scope width, and medium/high degree of interconnection → archetype: *"e-learning platform"*;
3. initiatives characterized by medium/high focus and scope width, and medium/high degree of interconnection → archetype: *"corporate university"*;
4. initiatives characterized by high focus and scope width and high degree of interconnection → archetype: *"Stakeholder University."*

We associated the width of scope and focus and the degree of interconnection of these archetypes to their value creation potential. Some considerations about the meaning of value are necessary now. In a

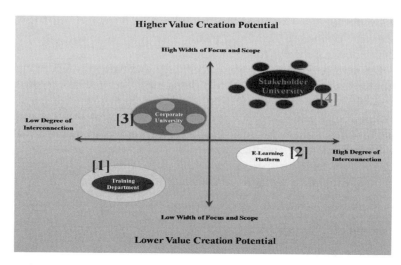

Figure 5.1 Key variables and corporate learning archetypes.

market economy, it is generally understood that companies should pursue economic profitability. They must be profitable to survive and earn a higher return on the shareholders' equity than would be gained through other investments. Profits enhance investors' trust and stock-prices, which makes it easier to grow the company further toward its long-term goals. In this perspective, profits are not only a result, but rather a source of competitive advantage.

However, the market perspective represents only one element. Another one, as already discussed in Chapter 3, is that companies are networks of parties and people working together toward a shared goal that is not merely economic. Human capital represents a major part of a company's value and a level of trust must be built with employees to motivate them to work for the interests of the company. Likewise, it is important to develop strong relationships between the organization and its external environment and this requires that all the stakehold-ers (customers, suppliers, partners, government, etc.) are taken into account.

In this perspective, the concept of value is not simply referring to an idea of shareholder value and thus profitability, economic and financial performance, but also to a *stakeholder value* view to emphasize responsibility besides profitability and see the success of the organiza-tion based on the satisfaction and development of all the "coalition" or network of actors being addressed. Building a strong motivation and citizenship in talented employees and nurturing all the parties surrounding the organization is the only strategy to ensure sustainable performance and competitive advantage.

The question at this point could be: "In what way are focus, scope and interconnection dimensions related to the higher value creation potential?" The answer is threefold. First, the stakeholder perspective, which goes beyond the pure shareholder and financial focus, enlarges the variety of actors addressed, resulting in a more extended *scope*; second, the concept of network that is implicit in the idea of the organization and its partners, suppliers, customers, etc., as a coalition, requires the mutual interactions and *interconnection* among the different actors; third, cultivating the interest of many parties involves enlarging the *focus* from a simple "education" perspective to a wider goal that includes aspects such as innovation, research and sharing of strategic knowledge. Where are the four archetypes positioned with respect to these variables?

The traditional *training department* was based on the 19th century model of corporate education and it is still used in many corporations. Training departments are characterized by a low focus width (specific skills and competencies are targeted and there are no strong links between business strategy and learning strategy), low scope width (only company employees and internal actors are involved), and low degree of interconnection (few actors, limited use of collaborative technologies).

The second archetype, the *e-learning platform*, is more recent and it has been the focus of ICT investments by companies in the last two decades. The reason is that the use of distance learning technologies can help organizations (above all multinationals) to reduce the costs (mainly for travel and accommodation) of face-to-face training while updating the skills of a larger number of employees. Technology-enhanced learning can facilitate *just in time*, *just in place* and *just appropriate* competency development, resulting in higher flexibility and compatibility with work schedules. The e-learning platform archetype is characterized by a medium/low focus width (sometimes different skills are targeted, though a wider perspective of organizational values and development is not addressed), medium/low scope width (employees located in different company sites can be involved easily but the participation of actors external to the organization is not common) and a medium/high degree of interconnection (through the use of collaborative technologies).

The *corporate university* archetype emerged in the 1990s to embrace a wide range of learning initiatives supported at different levels by ICT. This represents an important evolution with respect to the traditional training department as well as respect to the simple technology-enabled learning platform. The corporate university is characterized by a medium/ high focus width (different curricula and programs are implemented to support strategic business objectives and a wider organizational development and research focus is addressed sometimes), medium/high scope width (employees located in different company sites and also customers, suppliers, partners are involved in some of the initiatives) and a medium/ high degree of interconnection (due to many actors and the relevant use of knowledge management and e-learning systems).

One of the objectives of this chapter is to describe the emergence of a fourth archetype, the *Stakeholder University*. A brief background is needed related to previous definitions and applications of this concept. The stakeholder notion has been used in higher education to express the increasing accountability and responsiveness of higher education institutions in their environment, toward external actors. The rise of the stakeholder society in the 1960s took place when the state lost its position of prime authority in higher education (Neave, 2001). The shift from elite to mass education had profound consequences on redefining the purpose of higher education and the legitimacy of various actors and resulted in a change in the academic community. Stakeholders in higher education are specific groups of external actors that have a direct or indirect interest and cannot always be covered by the consumer-provider analogy (Maassen, 2000). Knight (1997) used the stakeholders' perspective when looking at the issue of internationalization of higher education and identified three main stakeholders having a central interest in this endeavour: government, academia and the private sector. Other authors distinguished students as key members of the academic community, and governments, businesses, social and cultural actors as well as other universities and higher education institutions as main stakeholders (EUA, 2003). In their work "*From the Entrepreneurial University to the Stakeholder University*" Jongbloed and Goedegebuure (2001) apply the stakeholder approach to demonstrate the need for changes in the university's structure and strategy needed to cope with the transforming environment and education needs.

Trends affecting the university today include mass individualization, the emergence of the knowledge society, social dynamics, information and communication technologies and globalization. In particular, the evolution in the socio-economic system and the transition from an industrial to a network economy forced higher education institutions to be in constant dialogue with their stakeholders. The Stakeholder University is thus a university in constant dialogue with its stakeholders, a learning archetype characterised by the largest focus, scope and interconnection, resulting in higher value potential. We associate the Stakeholder University with the following features:

- broad human capital development objectives are targeted, through an integration of research, competency development and knowledge management; as a consequence, the overall learning and development strategy is aligned with business strategy (*large focus*);
- the model is based on involvement of a wide range of an organization's stakeholders, recognizing the centrality of developing social capital and relationships besides human capital (*extended scope*); and
- networked learning, knowledge creation and innovation processes are founded on relationships and interactions among actors via a new generation of collaborative working and learning technologies (*rich interconnection*).

This chapter investigates the evolution of corporate university world as a central point in our discussion and assumes that training departments have evolved toward corporate university structures in which e-learning has been integrated in corporate learning initiatives. An exploration is presented through the analysis of seven key aspects that are considered with the ultimate goal of identifying the emerging trends and most innovative practices that are consititute the Stakeholder University archetype.

5.3 A deeper look in the Corporate University world

The phenomenon of corporate learning emerged into the 21st century as a fast growing sector of management education and human capital development. This is also because leading companies such as Motorola and Boeing have gradually transferred their successful business models and state-of-the-art technologies to serve the purposes of corporate education. This section focuses on the description of major trends that impact the corporate learning world, with a specific analysis of the Corporate University (CU) phenomenon. In particular, a qualitative and quantitative analysis is here illustrated based on the following *focus questions*:

- *Which strategic focus and scope characterizes a CU?*
- *How is the curriculum of a CU designed?*
- *What is the strategy for competency development that a CU adopts?*

- *Which role does ICT have in the launch and development of a CU?*
- *What are the drivers for the development and sustainability of a CU?*
- *Which organizational model works better for a CU?*
- *Which funding model works better for a CU?*
- *How is the performance and impact of a CU measured?*

The answer to these questions is grounded on different sources that have been used in our analysis. First, we did an extended review of CU literature and cases of successful companies (e.g. Motorola, Cisco, General Electric, Toyota, General Motors, McDonald's, Mc Kinsey and 3M). We considered the Sixth Annual Benchmarking Report 2007 (from now on "Benchmark") a study made by the *Corporate University Xchange* on 170 different corporate universities located worldwide and belonging to many industries. Finally, the "desk" part of the research was a survey we did at the *Corporate University Summit* in Las Vegas (May 2008) (referred to here as "Survey") involving 50 practitioners and participants of corporate learning.

5.3.1 Introduction: Stages of corporate learning

In the previous sections, we discussed aspects like the alignment of learning and business goals, the extension of learning processes outside company's boundaries, and a wider focus on competency development. Large companies like Motorola and Toyota achieved global leadership and excellence thanks to innovative development initiatives well beyond traditional job training, through the establishment of corporate education institutions that became real strategic partners, often working in conjunction with traditional educational institutions.

In the last decades, the corporate learning world has been characterized by a fast development supported by *five essential forces*:

- the emergence of flat and flexible organizations;
- the evolution of the economy into a knowledge economy;
- the shortened shelf life of knowledge;
- the focus on lifetime employability rather than lifetime employment; and
- the fundamental shift in the global education marketplace.

All these trends point to a new key vehicle for creating a sustainable competitive advantage: the company's commitment to employee education and development. This becomes the chief vehicle for disseminating an organization's culture and fostering the development of core workplace skills as learning-to-learn, leadership, creative thinking and problem-solving (Meister, 1998).

The effort made by companies to create their own CU (different definitions are reported in the Appendix) can be analyzed considering three stages of evolution of this phenomenon, corresponding to various degrees of maturity:

- Stage#1—Primitive or *training* phase (1920s–70s);
- Stage#2—Maturity or *corporate education* phase (1970s–90s); and
- Stage #3—Emerging or *networked learning* phase (1990s–. . .).

The *training* phase was characterized by conventional training and development activities, with organization-specific modules requiring classroom attendance and emphasis on the acquisition of corporate values (learning archetype #1). The customer was represented by the individual, the curriculum was based on business functions, the strategy based on knowledge transfer and there was an indirect link with business strategy. The use of technology was limited. Examples of this first wave are represented by the universities created by Disney.

The *corporate education* phase grew up to reflect a broader-based strategy toward promoting organizational change and learning (affirmation of the learning archetype #3). More than a physical and organizational entity, a CU is a strategic organizational process where all levels of employees are involved in continuous lifelong learning to improve their job performance. A CU has been conceived as an educational entity designed to assist an organization in achieving its mission by conducting activities that cultivate individual and organizational learning, knowledge and wisdom (Allen, 2002). Though the massive growth started in the 1970s, the introduction of the first CUs took place in the United States in 1955 with General Motors and in 1961 with McDonald's. This was when big American companies decided to create their *internal universities* to carry out the training more specific to them, rather than sending their employees to external universities. According to the Corporate University Xchange (CUX), in 1993 corporate universities existed in only 400 companies. In 2001, this number jumped to 2,000. Nelson Heller states that according to CUX, this number will grow to exceed 3,700 by 2010, which is more than the number of private United States universities (2000). Initially, 40 percent of the largest 500 America Companies cited by Fortune had their own

CU (e.g. Disney University, Crotonville Educational Center of General Electric, or McDonald's Hamburger University). Today, the market has expanded to include mid-size companies, and a recent survey of 100 CUs Deans found that 64 percent of universities are not on Fortune's list. Since in the Corporate University archetype the customer is the whole organization, the curriculum aims to develop leadership and skills through knowledge transfer and exchange, and there is a direct link between learning and business strategy. The use of technology is extended to incorporate web-learning applications (learning archetype #2). An example of this second wave is Toyota.

The primitive training and the corporate learning phases can be conceived as a transition phases toward the affirmation of *networked learning*, with a new generation of corporate learning processes (learning archetype #4) emerged as a strategy to go beyond the existing models, in two basic dimensions (Wheeler, 2005): (a) the academic and research emphasis and focus on valuing tacit knowledge; and (b) the value created for stakeholders in terms of solving organizational issues, attacking new areas, developing leadership and change management attitude. In this phase, learning becomes increasingly a strategic organizational process that is not company-bounded but rather arising within a community of organization's stakeholders. Learning supports the organization's ability to change and it is strongly linked with the strategic needs of the organization. For this purpose, companies transform their corporate learning processes to focus on leveraging new opportunities, enter global markets, develop deeper customer relationships and envision new scenarios for the future. Corporate learning becomes therefore a fundamental weapon to drive success in the long term based on a strong strategic purpose. In fact, it is impossible to have any real success in terms of adding value to the organization and making a difference when there is no real strategic intent behind the plan (Allen, 2007). For this purpose, the focus is more on learning strategies rather than tactics of training, on being proactive about changes, and moving from delivering classes to providing solutions and be strongly addressed to build organizations (Allen, 2002). Third stage corporate learning targets the integration of technology-oriented and management-oriented competencies and makes a substantial use of collaborative technologies to enhance networked learning. An example of advanced corporate learning is given by Motorola.

Table 5.1 synthesizes the three stages of evolution in terms of five key features: focus, link with strategy, scope, technology use (these last

Table 5.1 Stages of corporate education and main features

Aspect/Stage	Training (1920s—70s)	Corporate Education (1970s–90s)	Networked Learning (1990s–)
Focus	Individual competencies	Organizational change	Stakeholder value
Link with strategy	Indirect	Direct	Proactive
Scope	Individual	Organization	Network of stakeholders
ICT use	PC	Intranet and Internet, web-learning, multimedia	Collaborative learning, social computing, web 2.0
Curricula	Business topics and functions	Leadership and skills	Business processes
Example	Disney	Toyota	Motorola

two giving an idea of potential interconnections) and curricula. Three illustrative examples are also provided.

The next sections analyze the corporate university phenomenon based on the seven focus questions that were previously defined.

5.3.2 Which strategic directions and scope characterize a CU?

In the "Survey" we conducted in Las Vegas in May 2008 (Corporate University Summit) we asked to a sample of 50 academics and practitioners about the *scope* of a CU. In particular, we wanted to know their perception of the "internal" or "external" perspective of a corporate learning initiative. A slight majority of people interviewed (52%) reported the centrality of addressing the organization and its internal actors; 48 percent highlighted the importance of enlarging the scope of the CU to include also external stakeholders concerned or impacted by corporate learning initiatives.

The definition of the scope is strictly related to the *strategic direction* of the university. At this proposal, the *Benchmark* identifies five different directions:

1. *Skills and development*: The strategic driver is the qualification and development of people skills to drive excellence across specific disciplines or workplace competencies.
2. *Change management*: The university is aimed to drive organization transformation with a strong focus on business performance.

3. *External customer:* The driver is to deliver technical skills to customers, suppliers, partners, with the ultimate goal to increase loyalty and consolidate relationships with external parties belonging to the company's value network.
4. *Strategic business:* The senior management pushes strategy and corporate initiatives to move into territory that the organization has never explored.
5. *Academic research:* The university explores emerging areas and future needs as well as drivers of competitiveness.

Whereas skills and development and change management look mostly at the inside of the company, the last three options are more outside-oriented. Naturally, the strategic direction to follow is also dependent on the over-arching business goals of the company that vary, according to the *Benchmark,* from improved customer/service satisfaction (49%), to improved productivity (48%), reduced costs (45%), retained talented employees (42%) and increased revenues (40%). Related to the ultimate purpose of the CU, objectives mentioned as most important are to develop executives and high potential managers (65%), to measure the effectiveness of learning (55%), to implement/improve learning management systems (50%), and to reduce the fragmentation of learning within the organization (47%).

In our *Survey,* important roles emerged that are associated to the Corporate University, such as developing the ability of the company to invest in people, collecting good resources and constantly developing career paths, facilitating information flows and enhancing lateral knowledge sharing based on trust, openness, fairness and common values.

5.3.3   How is the curriculum of a CU designed?

Changing technologies, increased customer expectations and competitive pressures render the workplace a dynamic and interdependent environment where relevant decisions and actions must be undertaken by all employees. The key concern for workers is the shortened shelf life of the knowledge they hold, hence the need to constantly retool their skills. In our "Survey," 52 percent of respondents illustrate the importance for a CU to develop soft *skills* such as *communication and collaboration, creative thinking and problem solving, technology skills, leadership and change management.* 48 percent of people interviewed stressed the centrality of more *job-related competencies* such as customer relationship management and supply chain management.

The core curriculum delivered by a CU should cover a wide perspective and besides developing "workplace competencies," should address two broad areas (Meister, 1998):

- *Corporate citizenship*: to create a strong attachment to the company and to ensure the workforce is knowledgeable about the vision, history, culture, tradition and values of the company;
- *Contextual reference*: to provide learning opportunities about the company's products, services, and industry dynamics in the context of what competitors are offering in the marketplace and the industry best practices.

Interesting data emerged with reference to the criteria supporting the designing and delivery of curricula through a CU. In particular, only 28 percent of respondents in the "Survey" considered the importance of curricula strictly linked to business functions (i.e. marketing, finance, strategy, information systems, etc.), whereas the vast majority (72%) highlighted the importance of designing and providing more integrated curricula that embed different knowledge domains. Interdisciplinary curricula are indeed considered critical to develop competencies linked with the solution of real business problems and that have a visible impact on business performance.

5.3.4 What is the strategy for competency development that a CU adopts?

Transformations in managerial mindset and organizational settings determine the need to rethink how individual and corporate development is achieved. In particular, a new approach to developing competencies and skills is needed that is interdisciplinary and based on real problems and experiences as drivers of human and professional growth. A crucial paradigm shift emerges from traditional approaches based on *knowledge transfer* and *people shaping* (Baets and van der Linden, 2003) to learning strategies and methods that are highly learner-centric and experiential, based on simulations, projects, exercises with unpredictable outcomes, discussions and independent learning. Successful CUs focus on developing a set of competencies that can be applied to workplaces via experience and in *doing* rather than through purely theoretical knowledge transfer.

A variety of methods and tools are used to effectively support the processes of a CU: traditional classroom experience, web-based training, teamwork, projects and activities, simulations, self-study, reading, etc.

The choice of methods depends on different factors, including the skills of people, the availability of equipment and resources, the contents to be delivered, and the organization's familiarity with the chosen method.

In the *Survey*, 84 percent of respondents declared to be responsible for the management of employees' development and knowledge sharing activities that go beyond traditional classroom sessions. These include *hands-on sessions*, coaching, action learning, laboratory sessions and on the job training. Most of these initiatives are supported by technological platforms. Only 16 percent of respondents stressed the importance of traditional learning activities held in classroom, although if these are costly because of travel expenses for trainees, and complex to make, especially for multinational companies.

The concept of *learning laboratory* (Leonard-Barton, 1992) is particularly pertinent to describe the approach to address critical competencies through integrated problem solving, knowledge management, and experimentation through real or simulated organizational contexts. The ideal setting to developing workplace competencies is therefore a learning community engaging in the sharing in action of knowledge and experiences, a collaborative forum where different actors mutually develop new understanding, insights, approaches and perspectives.

5.3.5   What is the role of ICT in the launch and development of a CU?

There is a growing importance of technology infrastructures in learning delivery, also highlighted by evidence about the use of e-learning course completion as a measure of success (50%), and the promotion of e-learning through human resource management policies (38%). The technology infrastructure represents approximately the 9 percent of budget of the companies surveyed in the *Benchmark*. 70 percent of Corporate Universities studied had full responsibility for managing technology and only 24 percent outsourced this task. The *top three learning infrastructure tools* are:

- Learning Management Systems (77%);
- Authoring Tools (57%); and
- Virtual Collaboration Tools (55%).

In the *Survey*, 88 percent of respondents considered technological platforms as fundamental to developing and managing peoples' competencies as well as to optimizing knowledge sharing throughout the organization. ICT-based approaches to deliver learning are particularly adopted by multinational companies, with executives and employees distributed worldwide, and when "hands-on" strategies are prevalent in the delivery of curricula. The remaining 12 percent of managers interviewed in the "Survey" reported that the most of activities related to the development and delivery of courses are accomplished without using specific technologies. The adoption of many ICT tools such as Content and Learning Management Systems went up with the years of CUs' operation.

A relatively new trend in corporate education is the adoption of Web 2.0 applications such as wikis, blogs and folksonomies to stimulate exchange of ideas and expertise, systematize organizational knowledge, and facilitate intra and inter-organizational collaboration.

5.3.6   What are the drivers for the development of a CU?

In our "Survey," 80 percent of respondents reported that the main driver for building a sustainable CU program is a *strong initiative of the CEO*, from a top-down perspective. The continuous and active support of top and senior management is indeed one key success factor. Top management defines and supports the value creation drivers of the initiative (e.g. human capital development, integration of individual and organizational learning, change management). It is asked to promote and spread the learning mindset in terms of culture, models and strategies, to adapt and implement solutions, and to evaluate final performance at both business and learning level. The governing board of a CU is involved in very critical tasks such as identifying current and future organizational needs, approving strategic planning, promoting the CU within the company, defining its vision, mission and learning philosophy.

The majority of the interviewees reported the importance of *involving people at the bottom line* after the start-up phase and in the maturity stage of the initiative. Besides, implementing appropriate learning experiences requires teams endowed with lateral thinking, creativity and ability to analyze changes as well as strong knowledge and experience about the pedagogical and methodological approach.

Many CU initiatives fail because of the absence of a strong senior sponsorship, as well as because of the difficulty of integrating changes within the existing reality. At this purpose, a solution could be to focus on future leadership needs rather than bringing changes to the *as is*; for instance, by differentiating competence profiles and linking them to actionable decisions.

In the development and sustainability of the CU, the internal *marketing* strategy also plays an important role in that it reflects and reinforces the strategic function of the university. Improving marketing is of high or medium importance to 77 percent of all Corporate Universities, as reported by the *Benchmark*. Half of them have formal annual marketing and communication plans and 43 percent work with their company's marketing department. The three most important marketing and communication practices are to promote employees' learning as a recruitment/retention tool (79%), to feature learner testimonials in marketing material (70%) and to work closely with training vendors (52%).

For *promotional methods*, 84 percent of companies interviewed rely on the word of mouth, 81 percent depend on the university web site to deliver the message, 80 percent use e-mail marketing, 72 percent use a corporate website, 72 percent adopt presentations to align business managers and external clients, 63 percent use brochures and flyers, 56 percent resort to course catalogs, and 55 percent use company newsletters. Personal developments objectives represent the real reasons to motivate organization-wide participation in the CU (88% of respondents in our "Survey") whereas monetary-based motivation is only partially-seen as a motivation (12%).

5.3.7   Which organizational model works better for a CU?

Based on the "Survey", 76 percent of respondents reported that a CU should work to align learning with business goals. The ultimate objective is thus not just to train employees but to reach business goals and improve performance. Only 24 percent believed that CU manages competencies without considering long-term objectives. This is strongly reflected in the organizational level to which the CU is linked.

In fact, according to the *Benchmark*, young CUs (those launched and still building the credibility inside the organization) are more likely to report to Human Resource (64%) than established (51%), operating with a record of success and solid credibility, or expert CUs (61%) (the more consolidated CUs receiving benchmarking requests at least from five outside organizations each year). 14 percent of CUs report directly to the President/CEO, whereas the 10 percent report to Operations.

Established and expert CUs have just one level separating their CLOs from corporate leadership (54% and 64%, respectively) than young CUs (34%). This relationship supports the alignment of learning and development with organizational strategy and objectives, by ensuring that the CU leaders are active participants in the strategic planning for the organization as a whole.

Based on the *Survey*, 76% percent of respondents commented that a CU should have a structure different and separated from the HR function. Sometimes, employees could attend courses and events organized inside the CU and HR department. This is a quite new trend considering that in the early days CUs were born inside the HR department, starting with a delivery of occasional courses and seminars for employees and executives.

Related to the organizational structure adopted, three main models emerged based on the observation of real cases and the *Benchmark*:

1. *Centralized model*: Applied when training departments are small, organizations have fewer than 2,000 employees, charter is narrow and tightly defined, and there is a need for rapid change. This model works well in large organizations where there is a tightly defined purpose for the university.
2. *Decentralized model*: The organization is a conglomerate with little in common among divisions and it is globally dispersed with very different local needs, and there are profit centers with independent general managers.
3. *Federal model*: The organization is very big and global but there are common needs and the necessity to coordinate level of duplicated services or curricula.

One critical aspect related to the organizational model is the decision about the internalization or *outsourcing* of key design and implementation steps of the CU. According to the *Benchmark*, functions performed primarily by outsourcers are technology-enabled course delivery (32%), assessment/competency development (31%), classroom-based course delivery (30%), course design and development (27%) and leaning technology infrastructure (24%). The oldest corporate universities outsource very little of their learning and development activities, with 30 percent of the interviewed people responding that they use none of the mentioned suppliers. As a general trend, the design and implementation of a CU is increasingly accomplished by organizations in partnership with traditional universities and other learning partners who bring organization, structure, and faculty.

The organizational model also impacts on the governance. Critical stakeholders should be involved in the governance committee that is ideally composed by five/seven persons at high strategic level of the organization who can profess the organization's commitment to the program. The CU *executives* and the company's *Chief Learning Officer (CLO)* have to balance a wide range of responsibilities, such as to develop a vision for the role of learning in the company, build external alliances, develop learning processes that have a measurable impact on performance, identify business requirement and priorities, and achieve optimal impact within budget. 67 percent of CUs have governing boards consisting of senior executives and other managers having key roles such as identifying and prioritizing learning needs, approving strategic learning plans, promoting the university within the company, defining the corporate university vision and mission.

Staff is asked, at different levels, to ensure coaching, courses development, learning needs and skill gaps analysis, learning material design, training coordination. The number of Full Time Equivalent (FTE) staff employed by CU averages around 62 grouped per categories such as "management" (account/relationships management, delivery management, project management, learning technology management, vendor management), "instructional" (classroom-based and e-learning instructional design and development), "performance improvement" (consulting, measurement and evaluation) and "other" (back-office support, knowledge management, marketing and communication).

5.3.8   Which funding model works better for a CU?

The organization and governance aspects have relevant impact on the financial resources needed to carry out the initiative. Three key funding models are adopted in practice to back financially the Corporate University:

1. *Corporate allocation model*, when all the expenses are considered part of the general operating overhead of the firm, and costs are allocated to profit centers according to some internal procedures.
2. *Partial or full cost recovery model*, if the university charges individuals and departments for the costs they actually incur for training. This means that the education institution operates more or less as a business, itself.
3. *Profit center model*, a model that sells classes and programs to customers located both internally and externally to the company (for a profit). The training function of the university is not a cost for the company.

According to the companies surveyed in the *Benchmark*, CUs derive 65 percent of their funding from corporate allocation and, on average, 28 percent from charge-backs to business units. Only 5 percent of funding comes from tuition from customers, suppliers and other actors, and even smaller percentage (1% each) from governments' grants and other sources. As CUs evolve from beginner (CUs launched and operating, but still building the credibility within the company) to expert (CUs consolidated and well developed), their dependence on corporate allocation decreases. Expert CUs receive 49 percent of their funding from corporate allocation and 41 percent from charge-backs. These numbers have very clear patterns, with corporate allocation going down as CUs get older, the CU budget increase, and the number of employees increases. This makes sense as CUs start out with corporate allocations and shift to charge backs over time as they demonstrate the value of their services. There are significant differences between industries as well. Healthcare and professional services firms receive the largest percentage of corporate allocation (81% and 79% respectively), while telecom and manufacturing receive the least (53% and 55%). Information industry firms get a high 10 percent of their funding from tuition, and telecom has the highest level of charge backs at 43 percent. The CU budget covers 61 percent of the total training expenditure of companies, but that number varies from a low of 44 percent for very large companies to a high of 79 percent for companies in the professional service industry.

5.3.9   How does one measure the performance and impact of a CU?

Measurement is one of highest priorities for a CU. There are different complex issues in measuring business impact, such as identifying the recipient of measurements, creating a common language and standards, and gaining access to data such as sales figures, employee retention and production error rates. Respondents in our "Survey" highlighted that real job outcomes should be considered as the real output and performance measure for a CU (80%) whereas only 20 percent of people identified the achievement of competencies as the ultimate objective of the university.

The *Benchmark* reports the following *business impact metrics* as the ones most often used to evaluate the performance of the Corporate University:

- improved product service quality (70%);
- improved customer service (70%);
- reduced operating costs (59%);
- increased revenues (51%);
- improved sales efficiency (49%); and
- increased profits (48%).

The impact of learning can be evaluated at different levels. A CU ideally changes people's behavior and impacts consistently on company results. There is a big difference in approaching metrics for a CU compared to the old mindset. Indeed, the focus was historically on individuals whereas a CU addresses the whole organization. It is thus necessary, at the outset, to identify the different *metrics* of performance: for instance, cost and speed of competency development (efficiency), time to productivity of a new hired employee and reduction of manufacturing errors (effectiveness) could be relevant for management. Concerning employees, time to competence (efficiency), relevance of skills acquired and overall satisfaction (effectiveness) are relevant metrics.

5.4   The Stakeholder University: Features and cases

The data and insights emerged from our "Survey", the 2007 Corporate University Xchange Benchmark and the review of literature and cases reveal the emergence of some trends representing innovative features of advanced corporate learning. Table 5.2 reports these trends using the three aspects used to distinguish the learning archetypes (i.e. focus, scope and interconnection) as well the other aspects investigated in the previous section.

Once we isolated these trends, we identified some illustrative cases of leading organizations that have designed and implemented initiatives of corporate learning beyond the traditional Corporate University concept. The companies considered and the respective learning initiatives are the following:

1. Cisco → *Cisco Networking Academy;*
2. General Motors → *General Motors University;*
3. Motorola → *Motorola University.*

The presence in these initiatives of the innovative features identified above frames them in a more mature corporate learning archetype. A brief description is reported in the following paragraphs of these three success cases, trying to show the reasons why it is possible to talk of the presence of a Stakeholder University. The most of information reported has been obtained from the respective websites of companies, the specific university's sites and other web sources.

5.4.1   Cisco Networking Academy

Focus

Cisco created the Networking Academy Program in 1997 as a solution for schools that lacked the skills and resources needed to manage computer networks, and to prepare students for the Cisco certifications.

Table 5.2 Emerging trends in the Corporate University world

Aspect	Trend
#1 Focus	• Maximum alignment business goals—learning goals • Integration of organizational development and research • Integration of knowledge management and learning • Stakeholder value as ultimate purpose • Importance of customer satisfaction and service • Development of high potential managers
#2 Scope	• Network of stakeholders is the target • Global reach and multi-localization • Synergies with academic and industry partners
#3 Interconnection (and ICT use)	• Collaborative learning, research and innovation processes • ICT for managing content, competencies and communities • Social computing, open source and Web 2.0 applications
#4 Curricula (Design and Delivery)	• Holistic curricula address context, citizenship and competencies • Relevance of soft skills beside workplace competencies • Business processes driving curricula design • Integrated rather than functional/specialist knowledge • Hands-on, action and on-demand learning approaches
#5 Organization (and Development)	• CU as a separate entity respect to the HR function • Strategic and operational link with the business level • Top management fundamental for initial sponsorship • Bottom-line support requisite for the growth of the initiative • Personal development objectives overcome money rewards
#6 Performance	• Centrality of job outcomes and work performance • Personal development and career growth • Measurable impact on talent retention, productivity, efficiency

Today, the Networking Academy has expanded and is a comprehensive and innovative education initiative that delivers Information and Communication Technology skills to improve career and economic opportunities around the world. The Academy aims to educate the *"architects of the networked economy"* and help individuals develop the skills needed to fill ICT positions in virtually every type of industry.

Scope

The Academy trains teachers, staff and approximately 600,000 students each year in more than 165 countries. It forges alliances to deliver the services needed to build the global ICT workforce and promote socioeconomic development, above all in the world's underserved populations. The value of partners is strongly emphasized by Tae Yoo (Vice President of Corporate Affairs at Cisco) who states that "multi-stakeholder partnerships, which bring together public, private, nonprofit and multilateral organizations, each with their own unique perspective and expertise, result in greater impact and richer outcomes" (from Cisco website). Partners share these key values and commitment and actors include UN Organizations (e.g. United Nations Development Program—UNDP), Government Organizations (e.g. United States Agency for International Development—USAID), global businesses (e.g. Panduit), NGOs and private foundations (e.g. Cisco Learning Institute).

Interconnections

Cisco makes extensive use of technologies to train and develop people. Besides, to help facilitate connections across the human network of students, alumni, instructors and administrators that participate in the program, the interactive *NetSpace* website encourages members to showcase their talents and connect with others. The Cisco Learning Network is an on-line learning environment that provides access to training on Cisco product and technology information. The portal embeds the latest in social networking, certifications content, games, blogs, discussion forums and other tools and features.

Curricula

The Academy portfolio consists of 18 courses in nine different languages to help meet the diverse needs of students with different interests and objectives. All students receive high-quality education, supported by online content and assessment, performance tracking, and interactive learning tools. Curricula are designed to prepare at best students for career opportunities, continuing education, and globally-recognized certifications. Courses are offered at different entry, intermediate and advanced levels and several delivery options are available such as instructor-led training, virtual classroom, hands-on laboratory exercises and web-based teaching modes. Employees can choose from a database and a library a lot of video-on-demand materials, including subject matter expert recorded presentations. Also informal learning is widely diffused, through internal messaging system, *CiscoCast* (a push messaging system for executives), e-mail, projects and other. IT certification at associate, professional and expert level is delivered in various tracks such as *Routing and Switching*, *Network Security*, and *Service Providers*. In addition to general certifications, network professionals can enhance their core networking knowledge by achieving specialist certification in technologies such as security, IP telephony and wireless. Besides the Academy, many learning resources are available through authorized Cisco sources such as *Training From Cisco Learning Partners*, *Cisco on Cisco Technology Seminar Series*, *Technical Staff Development from Cisco Advanced Services*, *Partner Education Connection*, and *Cisco E-Service Training*.

Organization

The Comprehensive Learning Model of the Academy comprises four main functional areas: *Product* (design and delivery of courses and hands-on activities), *Relationships* (partnerships with public and private institutions), *Infrastructure* (data-management for on-line assessment supported by classroom instruction) and *Support and Design* (student progress and outcomes measurement, objectives identification, resource assessment and gap analysis, program offerings, adjustment and training and online support to instructors).

Performance

The e-learning strategy developed with a lot of partners (such as Oracle, Microsoft, and HP) allowed Cisco to save US$ 40 million in training costs (financial year 2002–3). For this reason, Cisco has been recognized as a pioneer using the Internet for its own business practices and for offering consulting services to help other organizations around the world through its Internet Business Solutions Group. In the 2003 fiscal year, Cisco saved US $2.1 billion by relying on the internet to provide customer support, offering employees services, selling products, managing finances and manufacturing process. Each year the company introduces new applications that enhance the Return on Investment ratios. The widely respected IT certification programs bring valuable, measurable rewards to network professionals, their managers, and the organizations that employ them. Besides more financial and technical aspects, the partnerships created by the Academy enable to develop initiatives that help bridge the digital divide and demonstrate how the Internet can be used to encourage socioeconomic gains in developing nations.

5.4.2   General Motors University

Focus

GM has a longstanding commitment to helping employees continue to grow the knowledge and skills required to fulfill the company's vision of being the world leader in transportation products and services. GM's policy is to educate workforce to achieve the highest standards, with a learning strategy deeply linked to business strategy and goals. The GM University (GMU) was established in 1997 to create a global network of learning resources and pursuit the vision to provide leading-edge learning resources for developing personal and professional excellence, resulting in technical and business leadership. GMU is today one of the largest corporate educational programs in the world. It was launched to create a culture of continuous learning and improvement for employees across the entire enterprise, to support GM's growth by building leadership capability and disseminating best practices and core values globally. GM new hires are paired with experienced GM team members with the primary objective to professionally transition and develop the new hires into the GM culture by enabling them to experience professional growth, corporate culture, new ideas and perspectives, while driving for business results.

Scope

GMU offers more than 3,200 courses to its executive, management, technical, and professional employees around the world. The offer includes traditional classroom training, web-based learning, Interactive Distance Learning and self-directed study. Regular active salaried employees are eligible for tuition assistance, a variety of graduate programs are available throughout GM, and a number of educational courses are offered in conjunction with educational institutions throughout the United States. In 2007, GMU provided over 1 million hours of learning to GM salaried and dealership participants. In particular, more than 60,600 GM salaried participants received nearly 823,000 hours with about 70 percent of the hours spent in traditional classrooms, 28 percent on web-based learning and 2 percent on interactive distance learning. GMU uses one dedicated classroom facility in the U.S. located at GM global headquarters in Detroit's Renaissance Center. In addition, GMU relies on affiliated sites and local accommodations in other parts of the globe. General Motors also offers programs in collaboration with Columbia Business School and Stanford University.

Interconnections

GMU manages costs by focusing on the development and delivery of courses that are critical to the business and by increasing the use of Distance Learning, e-Learning and 'blended' learning solutions. Distance Learning (DL) uses state-of-the-art equipment to train GM salary and dealership employees in North America, Canada and Mexico. DL uses a combination of live one-way video, two-way audio (for communication between the instructor and students), and an interactive keypad for quiz sessions. On average, 400 live video broadcasts covering a wide variety of subjects on a variety of functional topics are delivered monthly via satellite to GM salaried employees in over 200 GM facilities and more than 6,500 GM dealerships in North America, Canada and Mexico. DL is also used for communicating details about new product launches, as well as addressing new product issues that emerge during initial dealer rollouts. E-Learning uses GM's Intranet to improve the global access and availability of courses 24 hours a day, seven days a week. GMU gradually has been growing the percentage of e-learning courses over the last few years and has launched 600 global e-learning courses in multiple languages. In some instances, DL and/or e-Learning may be combined with classroom sessions to provide 'blended' learning that can make the overall approach more effective and efficient for certain topics.

Curricula

Curricula are designed in a way to help GM's executive, management, technical and professional employees to continuously improve their competitive performance. Some classes are lecture-based in a traditional classroom format and many classes are offered online, in multiple languages, so employees have the convenience and flexibility to initiate training when their schedule allows. At the same time, they eliminate the expense and inconvenience of travel to a classroom and promote common content across the globe. The top ten issues recognized from the executive managers of GM critical to business performance and leadership development are: *Benchmarking Leadership Development Programs, Creating Leaders at all Levels, Designing Effective Leadership Development Programs, Developing Managers into Leaders, Assessing Leadership Potential Skills, Leadership Models for Managing Change, Developing Coaching and Mentoring skills, Measuring the ROI of Leadership Development* and

Identifying and Developing Leadership Competencies. GM offers a variety of continuing education opportunities to support career development: foundation skill training (i.e. computer software, GM history and business orientation), functional specific skills and techniques, leadership and professional development, on-the-job training within each department. Mentoring is a critical strategy adopted to preparing the new hires of today to becoming the leaders for tomorrow.

Organization

GMU has 14 functional colleges (such as Communications, Engineering, Global Purchasing and Supply Chain, Manufacturing, Product Planning and Program Management, Quality) tied to GM's global processes that are charged with developing curricula tailored to the professional needs and unique challenges facing GM employees from a business sector, divisional or regional perspective. A "Dean" (typically an operating executive) is responsible for developing and delivering courses that improve results for that business function. The president of GMU, with the Council of Deans, oversees learning operations and GMU strategic direction.

Performance

GMU seeks to improve business performance by developing mission-critical professional skills and capabilities linked to performance and results, fostering faster learning that can be leveraged globally, developing leadership/executive programs that build capability tied to business results, enabling corporate-wide change initiatives to improve business results, helping develop a performance driven culture. GMU integrates employee development and performance under the GM's Performance Management Process (PMP), the annual process that helps employees to align their individual performance goals with overall business goals. Goal-setting, mid-year, and annual reviews provide opportunities to constructively discuss about performance, recognize accomplishments and help employees understand how their individual performance contributes to overall business results.

5.4.3   Motorola University

Focus

The University of Motorola was established in 1979 with the name of *Motorola Training and Education Center* and the goal to deliver quality training for workers and executives. In 1989 the Center was renamed Motorola University (MU) with the responsibility to satisfy all the learning needs of the company. Today, it is globally recognized as a leader in corporate education, the creator of Six Sigma, and provider of consistent and high-quality services. Cherishing the prestigious corporate culture of endless innovation, MU is to contribute to the company's sustained success by "adding values to customers." As the change enabler and culture communicator at Motorola, the University supports the company's continued development and breakthroughs in marketing, supply chain management and engineering by training people and optimizing quality. MU provides employees with curricula and learning initiatives aligned with real business goals such as to reduce product development cycle time. The University is committed to serving the business community with its professional insights and trendsetting concepts, becoming a driving force behind organizational change and growing into a full-fledged corporate education provider that leads the direction of business development.

Scope

Motorola customers, employees, suppliers, partners and other potential customers are part of the greater Motorola ecosystem to which the training, quality management and leadership development services are provided. MU builds partnerships with many well-known training and consulting firms, outstanding universities and business schools, as well as enterprise-based learning organizations. MU's training solutions have found extensive application at many customers in information technology, manufacturing, finance, petrochemical, fast-moving consumables and government sectors worldwide, contributing a lot to their performance improvement, management innovation and workforce empowerment. In the spirit of Six Sigma, the company proprietary courseware is continually improved by a team of experts including instructional designers and classroom instructors. This collaborative process leverages a deep statistical expertise, draws on perspectives beyond Motorola, incorporates participant feedback and ensures instructional integrity for every program delivered.

Interconnections

Since the costs to train employees according the traditional classroom learning in the different part of the world can be high, MU introduced the Self Direct Learning (SDL) into its learning strategy. In SDL mode employees were asked to identify their training needs and goals according their jobs and using the latest technologies including interactive video and satellite communication systems. In 1990 MU introduced the use of e-learning system to expedite the training process imparted to a large number of employees worldwide. At the core of the e-learning system there was the e-learning portal accessible in synchronous and asynchronous way. The employees could attend the on-line courses following six steps, from the skills gap analysis till to course's enrollment and attendance.

Curriculum

MU provides a variety of tailor-made programs, including business solutions for enterprises, certification and training for operators' management and technical forces, and soft skill training for college students. In the future, MU will, by sticking to its vision of "University Setup and Corporate Management," continuously perfect its organization, broaden its portfolio and expand into new disciplines. Motorola commits a significant investment each year to continuously improve the methodology and the Six Sigma consulting and training services it provides. Coherently, MU is an organization capable of providing professionally recognized Six Sigma certification, updated materials with lessons learned and best practices, and some of the most popular, expert and respected trainers in the industry. The instructors use MU's proprietary Six Sigma courseware, and are skilled in customizing learning initiatives to different industries, organizations' needs and geographic regions. They come from inside the company, and from the local and overseas academic institutions and universities. With abundant know-how and a wealth of experience in guiding business operations, they are capable of giving instructions in classrooms and providing consultation on real-world issues, especially in the areas of Performance Excellence and Quality Management.

Organization

MU has five institutes that offer a compelling spectrum of professional training and education programs in different areas of management such as *Leadership and Management, Quality, Go-To-Market, Supply Chain* and *Engineering*. The five institutes facilitate the development of competency models and curriculum development, and provide expertise with strategic learning solutions. The University also collaborates with some other training and consulting service bodies, such as prestigious universities and industry institution partners.

Performance

MU provides customers, employees, suppliers, partners and other potential customers with best-in-class practice and acts as a change agent through breakthrough performance improvement with sustainable financial results. The sales training program provided by the University are distinctive since do not focus only on marketing but provide sharp insights in finance industry. Some customers register a staggering 30:1 return on investment in the training at Motorola University. MU is really good at "Global Thinking and Local Execution" and its experts allow customers to successfully implement the Six Sigma system across their organizations.

5.4.4 A definition of Stakeholder University

Based on the preliminary desk and field investigation made and the analysis of the *Cisco Networking Academy, GM University* and *Motorola University* cases, we try to formulate a possible definition/characterization of the Stakeholder University as follows:

The Stakeholder University emerges as a new learning archetype which promotes and develops innovative learning and capability-building processes among globally distributed and integrated networks of employees, customers, suppliers, partners, as well as of academics, professionals, independent learners and other institutions. As a result of an increasing alignment among mental models of people, competency development plans and approaches, and supporting technological systems, the Stakeholder University becomes the key reason for continuous inter-organizational innovation and sustainable value creation.

The creation of a Stakeholder University is not an easy process and also large corporations can struggle with the implementation of an extended learning initiative that goes beyond the narrow training or competence development. The question at this point could thus be: "*What does it take to design and implement a successful initiative?*" In the following section, a purposeful roadmap is presented with some design and implementation guidelines. The roadmap uses all the discussion and the investigation contained in the previous sections as well as the evolution in human capital development dimensions discussed in Chapter 3.

5.5 A roadmap for implementing the Stakeholder University (SU)

The extended focus, scope and interconnections that characterize a Stakeholder University (SU) make its successful implementation a process that cannot happen overnight. In the perspective to come up with a holistic design and implementation model, the following questions should be posited at the outset of the initiative:

- *What are the value creation angles and strategic purposes?*
- *Who are the stakeholders to be addressed and involved?*
- *What knowledge domains and learning areas must be covered?*
- *How will the necessary knowledge and expertise be built?*
- *Which competencies and skills should be developed?*
- *How will peoples' development be ensured?*
- *Which processes should be activated to make the SU work?*
- *Which platform and technology applications have to be developed?*
- *How is the multifaceted impact of the SU measured?*

The answer to these questions implies defining the following components that characterize a SU:

1. the ultimate purpose and *strategic framework*;
2. the *development* issues, including people development and university development processes;
3. the underlying *learning* components, including learning base, learning technology platform and learning strategy; and
4. the *performance* achieved related with the purpose established for the SU.

These components can be also seen as the key activities to be included in the implementation plan of the Stakeholder University. Figure 5.2 shows the components and their relationships. A description follows right after, with the indication of the points in this chapter and Chapter 3 where some of the components mentioned have been already analyzed.

5.5.1   Strategic framework

Defining the purpose and strategic framework of the Stakeholder University is a key activity to undertake at the outset. Three aspects should be addressed: the *Strategic Direction* (i.e. the *focus* dimension that we have discussed and illustrated in Sections 5.2, 5.3.2 and 5.4); the *Target Stakeholders* (i.e. the *scope* analyzed in Sections 5.2, 5.3.2 and 5.4); and the *Networking Model* (i.e. the *interconnection* previously discussed in Sections 5.2, 5.3.5 and 5.4). These components provide the overall frame to the Stakeholder University and drive the implementation of processes aimed to develop the stakeholders and the university as a

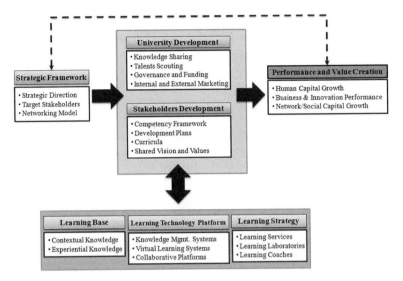

Figure 5.2   Components of a Stakeholder University.

whole to achieve the performance and value creation objectives coherent with the purpose.

5.5.2   Stakeholders and University core processes development

The strategic framework provides the compass that drives the development of stakeholders' capabilities and the growth of the University as a whole. Related to the first aspect, four components/activities are central: *Competency Framework* (i.e. the people competencies and skills critical for the success as illustrated in Sections 3.4 and in 5.3.3); *Development Plans* (i.e. the key stages of individual growth in the long term, in line with the career advancement policies of the organization); *Curricula* (i.e. the learning paths aimed to develop key competencies and skills as illustrated in Sections 3.5 and 5.3.4); and *Shared Vision and Values* (i.e. the common awareness about the University's present and future).

Related to the University Development, the components/processes critical are: *Talents Scouting* (i.e. actions aimed to attract and retain smart and outstanding people, a key organizational capability mentioned in Section 3.2); *Knowledge Sharing* (i.e. actions aimed to optimize the multi-directional flows of relevant information, a key organizational capability mentioned in Section 3.2 as well as throughout the whole book); *Governance and Funding* (i.e. the activities aimed to support, also financially, the operations and the growth of the Stakeholder University, as discussed in Sections 5.3.7 and 5.3.8); and the *Internal and External Marketing* (i.e. the promotion and nurturing of the initiative as commented in Section 5.3.7).

5.5.3   Learning components

Three key elements at the foundation of the SU development are an innovative learning strategy, a consistent learning base, and an integrated learning technology platform.

The Learning Strategy includes three interrelated issues: *Learning Laboratories* (i.e. the action learning "places" where to create new knowledge, experiment new approaches, and nurture innovation through a focus on linking workplace needs with the competency development process, as commented in Section 3.5); *Learning Services* (i.e. the whole activities aimed to ensure the implementation of curricula and development plans, as commented in Section 3.6); and the *Learning Coaches* (i.e. the mentors or expert individuals supporting and leading the learning process, as highlighted in Section 3.6).

The Learning Base includes the *Contextual Knowledge* (i.e. "static" knowledge about the business, industry trends, competition, etc.) and *Experiential Knowledge* (i.e. real life cases and experiences of practical applications of management concepts or solution of issues and problems).

Finally, the Learning Technology Platform includes three integrated subsystems: *Knowledge Management Systems* (i.e. the applications supporting collaborative and distributed processes of knowledge creation, sharing, search and application, as described in Section 3.8); *Collaborative Platforms* (i.e. the applications supporting the integrated management of collaborative work and projects, as described in Section 3.8); and *Virtual Learning Systems* (i.e. the applications supporting unstructured and just-in-time learning processes that deliver curricula and develop key competencies, as described in Section 3.8).

5.5.4   Performance and value creation

The implementation of the Stakeholder University requires a constant focus on monitoring the value generated in different dimensions. A comprehensive "dashboard" should consider the impact of the University at a threefold level. First, the native purpose of a University is to develop Human Capital. A first important set of metrics should be thus aimed at measuring the *Human Capital Growth* (i.e. the impact in terms of people competency level, time to competency, innovativeness, and talent retention). Second, the Stakeholder University is made up by a network that includes corporate stakeholders (interacting for business reasons such as suppliers, partners, and employees) and academic stakeholders (interacting in the design and delivery of learning services such as business schools, universities and educational institutions). The performance of the Stakeholder University should thus be measured in terms of *Network/Social Capital Growth* (i.e. the number of actors involved and the density of learning and innovation interactions arising within the network). However, the development of human and social capital is framed in a money making and business context of business and the University is expected also to support the achievement of business strategy. A third facet of performance is thus addressed to measure the *Business and Innovation Performance* (i.e. the impact of the Stakeholder University in terms of net revenues, productivity, overall efficiency, customer retention and satisfaction, etc., as discussed in Section 5.3.8).

5.6   Conclusion

The necessary alignment among strategic framework, learning components, development goals and approaches, and performance measures makes the Stakeholder University a powerful driver of inter-organizational learning and innovation to create value. In the first chapter of this book we introduced the concept of Open Business Innovation Leadership as the strategic capability of an organization to create sustainable value for its stakeholders based on networked innovation, learning and human capital development processes. We interpreted the Open Business Innovation Leadership also as Stakeholder Value Leadership.

The message underlying the title of this book is that the creation of a Stakeholder University can be the strategic route toward driving Open Business Innovation Leadership. The *federation* of ideas, goals and people becomes a key principle in organizing physical and virtual learning, innovation, knowledge creation and all the most strategic processes of companies in times of disruptive changes and increasing complexity.

In 1998, Marie-Claude Boudreau et al. highlighted how the *central feature of virtual organizations is their dependence on a federation of alliances and partnerships with other organizations . . . the practice of permeating organizational boundaries through partnerships and alliances has enabled virtual enterprises to realize tremendous advantages . . . virtual organizations use the federation concept as their primary principle of organizing.* Ten years have passed and the pressures to build networks of strategic alliances to drive competitiveness have still increased.

What is your organization's position regarding this concern? Are your current assumptions about management in-line with the transforming economy and business? Is your corporate learning and human capital development process actually incorporating a value-creation and stakeholder-oriented focus? Is your organizational configuration really able to foster people's potential and innovation in different forms? Ultimately, is your learning and innovation archetype enhancing the focus, the scope and the interconnections that should inform an open and boundary-less view of the organization?

In this book we tried to discuss all these points and support them with the analysis of cases and real data. In Chapter 1 we introduced the key drivers and assumptions at the basis of defining a different cultural framework in management. In Chapter 2 we moved from the analysis of the turbulent dynamics of today's markets and industries to show the need to go beyond the linear and deterministic approach to managing corporations. In Chapter 3 we illustrated how companies transform their learning and human capital development strategies and models to fit the new competitive landscape, with a specific focus on networked learning as a cause of stakeholder value. Chapter 4 provided a case-based response to the request of defining new approaches to developing social capital and new organizational models to stimulate creativity and innovativeness of organizations. Finally, in this fifth and last chapter we used the key conclusions of previous sections to start an analysis of major trends and evolution stages related to the phenomenon of corporate learning in the recent decades. The goal was to highlight how human capital development processes are today evolving to enhance the interconnections arising at intra and inter-organizational levels, along with the strategic focus and the scope of learning as a cause of competitiveness and value. The emergence of the Stakeholder University was introduced as a model capable of driving Open Business Innovation Leadership. A design and implementation roadmap has also been proposed.

We began this book with a clear idea in mind: the transforming dynamics of economy and business drive a "creative destruction" of existing cultural, strategic and organizational paradigms. New ideas and actions are needed in the way of strategizing, organizing, learning and innovating, and this demands, more than before, a holistic perspective to create value for an increasing variety and number of actors who are directly or indirectly concerned with their organization's success.

We believe that the Stakeholder University represents the philosophy, the method and the process to achieve that holistic view and be therefore the most promising strategy in the journey of pursuing leadership in an open world. A world of opportunities lies there waiting for those who decide to undertake that journey.

Appendix: Corporate University definitions

Definition	Author/Date
[T]he *strategic umbrella* for developing and educating employees, customers and suppliers in order to meet an organization's business strategies.	Meister, 1998
[A]n *overarching designation* for formal learning and knowledge creation activities and process in an organization.	Walton, 1999
[A]ll initiatives which are wholly owned by a parent work organization, have as their primary focus the provision of *learning opportunities* for employees of the parent organization (even though it may also offer learning to suppliers and customers), and utilize symbols and language from the educational sector.	Paton et al., 2000
[A] focus for the communications and facilitation of social, technological and organizational practices that support the *organization's learning* and knowledge creating process.	Prince and Beaver, 2001
[A]n educational entity that is a *strategic tool* designed to assist the parent organization in achieving its mission by conducting activities that cultivate individual and organizational learning, knowledge and wisdom.	Allen, 2002
[P]rocess through which organizations generate value from/to their intellectual and knowledge-based assets (explicit or tacit). The main goals of a CU are offer valuable training and education to employees, promoting continuous learning, starting and supporting change, getting the most out of the investment in education, bringing a common culture, loyalty, and belonging to a company, remaining competitive, retaining and promoting key employees.	Business Technology Leadership (www.cio.com)
[T]he organization responsible for managing the learning process and knowledge assets of the corporation for the purpose of increasing total *shareholder value*.	Tom McCarty, 2002
[A] central organization serving multiple constituencies that helps to develop the *employee capabilities* required for success.	Moore, 2002

(*continued*)

Appendix   continued

Definition	Author/Date
[A] function or department that is strategically oriented toward *integrating* the development of people as individuals with their performance as teams and ultimately as an entire organization by linking with suppliers, by conducting wide-ranging research, by facilitating the delivery of content, and leading the effort to build a superior leadership team.	Wheeler, 2003
[O]rganizational entity dedicated to turning business learning into action. It is designed, driven and intricately linked to the company's business strategy with the aim of achieving *corporate excellence* through improved staff performance and a company-wide culture in which innovation can thrive. In addition to generating value from their intellectual assets, it helps organizations to identify, retain and promote key employees, whilst at the same time providing valuable, work based learning and career development opportunities for staff.	ECUANET, 2006 (www.ecuanet. info/downloads/ 06Mar20_ ECUANET_ research.doc)
[A] process by which organizations integrate strategic, continuous, and *results-oriented learning* throughout their entire workforce chains.	CUE, 2007 (www.cuenterprise. com)

References

M. Allen (2007) *The Next Generation of Corporate University. Innovative Approaches for Developing People and Expanding Organizational Capabilities* (San Francisco, CA: Pfeiffer, John Wiley & Sons, Inc.)

M. Allen (2002) *The Corporate University Handbook* (New York, NY: AMACOM).

W. Baets and G. van der Linden (2003) *Virtual Corporate Universities: A Matrix of Knowledge and Learning for the New Digital Dawn* (Norwell, MA: Kluwer).

M. C. Boudreau, K. D. Loch, D. Robey and D. Straud (1998) "Going Global: Using Information Technology to Advance the Competitiveness of the Virtual Transnational Organization," *Academy of Management Executive*, 12(4), pp. 120–28.

Corporate University Xchange (2007) *Sixth Annual Benchmarking Report*.

CUE—Corporate University Enterprise (2007) " Corporate University Definition" (Retrieved at http://www.cuenterprise.com/777about/whatiscu.php).

ECUANET—The European Corporate Universities and Academies Network (2006) "ECUANET – An Overview of Corporate Universities" (Retrieved at www.ecuanet.info/downloads/06Mar20_ECUANET_research.doc).

EUA—European University Association (2003) "Response to the Communication from the Commission. The Role of the Universities in the Europe of Knowledge" (Retrieved at www.eua.be).

B. Jongbloed and L. Goedegebuure (2001) "From the Entrepreneurial University to the Stakeholder University," Proceedings of the Conference *Universities and Regional development in the Knowledge Society*, Universitat Politècnica de Catalunya Barcelona, 12–14 November.

J. Knight (1997) "A Shared Vision? Stakeholders' Perspectives on the Internationalization of Higher Education in Canada," *Journal of Studies in International Education*, Spring 1997, pp. 27–44.

D. Leonard-Barton (1992) "The Factory as a Learning Laboratory," *Sloan Management Review*, 34(1), pp. 23–38.

P. Maassen (2000) "Editorial," *European Journal of Education*, 4, pp. 377–83.

T. D. McCarty (2002) "The Corporate University as a Strategic Lever" in M. Allen (ed.) *The Corporate University Handbook* (New York, NY: AMACOM).

J. C. Meister (1998) *Corporate Universities: Lessons in Building a World-Class Work Force* (New York, NY: McGraw-Hill).

J. D. Moore (2002) "Running a Corporate University like a Business—A Financial Model" in M. Allen (ed.) *The Corporate University Handbook* (New York, NY: AMACOM).

G. Neave (2001) "The European Dimension in Higher Education: An Excursion into the Modern Use of Historical Analogues" in J. Huisman, P. Maassen and G. Neave (eds) *Higher Education and the Nation State* (Oxford: Pergamon Press) pp. 13–73.

R. Paton, G. Peters, J. Storey and S. Taylor (eds) (2000) *Handbook of Corporate University Development: Managing Strategic Learning Initiatives in Public and Private Domains* (Aldershot: Gower).

C. Prince and G. Beaver (2001) "Strategic Change and the Role of the Corporate University," *Strategic Change*, 10(3), pp. 189–99.

J. Walton (1999) "Human Resource Development and the Corporate University" in J. Walton (ed.) *Strategic Human Resource Development* (Harlow, UK: FT Prentice-Hall).

K. Wheeler (2005) *The Corporate University Workbook* (San Francisco, CA: Pfeiffer).

Glossary

Administrative theory: Theoretical approach to management developed at the beginning of the 20th century mainly based on the work of Weber and Fayol, who interpreted management as a universal set of functions (such as planning, organizing, coordinating and controlling) aimed to design effective organizations.

Alliance capitalism: A form of capitalism and organization of production based on the creation of strategic networks among companies.

"Ba": A shared context in which knowledge is created, shared, discussed, activated and exploited through an interaction among different actors.

Business concept innovation: "Meta-innovation" which goes beyond the pure incremental or radical innovation of a product, process or technology, to address the overall (concept of) business as the ultimate object of innovation.

Business innovation leadership: The capability to exploit the business opportunities deriving from technology and innovation, by reconfiguring the strategic assets of the organization, and particularly the components of intellectual capital.

Catalytic network: Emerging organizational form based on self-organization, flexibility of structure and a high rate of interactivity among internal and external agents, aimed at addressing the complexity of the external environment.

Centralized model (of Corporate University): An organizational model opportune when training departments are small, there are few employees and there is a need for rapid change or a tightly defined purpose for the university.

Collaboration platform: A technological platform supporting synchronous and asynchronous communication and collaborative work through a variety of channels, software components and services that enable participants to retrieve useful knowledge, locate experts, share effectively ideas and contents for the achievement of common goals.

Community of practice: A group of people working together over a period of time; different from a "team" or a "task force" as it is held together by a common sense of purpose and a desire to know what the other participants know.

Competence life cycle: All the phases of creation, development, maturity and decline (analogy with the life cycle of a product) which characterize the evolution of a given workplace competence possessed by an individual or relevant in a given industry.

Competency framework: Taxonomy and definition of workplace competencies and skills which are relevant for the success of an industry or a specific organization.

Complex Adaptive System (CAS): A dynamic network of interacting adaptive agents, characterized by dispersed and decentralized control, and by the emergence of a systemic behavior resulting from reaction, competition and cooperation among the agents.

Constructivism: A learning theory focused on knowledge as a personal construction of individuals and which stresses the subjective impact of the relationship between learners and knowledge sources for personal development, recognizing the importance of collaboration against isolation for the effectiveness of learning.

Core competencies: The most specialized and distinguishing company's expertise and features which contribute to strategically differentiate the organization from its competitors and lead the definition of future plans and positioning.

Corporate allocation model (of Corporate University): A funding model which consists in allocating all the university expenses as part of the general operating overhead of the firm.

Corporate citizenship: Individual awareness and identification with the company's culture, values, traditions and vision.

Corporate learning: An umbrella term used to indicate the personal and group development strategies and processes based on learning and aimed at developing the human capital of the organization.

Corporate University: See the appendix in Chapter 5 for different definitions.

Cost recovery model (for Corporate University): A funding model applied when the university charges individuals and departments for the costs they incur for training; it identifies situations in which the education institution operates more or less as a business organization.

Creative destruction: In its broadest sense, a process of transformation of business, economies and industries boosted by a radical innovation which leads to the emergence of a new economic structure.

Curriculum design: A process of design and organization of learning objectives, contents and assessment methods aimed at developing specific skills and competencies associated to the achievement of a target profile.

Decentralized model (of Corporate University): An organizational model opportune when the organization is a conglomerate of divisions with little in common; it is globally dispersed with very different local needs and has profit centers with independent general managers.

Distributed leadership: A collective and democratic capacity of people within an organization that initiates and sustains significant change.

Dynamic capability: An organizational capability that senses and seizes new opportunities; it reconfigures and protects knowledge assets, competencies and technologies in order to achieve a sustainable competitive advantage.

Entrepreneurial capitalism: A form of capitalism and organization of production based on single, small, fragmented companies focused on the exploitation of tangible assets.

Federal model (for Corporate University): An organizational model opportune when the organization is large and global but there are common core needs and a necessity to coordinate duplicated services or curricula while enhancing local flexibility.

Fitness landscape: An expression drawn from the evolutionary biology, where it is used to identify the relationship between genotypes and reproductive success; applied to the organization theory to refer to the complexity of the business environment of a company and its ability to adapt or prevent the changes that shape it.

Focus (of Corporate University): The strategic width that ranges from a narrow training purpose to broader forms of professional development and talent management as well as knowledge management and research.

Hierarchical capitalism: A form of capitalism; an organization of production based on oligopolies, focused on the exploitation of physical assets.

Holistic approach (to business): A systemic view of business based on the idea that the behavior of the whole system cannot be determined or explained by its components (the disciplines or functions) alone but rather through an integrated and cross-disciplinary framework.

Human capital: The stock of knowledge, skills and expertise held by the members of an organization.

Human capital development: Processes and strategies aimed at developing in the individuals of an organization the skills, competencies and expertise required to succeed in the competitive context.

Hypertextual curricula: The dynamic organization of learning objectives and content based on target competencies rather than traditional disciplines, business functions or knowledge areas.

Information and Communication Technology: An umbrella term that includes all technologies for the manipulation of information and communication flows.

Invisible hand: A metaphor associated with the economist Adam Smith, who in "The Wealth of Nations" referred to the capability of individuals acting in free markets to promote the good of the community by pursuing their own self-interest.

Job-related competence: The competence specific to a given job, organizational context or industry.

Knowledge management system: A technological system supporting the identification, transfer, creation, storage and distribution of individual and organizational knowledge.

Learning archetype: A model of corporate learning representing a specific stage of evolution in terms of focus and scope width and degree of interconnections.

Learning base: The overall contextual and experiential knowledge used to trigger individual and organizational learning processes which are at the bottom of competencies development.

Learning in action: A strategy by which a learner is intended to develop his/her competencies, not only by receiving pre-defined knowledge as a passive recipient but also by experimenting, interpreting and discovering new knowledge while setting the individual pace of learning.

Learning laboratory: A complex organizational system that integrates problem solving, internal knowledge, innovation and experimentation, and external information to address the development of critical workplace competencies.

Learning organization: An organization in which people continuously learn at both individual and group level, expanding their capacity to achieve the results targeted, and where new patterns of thinking are continually nurtured and collective aspiration is set free.

Learning strategy: An educational approach adopted to develop people competencies and skills.

Managerial competencies: The set of competencies necessary to bundle strategic resources and intellectual technologies underlying managerial roles in order to activate processes and apply practices to exploit them in a uniquely competitive way.

Managerial role: All the responsibilities and processes which characterise the manager of an organization at different levels.

Mass customization: A production system aimed at delivering goods and services resulting from the combination of a customer-oriented process of production with the efficiency of a mass production system.

Mass production: A production system aimed at manufacturing a large quantity of standardized products. Also called "flow" or "series" production, it is well represented by the Ford Model, applied by Henry Ford at the beginning of the 20th century.

Mechanistic organization: An organizational structure made up like a machine, where each component performs only what it is designed to do. It relies on efficiency and the predictability of the external environment, emphasized through specialization, standardization and formalization.

Networked learning: A collaborative, context-based, technology-enhanced learning process within networks of actors interacting to create value in different forms.

Open business innovation leadership: The strategic capability of an organization to create sustainable value for its stakeholders that relies on networked innovation, learning and human capital development processes.

Open innovation: The process of sourcing, integrating and developing new products and business systems, driven by external partnerships to benefit from the synergies created around joint investments in research investments.

Organic organization: An organizational form, logically counter-posed to the "mechanistic organization," which is suitable for unstable, turbulent and changing conditions, and characterized by flexibility, adaptation and job redefinition principles.

Organizational learning: The process through which an organization continuously learns and adapts to develop people and improve their performance.

Profit center model (for Corporate University): A funding model based on selling classes and programs to customers located both internally and externally to the company, with the final goal to gain profits.

Quantitative approach (to management): A rational approach founded on the application of mathematical, information and statistical models to solve business problems and support the decision-making process.

Resource-based view: A strategic management paradigm that sees in the resources and capabilities of a firm (and, in particular, in their heterogeneity and inimitability) the source of competitive and organizational advantage in the long term.

Scientific management: A theoretical approach to management that emerged at the end of the 19th century based on the work of Frederick Taylor, who developed a discipline containing the guiding principles for improving production efficiency through specialization and task orientation.

Scope (of Corporate University): The physical width (in terms of degree of involvement) of internal and external stakeholders, which can range from purely employee-oriented and site-specific actions to learning processes that address the whole organizational value network of actors dispersed geographically.

Skill: An ability acquired and developed through practice and the repeated application of knowledge.

Social capital: The overall set of relationships and connections within and between organizations, which drive collaborative work and creation of value based on shared goals.

Social network analysis: A set of methods for the analysis of social structures which aims at studying the linkages among social entities and the implications of these linkages.

Stakeholder University: An advanced learning archetype aimed at promoting and nurturing innovative learning and capability-building processes for globally distributed networks of employees, partners, customers, academics, professionals, independent learners and institutions.

Stakeholder value: A conceptualization of value that surpasses the economic and financial performance and aims at emphasizing a company's responsibility beyond mere profitability; it considers the success of the organization as the complex result of the satisfaction and development (the value) of many different actors.

Structural capital: All the explicit knowledge embedded in the organization's work processes and systems, or encoded in written policies, training documentation, or shared databases of "best practices." Also called "organizational capital," it includes intellectual property such as patents and copyrights.

Techno-economic paradigm: A combination of interrelated product, process, technical, organizational and managerial innovations, embodying a quantum jump in potential productivity, and opening up an unusually wide range of investment and profit opportunities.

Time to competence: The time necessary for an individual to acquire or develop a specific target competence at a given level of expertise.

Training department: The organization unit specifically devoted to plan, organize and deliver the education and training initiatives of a company.

Virtual learning community: A web-based environment experimenting with new instructional design and delivery methods, learning/knowledge management tools, and collaboration/interaction mechanisms and applications to enhance individual and team knowledge and competencies.

Virtual Learning System (VLS): A system designed to support a virtual learning environment through a set of tools for communication, content upload, peer assessment, profiles administration, evaluation tracking, etc.

Index